Computer
Support for
Co-operative
Work

Computer Support for Co-operative Work

Edited by

Kathy Spurr
Analysis Design Consultants, UK
Chairman, BCS CASE Specialist Group

Paul Layzell
UMIST, Manchester, UK

Leslie Jennison
TI Information Engineering UK Ltd, UK

Neil Richards
Neil Richards and Company, UK

JOHN WILEY & SONS
Chichester · New York · Brisbane · Toronto · Singapore

Other Wiley Editorial Offices

John Wiley & Sons, Inc., 605 Third Avenue,
New York, NY 10158-0012, USA

Jacaranda Wiley Ltd, 33 Park Road, Milton,
Queensland 4064, Australia

John Wiley & Sons (Canada) Ltd, 22 Worcester Road,
Rexdale, Ontario M9W 1L1, Canada

John Wiley & Sons (SEA) Pte Ltd, 37 Jalan Pemimpin #05-04,
Block B, Union Industrial Building, Singapore 2057

A catalogue record for this book is available from the British Library.

ISBN 0 471 95141 2

Typeset in 10/12pt Palatino from author's disks by Text Processing Deptartment, John Wiley & Sons Ltd, Chichester
Printed in Great Britain by Biddles of Guildford and King's Lynn

Contents

SECTION V
SELECTED SOFTWARE FOR SUPPORTING
CO-OPERATIVE WORK   **217**
Leslie Jennison

Preface

'Government and Co-operation are in all things the laws
of life; anarchy and competition the laws of death'
                                    John Ruskin 1819–1900

WHAT IS CSCW?

For centuries, humankind has been working together. The ability to
organise and work co-operatively is a defining characteristic of civilisation
as we know it. A variety of collaborative styles exist ranging from
hierarchical delegation, such as that found in the military, to more
egalitarian styles appropriate to leading-edge, task oriented organisations.

In recent years, globalisation of the market place has presented new
challenges for co-operative working. Multinational organisations need to
assemble team members, having varying skills and experiences, in widely
dispersed geographical locations. In addition, these teams may be focused
on one or more of several issues, dealing with overall strategy, analysis,
design, sales, marketing, general brainstorming or ongoing production
and administration.

There has been an explosion of high-technology solutions to
support collaborative endeavour. Teleconferencing, videoconferencing,
groupware, workflow automation, electronic mail, group scheduling and
network document management systems represent some of the advances
in this area. In this book, we assume that CSCW (Computer Support for
Co-operative Work) refers to any of these approaches. We take a catholic,
and eclectic interpretation, using the term to denote advances in computer
technology which will provide comprehensive support for co-operative
endeavour.

WHO SHOULD READ THIS BOOK?

This book is of interest to:

- managers and consultants concerned with gaining maximum competitive advantage through the use of CSCW
- professionals of any discipline who may wish to use CSCW in their everyday business
- IT practitioners who need to become effective contributors to the design and implementation of CSCW systems
- developers and vendors of CSCW tools, who need to understand the requirements and evolution of this growing market
- lecturers and students in business and computer studies who wish to understand the interplay of business need, techniques and tools in this key field of study
- IT practitioners who wish to use CSCW to support their own design and development work.

WHAT DOES THIS BOOK CONTAIN?

This book is based on papers presented at a one day seminar on CSCW, held at the London Business School in May 1994. The seminar was accompanied by an exhibition of CSCW tools, details of which appear in this book.

This book reflects the thoughts and experience of those concerned with the design and use of CSCW systems. Some are independent consultants, others represent some of the leading providers of CSCW services. They can guide us to some stimulating ideas and research.

THE BRITISH COMPUTER SOCIETY CASE GROUP

The seminar was organised by the British Computer Society CASE specialist group, formed in 1989, as an independent, non-partisan forum for debate on CASE and related issues. The group felt that it was an appropriate time to hold this seminar, because CSCW tools have been emerging and organisations are now seeking to gain maximum competitive advantage through the use of such tools.

This is the fourth book which has been published on behalf of the BCS CASE specialist group by John Wiley and Sons. The first two volumes, 'CASE on Trial' (1990) and 'CASE: Current Practice, Future Prospects' (1992) dealt directly with Computer Assistance for Software Engineering. The third book, 'Software Assistance for Business Re-Engineering' (1993) continued the software theme, but was directed more towards analytical techniques for understanding the business rather than direct production of a software solution. This and the current book broaden the scope of CASE to incorporate Computer Assistance for the wider activity of Systems Engineering. It is not a necessary prerequisite for the current book to have read the previous three volumes.

WHAT DOES CSCW MEAN FOR THE SOFTWARE DEVELOPMENT PRACTITIONER?

Since the activities of the BCS CASE group centre mainly around software production, one of the important issues raised by this book must concern the likely impact of CSCW on software development, and on participating developers.

This book will address the issues which concern software developers who wish to interact with business professionals in this area, either to design CSCW tools, or to use these tools as part of the overall development of business information technology solutions.

THANK YOU

The editors would like to thank those authors who submitted papers for the seminar. In all cases, the contributors had to work to very tight deadlines, in order to meet the publication date. Thanks also to the production staff at John Wiley and Sons for their patience and tolerance, and for unending good humour when the late delivery of contributions continually throws their production process into disarray.

Kathy Spurr
Paul Layzell
Leslie Jennison
Neil Richards
May 1994

CSCW: Introduction

THE WORKPLACE OF THE '90s

Team Based Operations

Business organisations in the United States and Europe are embarking on a revolutionary new era. For generations, the workplace has been structured around the hierarchy with control passed vertically from a narrow band of senior management at the top, to operational units lower down. Such an approach may have been suitable for traditional role cultures, such as government or the military, operating in a stable economic climate. However, this is not adequate for the rapidly changing technological and economic climate in which most businesses now compete.

Companies need the continual capability of fast response to an ever changing external environment, and in this sense, traditional workplace cultures are no longer appropriate. We are embarking on a revolutionary new era in the workplace, where capable, focused work teams are seen as a solution.

In addition, we now have the technology to provide more effective computer support for team-based operations. This book describes some products which can give active support in this area. It also raises issues and concerns in relation to the use of these products.

Evolution of the Workplace

Larry Greiner, in his excellent paper on organisational evolution, defined five phases of organisational growth (Greiner, 1972):

Table 1   Greiner's five phases of organisational growth

Phase	Evolutionary Growth Through	Crisis causing Revolution and movement to the next phase !!!
1	Creativity	Leadership
2	Direction	Autonomy
3	Delegation	Control
4	Co-ordination	Red tape
5	Collaboration	Psychological saturation??

In essence, Greiner was describing characteristics typical of individual organisations. However, his classification can be used equally well to describe the evolution of workplace culture in the Western world.

The organisation is 'born' in the first phase, with an emphasis on creating both a product and a market. This marks a period of highly creative, entrepreneurial activity. 'Management', as such, is seen as an irrelevance, since the company's founders are too busy targeting their energy towards making and selling a new product. Individualistic and innovative activities are necessary to get the company off the ground, but, as the company becomes more successful, it is apparent that larger production runs require more employees, and knowledge about the efficiencies of manufacturing. Increased numbers of employees cannot be managed through informal communication. A leadership crisis occurs, marking the onset of the first revolution.

Companies survive the first phase by installing capable business management, and then embark on a period of sustained growth under directive leadership. The new management and key supervisors take most of the responsibility for instituting direction, relegating lower level personnel to the role of functional specialists. This leads to an autonomy crisis, where lower level employees, knowledgeable about markets and machinery, wish to take action on their own initiative, yet find themselves restricted by cumbersome centralised control.

The delegation phase provides for heightened motivation at the lower levels. Decentralised managers have greater authority and incentive, enabling them to respond to customers faster, penetrate larger markets and develop new products. However, this will inevitably lead to a control crisis, where top executives feel that they are losing jurisdiction over a highly diversified operation.

The fourth phase is characterised by the use of formal systems to achieve greater co-ordination. Certain technical functions, such as information systems, are centralised at headquarters, while daily operating decisions remain unchanged. Local managers still retain a degree of autonomy, but need to justify their actions increasingly to the 'watchdog' audience at headquarters. This will lead to a 'red tape' crisis, where the proliferation of bureaucratic systems begins to exceed utility.

The way forward is to encourage collaboration, where the focus is on solving problems quickly through team action. Teams can be combined across groups for task-group activity, making use of a matrix or task style culture and assembling the right teams for the appropriate problems. The educational focus must be on encouraging managers to utilise behavioural skills to achieve better teamwork, and resolve conflicts. Real-time information systems need to be integrated into daily decision making.

Empowerment, Computer Technology and Mutual Adjustment (Mintzberg, 1979) are seen as being important factors for success. Since most innovative organisations find themselves in, or approaching phase 5, it is unpredictable as to what the terminating crisis will be. Greiner predicts 'psychological saturation' of employees who will grow physically and emotionally exhausted by the intensity of teamwork, and the heavy pressure for innovation.

CSCW IN THE WORKPLACE

The Need for CSCW

Organisations are realising the potential for radical change by utilising the potential offered by groupwork and computer technology. Businesses across the western world are undergoing radical re-engineering to focus more closely on customer needs, and to provide rapid response. CSCW (Computer Support for Co-operative Work) is one essential ingredient in the change process.

The new team-oriented workplace poses a challenge for those involved with the development and use of information technology. Now, for the first time it is feasible to make active use of computer technology in this area. We need CSCW to support the team-oriented workplace of the 1990s.

CSCW: What is It?

In this book, we discuss different ways in which computer technology offers support for co-operative endeavour.

Workflow computing (figure 1) is seen as providing control and support for tasks which need to be accomplished in some known sequence.

However, people can work in teams where the tasks are seen as being more concurrent than sequential (figure 2). 'Brainstorming' is one example

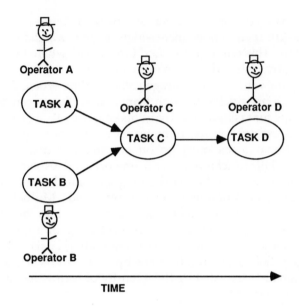

Figure 1 Workflow computing

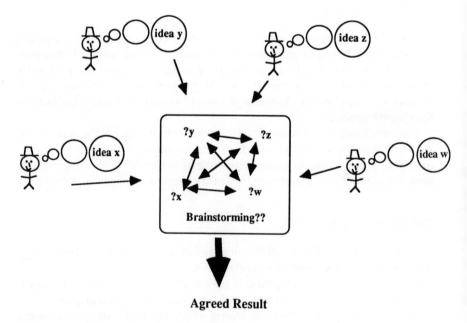

Figure 2 Concurrent groupwork: brainstorming

of concurrent group work. Teleconferencing and videoconferencing are possible technologies which can be adopted.

Iterative groupwork (figure 3) involves group members co-operating with one another to achieve an agreed goal, but not necessarily doing so in real time. Each participant can inject their own ideas/products/documents into the 'knowledge base' and some iteration will be necessary before the product is agreed and finalised.

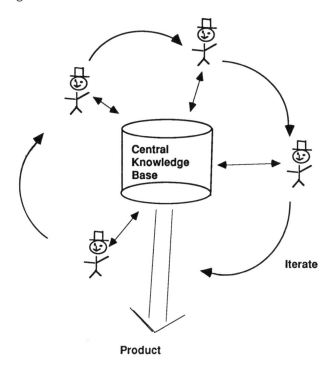

Figure 3   Iterative groupwork

Many of today's applications support this type of working, with a spectrum of attention to the peripheral details that ranges from little or none, to formal proposal and agreement.

THE PAPERS IN THIS BOOK

Section I, *Overview of CSCW* begins with a broad examination of computer aided support for co-operative working. Rose Lockwood's paper is taken from the recent Ovum report on Groupware (Ovum, 1993). The paper provides a useful overview of the groupware market, its products, suppliers and users, and describes a tool classification scheme similar to that shown in figures 1 and 2. Nigel Kirkham presents a management perspective on groupware and examines the drivers behind the role such technology has to play. David Hollingsworth completes the overview section by outlining a technical framework for co-operative working tools. His helpful classification of software infrastructure tools moves some way towards an understanding of the nature and purpose of co-operative working tools, suggesting that they support relatively unstructured processes and data and thus fall into the 'brainstorming' category of tools (figure 2).

Section II, *Use of CSCW* provides an insight into the application and experiences of using co-operative working tools and supporting methods. Clive Aldred's paper is firmly based around the integration of a set of tools to support workflow (figure 1) and the impact of a rule-based workflow scheme upon the organisation and individual. In contrast, Alan Fuller focuses upon a desktop conferencing facility from Fujitsu which is clearly designed to assist in greater concurrency of working by supporting group communication and brainstorming. Dan Diaper's paper is important in its attention to the design of co-operative working systems.

The role of individuals and management structures should never be underestimated when introducing a new technology. The papers by Carys Siemieniuch and Jack Cutts, in Section III, therefore address important Human and Organisational issues. The first of these papers examines the notion of concurrent engineering and in particular, the issues related to specifying, implementing and using co-operative work systems. The second paper provides a practical guide to the process of introducing co-operative working based upon the author's experiences at British Steel, in which Cutts examines the organisational benefits and pitfalls of technology such as Lotus Notes.

Section IV, *Future Issues for CSCW* examines some of the longer term issues. The paper by Gordon Blair and the team from Lancaster University recognises the role of multimedia in co-operative work and looks at the underlying support for the development of such systems. In contrast to the technology, Linda Macaulay's paper is based upon research and development aimed at the iterative groupwork model (figure 3). This work has addressed specifically the problem of co-operative requirements capture. Garth Shephard's paper looks to the future of groupware and co-operative working, recognising the challenge to develop the technological and methodological work outlined in the previous two papers.

Finally this book details, in Section V, some software for supporting co-operative work.

CSCW, THE BUSINESS AND THE IT PROFESSIONAL

The papers in this book outline the business opportunities provided by CSCW, and explore the implementation issues. However, we should remember that adoption of CSCW does not happen in isolation from other innovations. Instead this happens during times of extensive technical change (in network management, distributed data management, client/server computing and so on). From earlier and current developments in Information Technology, it is possible to foresee possible corresponding phases in the evolution of an organisation's use of CSCW.

Evolution of CSCW Use

A mature understanding of the dynamics of IT innovation acknowledges the need for partnership between Information Services and other business functions. Earlier in this Introduction we noted some characteristic phases of organisational growth. We hypothesise that these phases may be used also to throw some light on the possible course of collaboration between information services, functions and business professionals as shown in table 2.

Table 2 Evolution of the use of CSCW: five phases

Phase	Evolutionary Growth of Co-operative working through:	Crisis causing Revolution and movement to the next phase !!!
1	Creativity	Plethora of incompatible tools
2	Direction	Restrictive standards and autonomy
3	Delegation	Control: conflict and collisions
4	Co-ordination	Restrictions imposed by centralised information management facility: red tape
5	Collaboration	Psychological, physical, emotional saturation of employees?? Burn-out??

Phase 1: Creativity

IT practitioners provide client application support for user desktops giving access to data maintained on host servers. This allows groups to interact locally or via shared data on the servers, and to use whatever personal productivity tools and groupware seem appropriate for the task. Some of our contributors claim that applying co-operative working principles to existing data and procedures can also identify small changes to legacy systems, or simple additions to the technical infrastructure that can win early payback.

This approach initially provides learning opportunities and hopefully great satisfaction with what can be achieved by selected tools, sometimes used quite simply, by business professionals, with minimal support from IT practitioners. This will serve the creative and enthusiastic early adopter with compelling requirements and business benefits. Over time however, there is a danger that this may lead to a plethora of tools which don't all interact in the same way. As individuals move on to new teams and tasks, they may need to learn more and more tools.

Phase 2: Direction

The next approach is therefore to test and support a limited set of general purpose groupware and desktop tools, not necessarily all of them best of breed, but capable of exchanging data and working in broadly the same style. There is some agreement among the contributors to this book on the need for simplicity and for a technical architecture and standards. However, any restriction on use of tools by functional units will inevitably lead to a crisis of autonomy.

This more directive approach can avoid becoming too restrictive if new tools and facilities are added progressively as they are needed, providing they meet minimum criteria for interworking, and that selection criteria and usage guidelines are developed for the available tools. Several contributors identify relevant characteristics which may match applications with tools.

Phase 3: Delegation

These guidelines may develop into methods for developing point solutions which exploit personal productivity tools, groupware, and corporate databases. Groups of business people can become adept at developing and evolving new methods of working, without the need to involve IT practitioners in their application development.

As the use of groupware becomes widespread, collisions between different processes and uses of shared business data are likely to occur. Applications supported by groupware show a potential for rapid evolution. They are not always capable of being scaled up however. Later or reluctant adopters need more structure, and guidance in design and operation, than did their early pioneer colleagues. Auditors may express concern about the security and quality of corporate data which is mined and manipulated for an increasing variety of purposes. Servicing interrupts from communication mechanisms (paper mail, e-mail, voice mail, new orders queue) which are not properly integrated can contribute to communication overload for some individuals. Crises will be caused by collisions, conflict of interests and security concerns.

Phase 4: Coordination

Several contributors highlight the need for integration. Careful analysis and classification of objects (Shafer & Taylor, 1993), analysis of data use and communication patterns, together with the use of distributed database management technology, all promise to facilitate co-ordinated use of a spectrum of informal and formal working methods exploiting both unstructured and structured data.

Certain technical functions, such as database management, will need centralised control. While local users still retain a degree of freedom, they will need to justify their working practices increasingly to a 'watchdog' data administration role. This may lead to a 'red tape' crisis, and bottle-necks at the central information facility.

Phase 5: Collaboration

Collaboration must be achieved ideally without impairing the continued evolution (and revolution) of business processes. It should be possible to recognise an iterative life cycle of applications which support such process re-engineering, possibly like that of evolutionary prototyping, such as that shown in figure 4.

- The stages of this life cycle are: in Experimentation with closer, faster group working
- Elaboration of the use of tools and procedures
- Formulation of best practise and definitions to ensure control is applied only in necessary circumstances
- Partial integration with, or performance of tasks by, formal information systems
- Identification of further improvement opportunities, leading to conse-quent iterations of the life cycle, or new opportunities for group working.

Phase 5 is characterised by continual, ongoing collaboration between

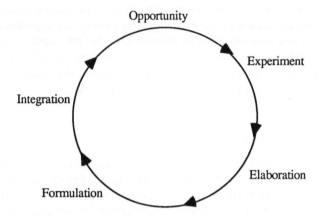

Figure 4   Stages of exploiting CSCW

information services, functions, and business professionals. What will the terminating crisis be? We can only hypothesise.

Innovation and change can present interesting and stimulating challenges. But, as with Griener's prediction, we may find that employees will become emotionally and physically exhausted by the intensity of collaboration and the constant requirement for creativity and innovative solutions. In order to avoid 'burn-out', there is a need for balance and mutual adjustment. As a community of business professionals, and information technologists, we lack the experience and knowledge with regard to overcoming these problems.

Evolution of Systems Engineering

On the systems engineering front, there is a need for improved techniques of modelling object states and transitions, roles and organisational inter-actions (Krackhardt & Hanson, 1993), as an aid to selection of groupware, design of workflow, and operational adjustment of roles to match changes in volume and business pressure.

Evolution of CASE Technology

Integrated CASE and lower CASE tools (those that perform detailed design and application generation) are making significant progress in hiding technical complexity from developers. This is especially important in the world of client/server computing. In so far as groupware products include application building facilities, they are at present 'point' solutions having little integration with mainstream CASE facilities. As CASE vendors accept the need for standards and interfacing, we hope to see CASE tools generating application components for both mainstream and CSCW environments. Object technology offers a promising mechanism for this line of evolution.

We also see the need to increase integration of traditional CASE repositories, the run-time controls used by some groupware, and business databases. This is a considerable technical challenge, but should improve control of the organisational structure and process information that these data stores have in common, and better support the continual adjustment of co-operative applications.

The need to respond to business re-engineering initiatives (Spurr et al., 1993) is already putting pressure on upper CASE tools to improve organisational modelling. These tools need also to support the evolving systems engineering techniques already mentioned.

The industry is still some way from CASE tools that can widely be used by business professionals. Will the evolution of CSCW tools drive CASE products in that direction?

The use of a CASE environment is itself a good example of group working. It corresponds to figure 3 above, (and occasionally to figure 2 when used in Joint Application Design workshops). There is however a potential for automating the active notification of interested parties affected by change, and general communication and explanation of proposals. Here CSCW techniques such as e-mail and workflow techniques offer interesting possibilities for improvement.

CONCLUSION

We hope that business and IT professionals alike will be stimulated and encouraged by the variety of views and accounts of CSCW represented by the papers in this book.

An awareness of the possibilities of CSCW technology, coupled with a mature understanding of the organisational and management issues, should enable most organisations to exploit an explosion of collaborative working experiments.

We believe it is possible to win the benefits of collective creativity and ingenuity without sacrificing any necessary control. We can certainly look forward to some interesting times as we attempt to maintain this dynamic equilibrium.

REFERENCES

Greiner, Larry E, *Evolution and Revolution as Organisations Grow*, The Harvard Business Review, July/August 1972

Krackhardt, D & Hanson, J, *Informal Networks: the Company behind the Chart*, Harvard Business Review, July–August 1993

Mintzberg, Henry, *The Structuring of Organisations*, Prentice Hall, 1979

Ovum, *Groupware* by Rose Lockwood, Mandy Lavery, Laurent Lachal, published by Ovum, September 1993

Shafer, D & Taylor, D *Transforming the Enterprise through Co-operation* Prentice Hall, 1993

Spurr, K, Layzell, P, Jennison, L & Richards, N *Software Assistance for Business Re-Engineering* Wiley, 1993

Authors' Addresses

EDITORS

Kathy Spurr

Analysis Design Consultants
Lyndhurst Lodge
41 Lyndhurst Road
Chichester
West Sussex
PO19 2LE

Paul Layzell

Department of Computation
UMIST
PO Box 88
Manchester
M60 1QD

Leslie Jennison

Frogmore House
Market Place
Box
Corsham
Wilts
SN14 9NZ

Neil Richards

Neil Richards and Company
Hobbits
Danesbury Park Road
Welwyn
Herts
AL6 9SS

AUTHORS

Clive Aldred

Managing Director
MS Technology Ltd
Quirrinal House
2 Aire Road
Wetherby
West Yorkshire
LS22 4UE

Jack Cutts

CMS, British Steel
PO Box 21
Aldwarke Lane
Rotherham
S65 3SQ

Dan Diaper

University of Liverpool
Department of Computer Science
PO Box 147
Liverpool
L69 3BX

Alan R. Fuller

Fujitsu Networks Industry Inc
2 Longwalk Road
Stockley Park
Uxbridge
UB11 1AB

David Hollingsworth and
Peter Wharton

ICL Wendy House
Beaumont
Burfield Road
Old Windsor
SL4 2JP

Nigel R. A. Kirkham

KPMG Management Consulting
PO Box 695
8 Salisbury Square
London
EC4Y 8BB

Rose Lockwood

Ovum Limited
1 Mortimer Street
London
W1N 7RH

Linda McAuley,
Greg O'Hare,
Paul Dongha and
Steve Viller

Department of Computation
UMIST
PO Box 88
Manchester
M60 1QD

Garth Shephard

TEKnowledge
The Little House
2 School Lane
Welwyn Village
AL6 9DZ

Carys Siemieniuch and
M. A. Sinclair

HUSAT Research Institute
Loughborough University of Technology
The Elms
Elm Grove
Loughborough
LE11 1RG

Neil Williams,
Gordon Blair,
Geoff Coulson,
Nigel Davies and
Tom Rodden

Department of Computing
Lancaster University
Lancaster
LA1 4YR

Trademarks

Motif is a trademark of Open Software Foundation, Inc.

Novell is a registered trademark of Novell, Inc.

Openframework is a trademark of ICL

ORACLE and ORACLE Card are registered trademarks of Oracle Corporation

PenAnalysis is a trademark of Hitachi Software Engineering Co., Ltd.

PenPoint is a trademark of GO Corporation

Post-it is a trademark of 3-M

Powerbuilder is a trademark of Powersoft Corporation

Saros and Mezzanine are registered marks of Saros Corporation

SmallTalk/V is a trademark of Digitalk, Inc.

Soft-Switch is a trademark of Soft-Switch Inc.

Staffware is a trademark of Staffware plc

Sybase is a trademark of Sybase, Inc.

TeamWorkStation and ClearBoard are trademarks of NTT Human Interface Labs

Turbo CAD is a trademark of IMSI

UNIX is a trademark of UNIX System Laboratories Inc.

Ventura is a trademark of Ventura Software Inc.

WACOM is a trademark of Wacom Co., Ltd

WordPerfect is a registered trademark of WordPerfect Corporation.

Section I

Overview of CSCW

1

The Groupware Market

Rose Lockwood

ABSTRACT

This paper is taken from the Management Summary of *Groupware: Market Strategies*, a report published by Ovum Ltd. The report studies the prospects for groupware as a generic and an enabling concept, showing how it has emerged from changes in the IT industry and in user's needs.

Groupware is considered as a set of products rather than as a technology; the history of the development of such products is briefly examined, in order to sketch their likely future development.

Drivers and inhibitors to take-up of groupware are discussed, as are the potential and actual motivations for companies to adopt it. The potential market for groupware is forecast to 1998.

GROUPWARE: A REAL MARKET

Groupware is truly a new desktop product market, with considerable revenue potential. The total product market is already around $700 million in the US and Europe and we expect it to grow to $2.2 billion by 1998.

The prospect of a groupware market emerged in the mid 1980s. Yet our research has shown that by 1993 no clear consensus has emerged about what constitutes the groupware market, what products or services are

---

Computer Support for Co-operative Work. Edited by Kathy Spurr, Paul Layzell,
Leslie Jennison and Neil Richards

included in groupware, and how big the opportunity will be to sell group-ware. At one extreme, the enthusiasts are fervently committed to the idea that groupware offers an entirely new—even revolutionary—approach to IT support for white-collar work. At the other, sceptics believe that group-ware is little more than a marketing strategy; at worst, a buzzword for a motley collection of products which are being repositioned by software vendors desperate to recover from the doldrums in the IT industry. There is some truth in both positions but we believe the enthusiasts are nearer the mark. We support this view by answering two fundamental questions— what exactly is groupware and why does it have such a market potential?

WHAT IS GROUPWARE?

Products Not Technology

Groupware is the generic term for software products that run on PC local-area networks (LANs), are interoperable with other types of software and support the co-ordination of office activities. Groupware is not a new technology. It is supported by innovation in the technical environment in which it operates (through operating system and network technology, for example) and in future will benefit from technologies such as high-speed communications and multimedia as they mature. Fundamentally, groupware is a product categorisation. It encompasses many different types of products that help coordinate work activities in the office (and the activities of workers who interact with offices but are based elsewhere). It also supports collaborative work of a more or less formal kind.

Because it supports co-ordination of work and collaboration of workers, groupware is as much about communications technology as it is about software applications. Indeed, some people define groupware in terms of its communications function, equating it with electronic mail, for instance. Other people focus on its capability to support the sharing of information in a systematic and controlled way, equating it with information management or databases. In our view, all these capabilities are part of groupware.

Categorising and positioning their products is one of the hardest tasks facing a groupware product supplier. We have categorised products into three major groups (see figure 1): workflow products, intelligent messag-ing products, and niche groupware applications. A fourth category, group-ware suites, represents those products which integrate sets of groupware functionality.

Workflow products have preceded groupware in the market by several years; as they are ported to desktop platforms and run on LANs, they

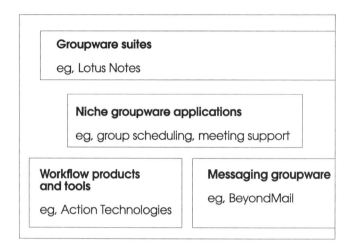

Figure 1   CSCW product categories

become mainstream groupware tools. Intelligent e-mail is a set of products that have revolutionised the LAN e-mail market by adding features similar to workflow, and other messaging management capabilities. In this report, these products are categorised as messaging groupware products, and represent threshold applications for many users. Niche applications are those products that have been designed to perform a specific function in support of the workgroup. Such products range from group scheduling, to sophisticated meeting-management tools which support and document decision-making processes.

Groupware suites integrate the services and functions provided by stand-alone products in each of the other categories. Within a relatively short time, we believe suites will become the dominant product category in the groupware market. As they replace office automation systems, they will deliver well-integrated features for basic workgroup functions such as messaging and information sharing. Because they will also represent the environment in which personal productivity tools are used, they will necessarily be highly flexible and modular.

Déjà Vu—Office Automation

One of the analysts who attended Groupware 92, an event which inaugurated the public face of groupware as an industry, remarked that the messages that came out of the conference were oddly familiar. They were, in fact, the same messages and claims about market prospects and user benefits which were common in the early 1980s, when the office automation industry was first established. These systems promised to eliminate repetitive and boring office work, to improve the productivity of white-collar workers (especially secretaries and clerks), and to improve the administration and control of paper-based processes. In fact, the office of the future was dedicated to the creation of the paperless office in which all information would be created, stored, shared and used electronically.

Needless to say, office automation products (or Integrated Office Systems, as they are sometimes called) did not fully deliver on these exaggerated promises. Ironically, word processing has created more, rather than less, paperwork. Work done by secretaries is, perhaps, more productive than it was ten years ago but the fact that there are fewer and fewer secretaries has little to do with office automation, and a lot to do with the arrival of personal computers on the desktop. In the intervening ten years, office automation has been derailed by the growth in the PC market and by changes in the business climate. Both these factors have influenced:

- the way organisations buy and use information technology
- organisational styles and structures.

Companies are moving away from terminals and towards PCs, away from central control of IT towards distributed and shared responsibility. Organisations are flatter, there are fewer levels of management, and there are also generally fewer support staff. As a result, the market for office automation products, in their original form, has been drastically reduced.

At the same time, markets for new kinds of office tools are growing daily. While the messages about groupware may sound similar to those made for office automation, they are in fact rather broader. The most important differences relate to target users, how they interact in the activities that support their work, and what kinds of technologies support them (see figure 2). Thus groupware:

- supports knowledge workers, as well as information workers in general
- is aimed at professionals and managers as well as the staff who work with and support them
- is used in cross-functional processes not just within the operational systems of single functional areas.

Groupware exists precisely because the infrastructure in the office has changed from centralised mainframe and mini-based systems to PC-LANs.

Office automation/integrated office systems	Groupware
Supports information workers	Supports knowledge workers and information workers
Targeted at support staff	Targeted at professional/managerial as well as support staff
Used within functional operations	Used in cross-functional processes as well as within departments
Employs a hierarchical architecture	Employs a client–server architecture
Based on mainframe or minicomputer hardware	Based on PC LAN hardware
Relies on closed, proprietary software	Designed for software interoperability

Figure 2   What is new about groupware?

THE POTENTIAL FOR THE GROUPWARE MARKET

Market Size

Figure 3 shows our forecasts for the groupware products and services market in the US and Europe to 1998. The market will more than double over this period and growth rates will remain very high for the period 1993–1995, after which more moderate, but extremely robust, rates of 15% per year can be expected.

In 1993, over a third of groupware revenue comes from workflow products. This will remain a significant part of the market. The most important product category, groupware suites, will replace older generations of products, both on the desktop and on host systems, and will grow from a third to nearly one half of product revenues by 1998. Stand-alone, intelligent e-mail products will correspondingly decline in significance over the forecast period, from $133 million (19%) to $216 million (10%) in 1998.

Groupware is a new type of desktop product and, as such, will need new channels and new marketing support if it is to succeed in the marketplace. One significant change that groupware will bring is the need for more comprehensive services from PC software suppliers. We expect that training and implementation will earn suppliers as much as $3.3 billion in 1998.

$ millions	1993	1994	1995	1996	1997	1998
US						
Total product revenues	480	656	825	1022	1162	1268
Training & implementation	720	985	1238	1533	1743	1902
Total US	1200	1641	2063	2554	2906	3170
Europe						
Total product revenues	215	341	466	608	738	930
Training & implementation	323	512	700	912	1107	1396
Total Europe	538	853	1166	1520	1845	2326
US & Europe						
Total product revenues	695	998	1291	1630	1900	2199
Training & implementation	1043	1497	1937	2445	2850	3298
Total	1738	2494	3229	4074	4751	5496

Figure 3   Market forecast: total groupware market, US & Europe, 1993–98

Market Drivers

Figure 4 summarises the forces that are driving and inhibiting the market for groupware products. Perhaps the most significant driver of the market is the fact that the installed base of PC-LANs has reached critical mass, covering a large proportion of office staff, particularly those who work in larger organisations. User surveys have clearly shown that the successful expansion of the LAN infrastructure is both a pre-requisite and an incentive for the adoption of groupware.

The market for groupware also benefits from the realisation that much of the existing investment in desktop IT equipment has not yielded significant improvements in the productivity of users. This, coupled with dramatic shifts in employment toward white-collar jobs and recent economic downturns, has opened up clear opportunities for products that can demonstrably deliver white-collar productivity. At the same time, companies have been revising their organisational structures, introducing quality programmes, and engaging in various degrees of business re-engineering, all of which can be supported by groupware products. Thus, organisational change and the need for more effective working practices are both significant drivers of the market for groupware.

The match between groupware functionality, and the changes in infrastructure and organisation cited above, has been identified by a few

Drivers	Inhibitors
A suitable infrastructure for client–server computing is being developed	Lack of a unified message on what groupware is
	• Misconceptions in the user base • Mixed messages • Realistic scenarios needed
Groupware delivers much-needed white-collar productivity	Budgetary constraints
	• Need to document cost/benefit • Link to business need
Important suppliers are promoting groupware	Product availability
	• No channels • Pricing strategies
Improvements in price/performance of hardware & software	IT dependency worries

Figure 4   Forces driving and inhibiting the uptake of groupware

of the pioneering promoters of groupware, and by Lotus Development Corporation in particular. It would be fair to say that all the major independent software vendors (ISVs) are now strongly promoting products which support workgroup computing. Thus, consciousness of products in the market has been greatly improved by the activities of the vendors. While such activities are not enough to create a market in themselves, when they are combined with the changes in the market, and the urgent needs of users, they can be a powerful driving force.

Finally, the market will continue to benefit from improvements in price/performance of both hardware and software. The expansion of the LAN infrastructure is, of course, partially due to significant decreases in costs over the last five years. The same kind of commoditisation is now taking hold in the software market, where some packaged products for the desktop are cheaper, by several factors, than they were only two years ago. In short, users can get much more functionality for much less money. As these products are enabled and engineered for use by work-groups on LANs, the cost/benefit calculations of users will be increasingly favourable. This will prove to be an important factor in driving the market over the next two to three years, as groupware establishes itself in the user base.

Inhibitors to the Groupware Market

The most obvious barrier to the take-off of groupware products has been the difficulty vendors have had in positioning these products in the market. Messages to users about groupware products have not been consistent, and some users are confused both about what groupware is, and about how groupware is related to their needs. They do not always see how groupware is different from existing products, and equally they do not see clear strategies for handling groupware within their existing IT systems and infrastructure.

The fact is that suppliers have created some confusion in the market by issuing contradictory and/or incomprehensible messages. Inconsistency in the groupware story has come from the strong competitive value which ISVs are placing on this new category of product; vendors are tempted to characterise their own approach as the definitive path to workgroup computing. In fact, in our view there are many paths and this should be made clear.

Incomprehensibility in the market is due largely to the fact that groupware is very hard to define. It is much easier to see the benefits from groupware once you are using it, than to predict in advance what the benefits will be. We believe this is certainly true, but that it need not continue to muddle the market image of groupware. Realistic and well-documented user scenarios, such as those developed by Lotus with the help of Telesis, are necessary to help clarify what groupware can do for users.

A second area of constraint in the market is financial. Spending for IT systems is, on the whole, much more closely controlled in user organisations than was the case ten years ago. This fact has arisen from a variety of causes, partly macro-economic circumstances, and partly disillusionment with the results of large IT budgets in the 1980s. Users are increasingly aware that costs in the IT industry have plummeted, and they expect to spend less for more. Furthermore, users expect to be able to make cost/benefit calculations for their IT purchases, and until good procedures are in place for doing this with groupware, there will be reluctance to embrace this new approach to IT spending. This will require a better understanding of techniques for measuring benefit, and creative approaches to the assessment of the value of groupware. In turn, this implies that groupware must be seen in relation to business needs, and not just as a technology solution in itself.

A third area of constraint is related to the structure of the software industry in general. We view groupware as a transitional product category, which will begin a new era where packaged software solutions for the desktop are the basis for enterprise-level computing systems. This implies that existing channels for corporate IT solutions will need to absorb group-ware, and equally that groupware suppliers will need to develop sales channels which are appropriate to these types of products. Neither of these things has happened yet.

The major suppliers of personal productivity tools for the desktop are still struggling to develop relationships with large users, and with systems integrators and consultants who service those users, as well as to set policies on licensing, pricing, support, and the complexities of servicing a corporate customer base. However, we discovered in the course of our research with users that sales channels for traditional systems suppliers are sometimes not even aware that their companies have groupware products to sell.

Until channels are better developed, there will continue to be difficulty in getting the message to users, and in getting products into the market. The solution to this bottleneck will come, at least in part, through an unprecedented level of co-operative marketing and strategic alliances among suppliers. This will help develop new, refined channels for group-ware products. Pricing strategies must be developed in the light of the emergence of these new relationships, and of the role groupware will play as a central pillar of office-based IT. At the moment, prices are in flux and users are not sure what they get for their investment. Some stability in pricing which we believe will be achieved in the next two years will be necessary for groupware sales to take off.

Some users are sceptical about the capability of IT solutions to serve as a reliable support structure for their work. This arises from two opposite influences. Experience with centralised IT solutions has shown users the risks of total dependence on electronic solutions; when things go wrong, they go badly wrong. However, many user organisations are, as yet, quite uninformed about the innovations which groupware could bring in their working environments, and have little understanding of the degree to which groupware products can put control of processes and activities back in the hands of users. In short, while groupware offers the possibility of truly bridging the gap between users and IT specialists in user organisations, there is little understanding of this in the market; this is one of the key messages which should, we believe, help the market for groupware to grow.

During our research we identified some users who are worried about the potentially intrusive aspects of groupware. Some expressed worries about process automation tools and their ability to automate tasks and monitor worker output. Others expressed the view that decision support tools would lead to an unhealthy over-dependence on computer technology. What is very clear is that groupware can bring significant changes in the way people are asked to perform their jobs. Resistance to this change is the most common cause of the failure of groupware, and must be addressed as groupware applications become more widespread.

THE USERS

Who uses groupware? The simple answer to this question is that any organisation in which people must work together, relying on information to help them do so, can use groupware. It is important to make this rather unsubtle point, if only to support our contention that groupware, as a product category, will come to be pervasive. It will be as significant in the next five years as stand-alone desktop software products have been in the last five years.

One of the main messages of this report is that groupware will, on the whole, be used to do the same kinds of things that are already being done in offices. The fundamental goal is to do these things better. In the course of exploring how groupware can solve one problem, or make one business process more efficient, users often find that other opportunities present themselves.

For example, at Amadeus, an implementation that started with a database to support troubleshooting has grown into dozens of *ad hoc* groupware applications developed by end users in Notes. This characteristic is one of the most interesting features of groupware products. They are difficult to define and categorise precisely because they are so flexible.

We have identified three broad approaches that are typical of the early adopters' use of groupware (see figure 5):

- systems aimed at improving operational effectiveness; within the organisation department at Stadt Bochum, for example, networked PCs are helping eliminate bottlenecks in the administration of the city's business

- systems aimed at helping organisations pursue strategic business goals, such as the system being developed at Banque Hervet, to enable professionals to devote more time to risk-assessment for the bank

- systems aimed at improving the systems development process, such as the implementation at Stromberg Drives, where a groupware solution is being used to support a long-term re-engineering drive, integrating cross-functional business processes.

These broad categories contain a rich variety of specific approaches to

Goal	Method
Improve operational effectiveness	
Through improved quality	More accurate work
	More consistent work
	Retention of group and individual
	experience (corporate memory)
	More timely work
Through cost control	Saving time
	Minimising paper workflows
	Improving staffing efficiency
	Reducing costs directly
	Eliminating redundancy
	Better control of processes
	Fewer meetings
Pursue strategic business goals	
Through operational innovation	Quality programmes
	Customer culture
	Regulatory compliance
	Market integration
	Cross-functional integration
	Geographic integration
Through revenue generation	Defining an unique selling position
	Greater revenue from professionals
	Better marketing support
Solve systems development problems	Rapid prototyping/development
	Effective use of pilots
	Integrating resources
	Integrating applications
	Improving co-ordination with users
	Supporting rightsizing

Figure 5   Forces driving and inhibiting the uptake of groupware

solving problems through groupware. Each of these main approaches will continue to be important as the market develops. All companies will be looking to solve operational problems and to support progress in their development of business strategy, and these tasks will increasingly be supported by groupware products. On the technical side, we believe groupware will have a significant impact on the evolution of IT within user organisations, as users and IT staff collaborate on the development of process- and problem-oriented systems. In the future, we believe groupware will be the technological link between systems developers and end users.

THE SUPPLIERS

Who Will Supply Groupware?

The emerging market for groupware is serving to highlight a number of systematic problems in the software market generally. First, computer systems companies such as IBM and Digital, which have traditionally dominated software markets through their control of the supply of hardware, are in trouble. Groupware is providing them with a new focus for software which is less proprietary and more open to interoperability with the products of other suppliers.

The major Independent Software Vendors, such as Microsoft and Lotus, are now suppliers of packaged products, mainly for the desktop. Some markets are near saturation, and prices are approaching commodity levels. Groupware offers these suppliers a way to leverage existing products and move into new levels of corporate sales. Large systems integrators, such as Andersen, are struggling to move with the tide towards client–server architectures and provide large-scale solutions in a cost-conscious market. Groupware (and particularly groupware development tools) will be important technical resources for these companies.

Small integrators and value-added resellers such as the extensive network developed by Novell for the PC-LAN market, have ridden the wave of LAN networking which has supported the rapid expansion of this supply chain. Groupware provides the tools to enhance the applications that can be built on LANs and allows these suppliers to develop more functional and targeted solutions.

Finally, niche suppliers such as Ventana and Beyond can no longer rely on an ample stream of venture capital to support their development of innovative products. Groupware tools and products are the ideal basis for strategic partnerships within the existing supply chain, providing investment for innovative research and development and natural channels for new products.

Figure 6 highlights the approach each type of supplier is taking to the groupware market.

Competitive Issues

Competitive issues in the groupware market will be related to the strategic positioning of products and channels as much as the functionality or performance of products. There are several arenas in which these competitive issues will be played out:

Type of supplier	Approach
Niche technology suppliers • Process automation • Group scheduling • Team productivity	Supply niche groupware technologies and products to end users and/or OEM to other suppliers
Computer systems companies Independent software vendors	Provide groupware suites as well as stand-alone groupware products
Systems integrators • Large, global systems integrators • Small, national systems integrators	Supply solutions, including group-ware elements, for specialised or custom applications

Figure 6   Supplier scenarios in the groupware market

- Platform: The desktop platform will be the groupware platform; what products succeed in the market for next-generation operating systems and network operating systems will shape the market for applications

- Interoperability: The development of standards such as messaging, database and other application interfaces will determine the extent to which the confusing range of products will become an ordered range of modular choices which users can mix and match

- Heterogeneity: No single vendor will own this market, because there will be no single platform and no single network environment; the ability to thrive in an atmosphere of heterogeneity, especially through partnerships with other vendors, will be a key competitive requirement for suppliers

- Functional richness: Functionality on the desktop is getting richer by the day; competition for markets will centre on the ability to deliver better and more functional products in appropriate formats, with the potential to evolve with the infrastructure that supports groupware.

MESSAGES TO SUPPLIERS

If groupware is to become a new standard for office computing, as we believe it will, suppliers will need to consider the following issues.

The need for a clearer definition of groupware

Groupware suite suppliers should be more willing to agree to, and publicise, a more generic definition now that their groupware toolsets are more complete.

The opportunities in Europe

US-based groupware companies need to establish themselves, and make their products available in Europe. European suppliers need to position their products in the same context as those being developed in the US. The Unix market and the trend towards downsizing are stronger in Europe. US groupware suppliers must take this difference into account in their plans for Europe, and European suppliers should look on this as a potential competitive advantage. US companies should, however, be careful whom they choose as partners when they enter the European market. The wrong partner (inexperience, low quality support structure) could damage them immeasurably in the eyes of users.

The need for modularity

Suite suppliers, in particular, must provide the e-mail system, workflow solutions and tools that users want, rather than being limited to proprietary offerings. Niche and application suppliers should strive to develop products for standard environments. Suppliers interfaces must be generic and customisable at the same time.

The need for integration

This is particularly true of what are currently stand-alone team productivity tools. Vendors need to integrate them within groupware suites. If team productivity groupware is to become widely used, it needs to support commonly used word processing tools, spreadsheets and graphics tools, as well as a windowing interface. Product prices must also fall.

The need for user support

There is a need for all suite suppliers to provide some form of consultancy service to users to enable them to get the most out of their group-ware toolsets. Digital, for example, has its own 200-strong management consultancy and change management group for this. Other suppliers, such as Olivetti and IBM are forming stronger links with management consultancies. The presence of such consultancy is particulary essential in those solutions that suppliers wish to evolve to enterprise coverage.

CONCLUSION: MESSAGES TO USERS

The experience of early adopters has revealed some clear guidelines for the successful use of groupware products. These are summarised below.

The need for orderly development of infrastructure

The expansion of LANs should now be undertaken with groupware in mind. Inter-LAN communication will be vital if large-scale groupware implementations are to work effectively. This implies a systematic and strategic approach to the expansion of networking.

Re-engineering is desirable

Although we do not believe all businesses need to be re-engineered from the ground up (and indeed feel that this may not even be desirable in many circumstances), there is no question that the introduction of group-ware offers many opportunities for assessing the effectiveness of office practices and white-collar systems. Groupware implementations should be the occasion for considering issues of effectiveness and process efficiency.

Management of the take-up of groupware is vital

Many users have implemented groupware in an *ad hoc* way, leaving most decisions about what systems are developed and how they are administered up to end users. We feel that this approach is dangerous and likely to lead to the same kinds of dysfunctions which have dogged the desktop world for a decade. We strongly believe that distributed planning and execution can be carried out within managed strategies for developing groupware applications and systems.

Training is essential

One of the differences between personal productivity and group pro-ductivity tools is that ineffective training in the latter has serious implications for the effectiveness of the entire workgroup. Groupware actually exposes weaknesses in the workgroup. Effective training of all levels of staff is necessary, including end users, user–developers, and technical IT staff who may be involved in customisation of larger implementations.

Quantify the benefits of groupware

It is perfectly feasible to measure the effects of groupware within an organisation if plans are made to do so in advance of, or as part of, the planning and implementation of groupware systems. Users should strive to master the techniques which permit such cost/benefit analysis to be conducted. Groupware can be justified on the basis of cost as well as improved effectiveness, and users should take care to do so, to preserve their investments in systems and provide guidance for system development.

2

The Management Issues of Groupware

Nigel R. A. Kirkham

ABSTRACT

Whilst many companies have been wrestling with the technical intricacies of implementing "groupware" products to support collaborative computing, some of the most difficult hurdles they are facing have little to do with the technology itself. Harder to overcome are the fundamental issues surrounding people, process, organisation and culture. Understanding the balance and interaction between these issues is key to the successful deployment of workgroup computing. Our activities with clients in this area has revealed the drivers behind the role groupware has to play, the benefits that can be achieved and the pitfalls faced during implementation. This paper discusses the broad reasons why groupware has evolved, the benefits and pitfalls, and the key management issues facing organisations implementing groupware technology. The terms groupware and workgroup computing are used interchangeably.

WHY WORKGROUP COMPUTING?

A brief look at the reasons why workgroup computing has evolved will help us to understand some of the thornier issues of implementation.

Computer Support for Co-operative Work. Edited by Kathy Spurr, Paul Layzell,
Leslie Jennison and Neil Richards
© 1994 John Wiley & Sons Ltd

Today's businesses are being effected in major ways by change brought about predominantly by political and economic factors (figure 1). Changes in Europe have brought uncertainty; emerging economies in the Far East are causing businesses in the West to look long and hard at their ability to compete; GATT has signalled a global marketplace that will allow global business to compete and operate as never before. Closer to home, the UK's international businesses have been pre-occupied with managing the effects of one of the longest recessions they have encountered.

Rapid change is affecting all businesses

KPMG Management Consulting, (1993)

Figure 1

For many organisations, these influences have convinced them of the need for change. But external change is happening faster than many organisations can manage. The change is also unpredictable. The key challenge, and indeed priority, is to organise better. It is necessary to respond more quickly and with flexibility to the influences such changes bring about.

For many companies, this has meant introducing programmes of change around their key business processes, and programmes for continuous improvement. Businesses are saying they need a culture which will unify. They want a common way of doing things wherever they are located internationally. They are saying they need to invest more in people. They speak of empowerment, driving decision making to the point in the organisation where the decision can be made most quickly and with the most appropriate information; and they speak of teamwork—people working together irrespective of whether the team members come from different disciplines, locations or business units.

Organisations are seeking to improve their customer responsiveness; sharpening their business processes and reducing the lead time in servicing them; managing their geography better to streamline activities across locations and across business units; delayering the Head Office function to focus on core activities and reduce the cost base. So top priorities are improved competitiveness, improved efficiency and improved management information.

In order to adapt to such change, the systems supporting the organisation must similarly provide the utmost flexibility. Most businesses have implemented systems which support specific applications, specific people in the business and structured activities. But in order to support the drivers of change already mentioned, they need systems that support key business processes, multi-disciplinary teams, multi-business unit activities, and unstructured activities. They need systems that can help deliver information to people across the organisation irrespective of where they reside.

The conclusion from all this should be that the introduction of groupware can help solve many of the problems associated with such change programmes. Indeed, there are many sound, well publicised examples of beneficial groupware applications. In their paper on "The Impact of Lotus Notes on Organizational Productivity", Henry, Blum and Salloway (1992) provide several case studies of companies who have implemented this archetypal groupware application. Their research shows returns on investment ranging from a modest 33% in an electronics company partner tracking application, to a massive 2,480% ROI in a government agency for their customer support application. But although these represent impressive findings, the majority of cases relate to implementations within specific business units rather than across the entire organisation.

Such change programmes involve complex and far reaching business management issues, as well as deep-rooted cultural ones. These are often far more difficult to resolve than the technical problems associated with the implementation of any new technology.

THE BENEFITS AND PITFALLS OF WORKGROUP COMPUTING

Much has been written and many examples cited on the benefits of workgroup computing. To understand the benefits, and indeed pitfalls, it is perhaps useful to consider a basic definition of the term. Workgroup computing or groupware can be regarded as a set of tools that allow groups or teams of people to share knowledge or information with each other across computer networks, irrespective of where they are physically based. In this sense, basic electronic messaging (e-mail) could be regarded as groupware. But what makes true groupware products different is the ability for "many-to-many" communication, rather than the "one-to-many" communication available through basic e-mail. So groupware makes it possible for many members of a team to discuss, share ideas, and share opinions on a particular topic with many others. Although there are over 300 products that classify themselves as groupware, there are broadly three main categories:

- Discussion databases, where users can read and contribute to on-going discussions around a particular topic, such as a problem with a supplier, or progress on a customer account.

- Workflow software which attempts to streamline business processes, routing work automatically from employee to employee.

- Meeting software, which allows those participating in face-to-face meetings or videoconferences to type their comments simultaneously into their PC.

Our work at KPMG has uncovered many examples of beneficial groupware applications, gathered through feasibility studies, research, and client projects. The main benefits are perceived to be the ease with which information can be shared and the ease with which people can communicate across sites and country borders. Groupware is also seen to facilitate changes in processes and reduce the bureaucracy often associated with people working together across disciplines, departments and business units. Key examples of this include the process of bid management where a business is competing for large contracts on an international basis. In order to win the bid, the best bid team has to be pulled together from across locations, and often from across its own sub-contractors. Such a team has to work to tight time scales, sharing and gathering information from a wide variety of sources. Once successful, such contracts then often run across locations and the customer team needs to share information to manage its relationship with the customer.

So bid management, project management and account management all rely increasingly on international teams that can be supported by work-group computing.

Both the benefits and pitfalls of workgroup computing can be broadly categorised into three areas (figure 2): organisation/people issues,

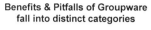

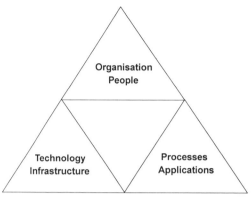

Figure 2

technology/infrastructure issues and processes/applications issues.

A recent survey conducted by KPMG showed the types of benefits attained by large corporate users of the groupware product Lotus Notes (KPMG Management Consulting, 1993). The survey was conducted amongst the members of the UK Lotus Notes User Group, and attempted to ascertain the main issues, benefits and pitfalls companies face when implementing this groupware product. Some 38 companies responded representing most business sectors; banking & finance, oil, consumer goods, insurance, publishing, manufacturing, education, government, utilities, pharmaceuticals. Significant benefits fell into the organisation/people category. The most often quoted benefits included:

- "sharing knowledge around the whole organisation",
- breaking down divisional barriers,
- empowering teams and individuals.

Similarly, business processes have been impacted, with benefits quoted including;

- improvement and stream-lining of workflow,
- facilitation of workflow management in complex business, given high rates of business re-organisation.

Interestingly, it did not appear that one particular type of application dominated, although discussion and tracking applications were reported as being of key significance. Discussion applications are those in which the technology is used to support "free-form" discussions around a particular topic: one example from the survey was where individual members of a client service team from a large insurance company share ideas and knowledge on their clients, how best to service them, products that may be of interest to them and so on, irrespective of where the individual team members are located. An example of a tracking application was where a large bank uses Notes to support the credit approval process, with the technology automatically routing the necessary approval forms to the next person in the process.

But such successes do not come easily, especially in the largest organisations, where the pitfalls and problems faced are magnified due to sheer numbers of people and complexity of business processes. The culture of the organisation also plays a significant part. The more open the culture, the more likely the success. There are a raft of management issues that need to be addressed, surprisingly few related to the technical aspects of implementation.

Without addressing the key issues, the scale of the success is reduced. It is widely believed that workgroup computing, when adopted corporate-wide, and when used to support changes to critical business processes, can lead to benefits of a magnitude all too rarely seen. The KPMG/Nolan Norton & Co "S-curves" of user-driven computing (figure 3) show the various stages of development, from the traditional DP era of the 70's, the PC era of the 80's with the automation of individual or stand-alone tasks, to networked technologies and applications, supporting process and business transformation.

This shows the stages of evolution that most organisations go through in their adoption of technology and the potential for payback the further they get up the learning curves. The horizontal axis shows the extent to which the organisation is impacted by each phase of technology. The initial phase (DP) shows the computerisation of company procedures, like payroll, ledgers and so on. With the introduction of the PC (the Task Automation phase), individual end-users found that they could now "own their own" applications, albeit on a relatively isolated and small scale. The advent of the Local Area Network and with it the mechanism for sharing information provided the potential to transform processes.

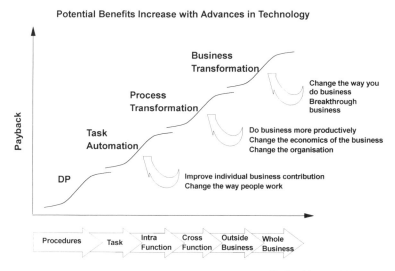

Potential Benefits Increase with Advances in Technology

Figure 3

What characterises the latter stages is the use of technology to do business more productively, or even support changes to the way business is carried out. Workgroup computing can be seen as one of the key drivers behind process and business transformation. For those getting it right, the payback is substantial. The danger for those that haven't addressed the key issues, is that they are spending greater amounts for comparatively minor paybacks. In his recent study of groupware use amongst international organisations (Holtham, 1992), Professor Clive Holtham of City University Business School found that roughly 80% of those companies implementing groupware were using it to achieve tactical goals such as cutting operational costs. Only 20% were actually using the technology for strategic advantage to improve customer relationship or re-engineer key business processes.

So what are the key barriers? The main causes for the lack of impact of groupware on the business priorities lie in both the user community and within the IT community and success relies heavily on the ability of these two communities to work together and focus on the alignment of IT with the business imperatives. Also from the KPMG survey of Lotus Notes users, the most often quoted pitfalls fell predominantly into the organisation/people triangle (figure 2) and included;

- understanding the potential of groupware,
- accepting the concept,
- senior management sponsorship,
- selecting the right applications.

The whole area of business sponsorship is key. It gets to the heart of any successful change programme. Without sponsorship at a senior level, any change programme is likely to falter, reduce its effectiveness, and ultimately even fail altogether. The nature of workgroup computing, and the evidence of high payback from organisation-wide use makes it vital that senior sponsorship is sought and gained. Furthermore, this sponsorship must not just be "lip-service" sponsorship, but must be solid and sustained. Organisations implementing workgroup computing applications globally are finding the need for multiple sponsors; senior, respected figures in diverse locations who all buy-in to the corporate mission of using the technology to support business processes.

Conversely, many organisations who have not managed to gain such sponsorship have found their experimentation with groupware and work-group computing confined to specific tasks or departments.

But attaining senior sponsorship in the first place is no easy task. The main problem is understanding the potential and the concepts of group-ware and indeed having the time and interest to invest in gaining such an understanding. The difficulty is that senior management are pre-occupied with handling the uncertainty and speed of change in their marketplace. They are sceptical as to the payback and benefits they have received from IT in the past and they are now in need of a quicker and more flexible response to help them manage this change. In many organisations they are overloaded with initiatives; change programmes, downsizing, new products, new working methods. Getting and sustaining their attention, involvement and crucially their participation in new implementation projects is difficult. The problem is further compounded by the difficulty in explaining the concepts and application of groupware. This is somewhat ironical however, as a key plus point of groupware applications is their flexible nature and the speed with which applications can be prototyped, tried, improved and implemented. Similarly, as many organisations grapple with issues of process re-engineering, groupware applications offer a very attractive way to support such change programmes.

Closely related to the whole area of sponsorship is an organisations' culture, which is one of the greatest hurdles it faces when implementing groupware. Culture in this context means the openness with which the employees share their knowledge and ideas. As the majority of workgroup computing applications involve a high degree of information or knowledge sharing, the extent and more crucially, the ease with which this happens is of paramount importance. To many people, their knowledge is their security; it is what keeps them employed. Being asked to share this knowledge with others through workgroup computing is tantamount to diluting their power. Many organisations admit that they are extremely bad at team working, yet it is this very behaviour that they are seeking to encourage by the implementation of groupware applications.

The KPMG survey found that culture plays a significant part in both the speed of acceptance of workgroup computing and the extent to which it is deployed across an organisation (figure 4). The figure on the left shows the speed with which the groupware product Lotus Notes has been taken-up within organisations, the choices being slow, steady or rapid. The figure on the right shows the extent of the spread of Lotus Notes within organisations, the choices being a few areas, many areas or all areas.

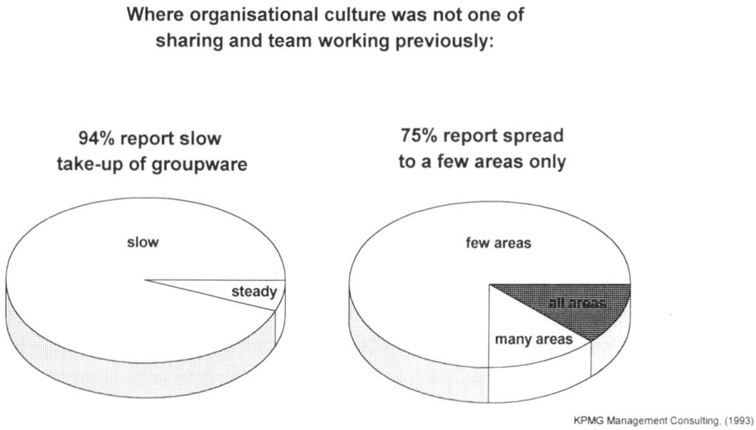

Where organisational culture was not one of sharing and team working previously:

94% report slow
take-up of groupware

75% report spread
to a few areas only

slow

steady

few areas

all areas

many areas

KPMG Management Consulting. (1993)

Figure 4

Where the culture of the organisation was not deemed to be one of team-working, the vast majority of companies reported a slow acceptance of groupware, and the spread of the technology to a few areas of the business. Conversely, in those organisations where team-working and an openness to knowledge sharing were the norm, a very different picture emerged (figure 5).

The majority of companies indicate that take-up has been steady or rapid, and applications have been embraced in many or all areas of the

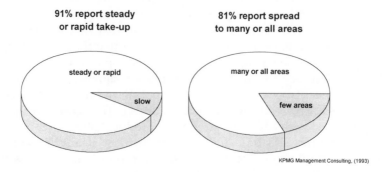

Figure 5

business. Overcoming cultural barriers requires strong change management and communication processes, touched on later.

The next major pitfall is the IT infrastructure of an organisation. It is the job of the IT professionals to design, plan and manage this infrastructure. It is no longer simply the data centre, but it includes telecommunications, the PCs and the local networks. In recent years IT infrastructures have become more critical; organisations depend on them more and they have become more complex; they are multi-vendor and more distributed. Problems can arise for which there is no precedent. Managing such environments demand new techniques and new skills compared to managing a more centralised environment. To run groupware successfully an organisation needs a cohesive integrated infrastructure which enable people to work together and share information across locations. In many international organisations the IT infrastructure will have been developed independently across regions directed by such factors as local supply and local needs. User driven projects and new pplications have a tendency to fragment the infrastructure rather than pull it together and investment in infrastructure alone is difficult to justify.

So what are some of the solutions?

KEY MANAGEMENT ISSUES

In the work that KPMG has carried out with clients, it is clear that the successful examples of workgroup computing have a number of key attributes in common.

Change management

Change management techniques should help to develop the crucial senior sponsorship. But senior management need to understand the role group-ware can play in supporting or helping change business processes, and be prepared to exploit such innovative technology. Identifying the attributes that make up the key processes can help explain to senior management just how the technology can support the business. We use the term "do-wells" to identify those key activities that must be done supremely well in order for the activity or process to be deemed successful. An example of a do-well in a firm like KPMG would be pulling together a team of consultants with the skills and experience relevant to a client's needs. The success or failure to win a new client engagement is often dependent on both the ability to find the right resources, and the speed with which they are found. Applying technology to support this do-well may help to speed the process.

Mapping the current use of IT against these "do-wells" (figure 6) dramatically shows the effect even marginal changes in use can have. The bid management process, mentioned earlier, included such do-wells as searching for information on the prospective client, pulling a bid team

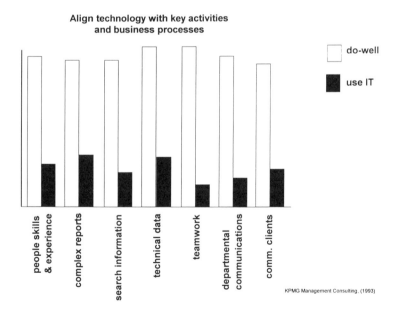

Figure 6

together with the best possible skills and experiences, producing complex bid reports and a number of others.

What this particular example shows is how technology currently supports the key do-wells for the bid team of one specific client. The height of the bars represents the importance of the activity (the "do-well" bars) against the current use of technology to support the team in these activities (the "use IT" bars).

The change management process confirmed that for the majority of people involved, these were the key activities that they had to get right. But the use of IT to support these activities was extremely low. The facts that groupware could help greatly in each instance, and that by speeding the process could win more bids, served to convince the senior management that this was something worth sponsoring. Finding the critical use for groupware, the "killer application", is no easy task. Some argue that because groupware is a difficult concept to grasp, it is hard to determine whether critical business processes can benefit by its support. They would advocate automating smaller, less critical tasks first as part of the learning period of the organisation. Whichever approach you adopt, one common factor persists: that to enable the corporate-wide implementation of groupware solutions, a key application will need to be found. Senior management need to be convinced of the value before they will sponsor on a large scale. Acts of faith are all too rare these days.

Change management techniques will also help identify the areas of resistance to change amongst the users. Remedial action can then be planned early to get the user community signed up to new methods of working. Involving staff in decisions that directly affect them is the surest route to acceptance.

Training and communication programmes

Training and communication programmes are vital to ensure that the users are not only familiar with the use of the technology, but understand the reasons why they are being asked to use it in the first place. Training is therefore more than just providing skills. This will only deal with the ability to use the system; vitally important are the willingness issues. Exactly why they should use it can only be addressed by looking at and communicating the benefits: benefits for the organisation as a whole and the benefits for the individual, their "personal rewards". Remuneration policies often need to be addressed: how is an employee rewarded? The chances are that such policies will need to change, especially when groupware applications are asking employees to be more open and sharing: why should they? Training programmes also need to teach the use of the technology in relation to the user's day-to-day activities. It is not enough to base training programmes around the functions of the technology.

The role of IT

The role of IT is changing. For groupware to be successful, projects must be user led and user driven. The role of the IT professional is increasingly to design and manage the supporting IT infrastructure, but to do that, technical excellence is not enough. The IT professional needs to adopt a more pro-active and consultative approach to their users. They need to work in partnership (figure 7) with the business to help senior management move forward with these new applications whilst at the same time preserving the cohesion necessary to support the implementation of groupware and manage the cost base of the infrastructure. They need to be able to explain in business terms the benefits of these new applications to win the attention, participation and sponsorship of the user community.

Programmes of education need to be provided for practitioners, users and IT to ensure both parties understand the roles they need to fulfil.

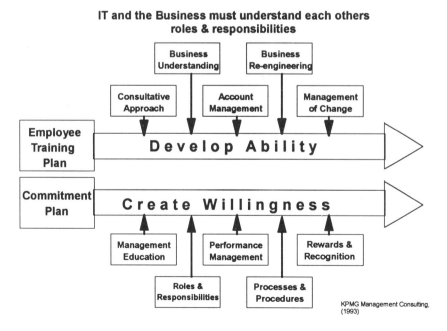

Figure 7

Such programmes must concentrate not only on skills and ability but also provide a willingness and commitment to change.

CONCLUSIONS

With continual technological advances, workgroup computing will continue to become a compelling method for organisational knowledge sharing and communications. Similarly, as more companies attempt to re-engineer their business processes, workgroup computing will provide an attractive method for supporting, and in some cases driving, such changes. Technical issues, particularly those to do with the integration of workgroup computing with existing corporate systems, will continue to be taxing. But the most difficult issues organisations face will remain people ones; understanding the concept, buying in to the benefits, finding the critical processes, changing working patterns and behaviour, sharing knowledge.

For those companies that have addressed these vital issues, the rewards are becoming substantial. For those who do not, benefits on a small scale are likely to be experienced, but the big payback will be more difficult to achieve.

REFERENCES

KPMG Management Consulting/Lotus Notes User Group—*Survey 1993*.
Holtham C. 1992. *Improving the Performance of Workgroups through Information Technology*
Henry J S, Blum P, Salloway E—*The Impact of Lotus Notes on Organizational Productivity, Evidence from Customers, Final Paper November 1992*

3

An Architecture for Developing CSCW

David Hollingsworth, Peter Wharton

ABSTRACT

The flatter, distributed and team oriented organisations of the 1990s offer new opportunities for the exploitation of CSCW. Two particular trends are discussed; the increasing use of document centred information and the move towards distributed, rather than centralised, control of process. CSCW application are analysed in terms of the nature of the processes involved—formal or informal—and the nature of the information in use—structured or unstructured.

The paper discusses the key software components to support this range of applications—Transaction Processing, Workflow, and office groupware—and their relationship with emerging client-server infrastructures. It draws together the important functions from each of these environments and discusses the opportunities for developing a long term architecture which brings the different application environments into a single cohesive infrastructure.

Computer Support for Co-operative Work. Edited by Kathy Spurr, Paul Layzell, Leslie Jennison and Neil Richards
© 1994 John Wiley & Sons Ltd

INTRODUCTION

Computer Support for Co-operative Work is not a new subject, but one in which there has been increasing interest as the flatter, more distributed organisations of the 1990s have placed greater emphasis on working group interactions and their relationship to business processes.

There is no universally accepted boundary as to what separates CSCW from other types of application, nor definition of which categories of software products are covered by the related term "Groupware". Much of the software labelled by the industry as Groupware is actually focussed on document-centred office applications; whereas a more general definition would include any class of software designed to support groups of users work together more effectively. This paper takes a deliberately broad view of CSCW in the belief that almost all Information Systems involve cooperative interaction between individuals at some level, either directly or via manipulation of shared information. Furthermore, few of the newer applications directly focussed on workgroup cooperation are able to exist in isolation from "legacy" applications and databases established during the 1970s and 1980s, so an effective architecture must address these wider aspects of integration.

BACKGROUND—TECHNICAL AND BUSINESS TRENDS

As noted above, IT systems supporting cooperative working are not new; traditional Transaction Processing systems have provided a framework for such applications for many years. What has changed is the business environment and the wider range of information technology available to support this business environment.

Two trends have been of particular importance in recent years, broadening the range of infrastructure available and opening up new requirements for, and approaches to, the design of CSCW applications.

Distribution of Process Control

Most applications developed in the 1970s and 1980s exploited centralised control of the operational business process, embodied within the computer application. The sequencing of activities within a process was typically reflected within the application logic as phases within a transaction. This type of architecture particularly suits processes which have a strong hierarchical control pattern, and is characterised by the system controlling dialogue with the end-user in a prescriptive manner.

Such systems may well be distributed in terms of the placement of functional components such as user interface, data access logic, etc, but the business process logic is essentially centralised and static—embodied within the programming of the application.

The business trends which have lead to distribution of process control have been founded on the increasing autonomy of operation and local empowerment at all levels within the organisation. Equally important have been the trends towards increasing integration of supply and distribution activities into global business processes using electronic information interchange. These have been discussed in various other publications (e.g. Scott Morton, 1991); one important factor arising from them is the movement towards the use of IT as a supportive infrastructure to facilitate flexible and dynamically evolving business processes rather than as a vehicle to impose centralised control.

Recent developments in the area of workflow software and support for distributed Transaction Processing and database operations have enabled progress towards distributed control of process in applications supporting formal rather than informal business processes which are supported by much of the common office groupware.

Document Centred Information Models

Another significant trend over the past decade has been the increasing use of document based information, fuelled by the growth in PCs and office automation software. Continuing developments in software and applications to support efficient handling of office information have greatly increased the role for document centred information. Full text and keyword searching software represented an early step towards processable text; standards to support compound documents and the linking and embedding of information within documents have increased the flexibility of electronically processable office information. Software to extract and convert structured information held in relational databases has allowed a measure of information interchange between office systems and data processing applications. Further developments will take the document concept into the area of dynamic multimedia information.

This movement has made the greatest progress in the area of office systems where the ability to link together desktop information systems has enabled co-operative working via applications such as messaging, shared document libraries, access to common information bulletin boards and so on. Many of the business processes underlying these applications are essentially informal, or unstructured in nature, rather than the formal, often mission critical, processes embodied in the earlier generation of applications founded on Transaction Processing and structured database infrastructure.

THE USER APPLICATION ENVIRONMENT

The available software and development tools to support CSCW applications are now wide ranging. In assessing this variety, we have found it useful to classify CSCW applications, along with the appropriate infrastructure, against two criteria:

- The nature of the business processes being undertaken—ranging from well-defined and formally controlled, enacted by the IT system through to informal and enacted outside the IT system (although possibly supported by IT infrastructure such as mail or database information access)

- The nature of the information associated with the application—ranging from highly structured (typically relational or codasyl database centred) to unstructured , multi-media (typically document centred).

This is illustrated in figure 1, which identifies the principal software infrastructure tools available to support applications in the 4 quadrants.

This simple classification is a useful starting point for discussion and reflects the way in which most co-operative applications have been viewed historically. It is particularly interesting to note that many of the development tools and run-time software environments used to construct CSCW applications are strongly focussed towards one particular quadrant and often provide very limited integration with other application areas.

For example, very few TP systems have convenient interfaces to handle the integration of even simple document based tasks. This is not just a question of defining interfaces to transfer data between the two environments. There are major, almost philosophical, differences in design approach to aspects such as data ownership, security, integrity, backup, etc. The TP environment is very much the province of the MIS function where the data is regarded as a corporate asset, whereas the electronic office environment is much more the (collective) environment of end-users. The industry is only just beginning to address the emerging issues of security, integrity and availability of document-centred information as a corporate asset.

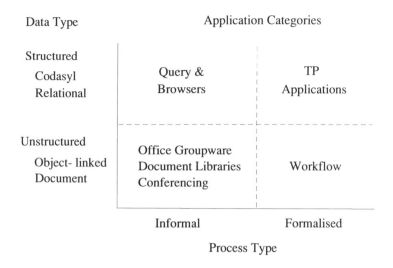

Figure 1   CSCW application environments

Improved integration between applications with such different characteristics and support for applications embracing a mix of structured and unstructured data and varying degrees of process formality is a goal of the target CSCW architecture. The evolution of existing TP applications to incorporate document based functions and adapt to changing business processes are regarded as important, particularly in view of the scale of existing investment in mission critical TP applications.

Formal process/structured data

This has traditionally been the preserve of TP based applications which can exploit the formalised design approach and support for qualities such as security, data integrity, resilience and performance, responsiveness and throughput. The traditional, centrally controlled applications are now beginning to give way to newer distributed systems which can co-operate together to process a particular business transaction, whilst retaining support for high levels of data integrity. Recent standards developed by the ISO (1992) and X/Open Group (1991 et seq.) have paved the way for heterogeneous systems to co-operate in this way, in the context of a top level design which identifies the "rules" by which such co-operative inter-actions are regulated. These rules identify also specific runtime protocols to delineate transaction boundaries and handle the 2-phase commit process to maintain data integrity.

Formal process/unstructured data

Workflow applications, integrated with document-based office automation tools have been generally promoted as the solution to this type of requirement. A wide range of tools are available to support the analysis, definition and modelling of business process; often they may be linked to a specific workflow runtime package. The workflow application handles the creation and control of the process, passing the thread of execution for individual activities to local users via e-mail or a real-time message passing interface. Local application tools, typically PC based, may be used to manipulate information at the individual activity steps under the control of the user responsible for each particular step. Many types of workflow applications are also able to invoke particular application programs directly without user involvement. This allows workflow based applications to be constructed which can support a measure of integration with existing TP systems. Work has recently started within the industry on the definition of an open architecture and interchange standards to support workflow interoperability and applications integration.

Informal process/structured data

Where structured data is used in an informal process environment (for example to support ad hoc management information needs or for informal review and comments) the typical approach has been to extract the data using browsers or query tools, possibly importing the data into local document based systems for further distribution. A variety of tools are now available to support this process, particularly to extract data from relational tables into spreadsheets or word processing documents.

Informal process/unstructured data

This is the focus of a great many office based groupware products, providing supportive services for informal co-operative working—electronic message passing, access to shared document stores, bulletin boards, interactive conferencing, etc. Often there is no application development as such, rather a process of integrating and customising a number of application tools to collectively deliver the information system.

The scope for integrating these different types of applications varies considerably. In developing an overall architecture for CSCW we look for a framework which can encompass all aspects of cooperative working without significant restrictions on application and data integration and which can incorporate as much as possible of today's existing applications and computer infrastructure.

FUNCTIONAL COMPONENTS OF THE ARCHITECTURE

The aim of the long term architecture is to consolidate the key functional components from the existing environments into a cohesive framework which can support the evolution and integration of existing applications and data whilst offering the ability to exploit new technology areas such as client-server and object technology. Three particular areas are considered in the following sections: Workflow, TP and Client-Server/Office

Workflow

We have taken as a starting point current work on a top level model being developed by the recently formed Workflow Management Coalition (1993). This starts with the concept of a business process, which can be expressed as a series of inter-related activities, which may each involve a combination of human and IT resources to satisfy the associated business processing. The model, illustrated in figure 2, provides separation between:

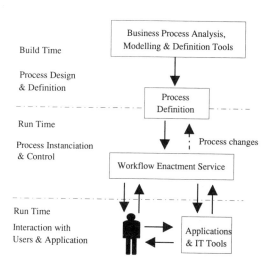

Figure 2   Workflow system characteristics

- the Build-time functions, concerned with analysis and modelling of the business process and defining the activities embodied within it

- the Run-time control functions concerned with managing the processes (creation/deletion, activation/suspension, provision of statistics and metrics, etc) and sequencing the various activities to be handled as part of each process

- the Run-time interactions with human users and IT applications and tools for processing the various activity steps.

Build-time functions

The Build-time functions are those which result in a computerised definition of a business process. That is, a business process is translated from the real world into a formal, computer processable definition by the use of one or more analysis, modelling and system definition techniques. The resulting definition is sometimes called a process model, a process template, process metadata, or a process definition. For purposes of this document, the term "process definition" will be used. Such a process definition normally comprises a number of discrete activity steps, with associated computer and/or human operations and rules governing the progression of the process through the various activity steps. It may be expressed in textual or graphical form or in a formal language notation.

Run-time process control functions

At run-time the process definition is interpreted by software which is responsible for creating and controlling operational instances of the process, scheduling the various activities and interactions within the process, invoking the appropriate human and IT application resources as necessary. The core component is the basic workflow process management control software (or "engine"), responsible for process creation and deletion, control of the activity scheduling within an operational process and interaction with application tools or human resources. This software is often distributed across a number of computer platforms to cope with processes which operate over a wide geographic basis.

Run-time activity interactions

Individual activities within a workflow process are typically concerned with human operations, often realised in conjunction with the use of a particular IT tool (for example, form filling), or with information processing operations requiring a particular application program to operate on some defined information (for example, updating an orders database with a new record). Interaction with the process control software is necessary to transfer control between activities, to ascertain the operational status of processes, to invoke application tools and pass the appropriate data, etc. There are several benefits in having a standardised framework for supporting this type of interaction, including the use of a consistent interface to multiple workflow systems and the ability to develop common application tools to work with different workflow products.

The model separates a user interface component, interacting with the process control engine via a worklist—a set of individual user tasks queued for the attention of the user. The user may process these tasks using local personal application tools, or retrieving and manipulating information from elsewhere in the system, or by manual processes outside the scope of the IT system.

Similarly, an application interface with the process control engine is identified, which may use a (proposed) standardised set of API calls, or may be customised to any particular application type via an "application agent". This is envisaged as a very general interface which could be used for launching a PC or office groupware application, initiating a TP transaction, etc.

System interfaces

The aim of the Workflow Management Coalition is to define a set of industry standard interfaces between the major functional components of the model to facilitate interworking between workflow applications and with standard industry infrastructure. The interfaces as currently proposed are shown in figure 3 and cover:

- interchange of process definition data between build-time tools and the run-time process control engines
- interaction with users via a worklist
- invocation and interfacing to applications
- interoperability between different process engines
- provision of monitoring information and process metrics.

The workflow model does not (yet) define in detail how the various functional components and interfaces may be distributed across the range of existing and emerging infrastructure, although it is possible to envisage

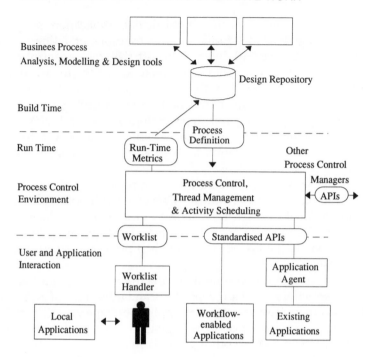

Figure 3   System interfaces within the workflow model

a layer of middleware between the process control function and the applications and user interface to support this distribution. Future work by the Workflow Management Coalition is expected to cover mapping the information and control flows onto different distributed computing models, including electronic mail, remote procedure call and shared document access.

Another significant area which is not specifically addressed by the model is coordination of data access and provision of data integrity semantics for the set of applications or user activities invoked during the life of a business process instance. This contrasts, for example, with the specific design and implementation features provided within the TP environment to provide support for the ACID properties (Atomicity, Consistency, Isolation and Durability).

Both these subjects are further considered in the following sections.

Transaction Processing

There are a number of reasons for considering the specific characteristics of TP within the architectural framework. Firstly, the large installed base of such systems merits specific analysis of the key characteristics of the environment to establish a forward path for the user community. Secondly, the TP environment has historically been optimised towards important functionality requirements for mission critical systems, in particular high levels of data integrity, resilience and security. These requirements will continue and pervade newer forms of CSCW applications. Thirdly, industry work on an overall architecture for TP is reasonably well advanced, covering specifications for application programming interfaces and protocols to support distributed operation between heterogeneous TP systems. This work is the foundation for the TP model used within ICL and shown in figure 4.

There are a number of similarities between the TP model and the Workflow model considered earlier. Both provide facilities for invoking applications in response to a particular (user-driven) event; both provide support for sequencing a process instance through a series of activity steps involving various user interactions as part of the processing of a business operation. If one equates a business process instance to a transaction instance, they appear logically equivalent at the highest level. However, there are several important differences which are considered below.

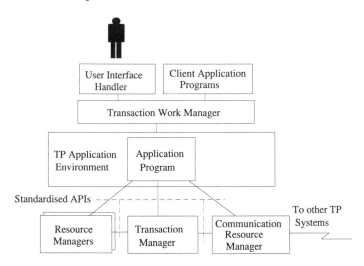

Figure 4   TP architectural model

Transaction coordination

An important aspect of the Transaction Management Architecture is that a distributed transaction can be implemented with parts being executed on several different systems, yet the whole transaction will either succeed or fail as an atomic unit. In the latter case the transaction is rolled back leaving any associated data files in a consistent (and unchanged) state. This coordination is organised by system software within the Transaction Manager component and is supported in the model by specific interactions to delineate transactions, preserve partial results between sub-transaction phases, apply and release data locks, handle 2-phase commitment protocol, etc.

If the data coordination facility is not implemented (i.e. leaving the individual applications to handle coordination without any specific supporting system services), the model is functionally similar to the work-flow model discussed earlier, although the design optimisation of the various system qualities is quite different.

Semantic transactions

When coordination is supported within the distributed TP application model, data locks must be applied to portions of the (distributed) data base(s) during the life of the transaction. As business operations become more distributed and the life of transactions (or processes) extends, this may become an increasing problem with lock life extending to hours or even days. Conventional design seeks to reduce this impact by minimising the amount of data locked, although even this may not be adequate in CSCW applications involving lengthy transactions. An approach based on "Semantic Transactions" has been described by Veijalainen et al (1991), founded on the principle that in many practical situations global consistency of distributed data may be sacrificed for periods as long as inconsistencies resulting from multiple updates can be detected and compensating transactions applied. The compensating transaction may be applied by system software or ultimately by human intervention. A similar approach is often followed in many office groupware applications, where documents or spreadsheets (possibly containing quite significant amounts of information) may be replicated around a distributed system without any global access lock. Version control is often employed to maintain and detect inconsistencies which are then resolved manually. Support for both transaction coordination and semantic transactions are important concepts which we expect to see incorporated into the emerging long term architecture to support CSCW. Ultimately these will need to be incorporated within a business process model, enabling the system design to invoke either (or both) capabilities to support the appropriate needs for integrity across distributed information used within the business process.

Application program environment

Within the TP model specific APIs are defined for the dialogue between an application program and other system components such as the Transaction Manager. These APIs reflect the specific nature of transactional working, including the need to achieve coordination between distributed application components. An application operating within the TP model is constrained to interface to the infrastructure in this way and must have been developed to this approach. It can thus be considered to operate within a specific application program environment optimised for transactional processing.

This is in contrast to the workflow model, which defines a more general approach to the application environment, envisaging a number of alternative infrastructure scenarios for application invocation and launch, making no specific assumptions about application support for transactional semantics. In this scenario the emphasis is on integrating existing applications, including general purpose office tools, via adaptable interfaces within application agents or under user control. One price of this increased generality is, of course, less performance optimisation, when compared to the (more constrained) TP environment.

CASE tool support

The simple TP model described above makes no reference to development tools to support the construction of applications; in practical terms, however, most TP software systems are supported by a specific, well integrated set of development tools to provide functions such as:

- programming of the application logic (usually by means of a 4GL code generator)

- definition of database subschemas and data manipulation operations

- definition of steering parameters to the TP software to control transaction queuing, sequencing, etc

- definition of dialogue with the end user based on screen templates or forms, often optimised to particular data communications protocols.

Work has been undertaken within the industry on architecture to support the integration of development toolsets, for example the Reference Model developed by the ECMA PCTE group (1991) and work undertaken by the industry based Case Communique group. Our long term architecture envisages a flexible environment to integrate development tools, enabling individual tools to analyse and specify business process definitions, activity definitions and application logic, data transformations, user dialogues independently of the target application execution environment

Client-Server and Office Infrastructure

Both Transaction Processing and workflow models have focussed principally on server functionality; this section considers the infrastructure to facilitate client-server interaction.

Client-server working has gained steadily in functionality and popularity as the PC and Local Area Network have become the accepted approach to organising local workgroup or departmental computing. However, a true groupware architecture needs to span a much wider domain than local workgroup, potentially embracing the enterprise and, in some cases, inter-enterprise relationships. When consider this wider distribution of workgroups, it is important to establish a range of global infrastructure which can support a range of CSCW applications in a heterogeneous product environment. The major components of this infrastructure are shown below.

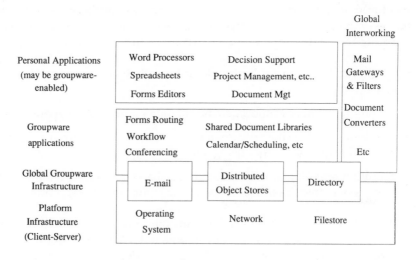

Figure 5   Office groupware infrastructure

Platform infrastructure

The platform and network infrastructure provides the basic distributed computing framework on which the various local client-server applications are built. To date this infrastructure has tended to provide distribution and transparency mechanisms local to the server and to its immediately connected population of clients—typically a logical PC-LAN group. Current products typically provide facilities such as file and printer sharing, procedure calls or message passing to support distributed applications, local e-mail and a measure of workgroup administration. Across an enterprise, there will often be many such local workgroups, possibly using different vendor's products. Wider co-operative working across an enterprise thus requires some common services which can operate globally across the different workgroup communities; we have termed this "global groupware infrastructure". To support this global workgroup environment, three functions in particular have emerged as core building blocks; these are briefly considered below.

Electronic mail

Electronic messaging has already established itself as an important component of the IT infrastructure. One key to its success is the "store and forward" nature of its service, enabling effective communication between users irrespective of time zones and working patterns. Gateways to facsimile and physical delivery services extend its capabilities into wider communications environments. However, its real value goes far beyond simple transfer of messages:

• It can support the interchange of a wide variety of information types as attachments—forms, tables, word processing documents, spreadsheets, image data, audio or video clips, software programs, application defined message formats, directory information, etc. Its only inherent constraint is one of message size; it is relatively expensive (and slow) for small messages of a few characters and limited to a maximum size (nominally 2Mb in X.400) due to storage constraints at intermediate transfer nodes.

• It can support delivery to multiple recipients and distribution lists (normally maintained in a directory), providing an important foundation for information transfer between defined workgroups.

The recent definition by the XAPIA (1993) of industry standard APIs to access electronic mail services has enabled the development of "mail-enabled" applications, to exploit e-mail as a vehicle for distributing information between applications as well as individuals.

Distributed object stores

Whilst electronic mail provides an excellent framework for delivering information individually to users located around an organisation, it does not enable users to share information directly. Electronic mail distributes multiple copies of information; effective sharing depends upon some higher level coordination mechanism to control and propagate changes. Providing remote access to shared multi-media information held as a single copy at a particular physical location within the office network is often impractical due to the physical characteristics of the network and the complexities of configuring the logical access paths.

The solution to this requirement which has emerged is a shared object store which is replicated, in whole or part, across a community of servers, providing each user with a single image of the information, maintained at the local server. The object store may then be used to support groupware applications such as conferencing or shared document libraries. Important characteristics of such products are:

- A directory (which itself may be distributed using replication) is used to maintain global information about users, their access permissions and server locations

- Changes to the object store information are replicated across servers as necessary using e-mail or other communications service.

Data consistency is maintained by periodic synchronisation of changes between servers; in a global network with relatively large and dynamic objects this can impose a significant overhead. Object updating is usually handled via version control; inconsistencies arising from multiple updates of replicated copies are resolved manually or via specially written recovery routines. Where such transitory inconsistencies are unacceptable in a particular application context, it is sometimes possible to use a single global update right (which may be dynamically reassigned amongst users) to lock the object against access by other users; 2-phase commitment is not usually supported by products of this type.

Directory

Electronic mail and distributed object stores both depend upon a global directory mechanism to maintain information about user's names and addresses, server location, access rights, membership of distribution lists, etc. Other groupware applications also may need to maintain further user information such as preferred document or terminal formats, passwords or application privileges, roles within a workflow process, etc. As the scope of co-operative working grows, so does the importance of a directory service to administer and co-ordinate information about users and services. For administrative convenience, the directory needs to be distributed in all except the most simple networks.

Most products today, from Transaction Processing systems down to office applications, maintain their own user information in local directories associated with the individual products, making administration of co-operative working complex, with significant information duplication and often using alternative naming conventions. There are significant benefits in administration and management by locating this information in a general purpose directory accessible to all such applications (and extensible by new applications). This is an important goal of the long term architecture. The X.500 standard (1988, 1992) models the directory in object-oriented terms with attributes grouped into class hierarchies; it also contains provision for the replication of directory information. Open APIs to access directory information have been published by the X/Open Group (1992).

Interchange gateways and converters

The growth in office applications, particularly in the PC area, has led to many different, often incompatible formats and interfaces in areas such as mail interchange, revisable and compound document standards, directory information and office groupware applications. To overcome some of these limitations, specialist vendors have developed e-mail/directory gateways and document conversion products; until common industry standards are more widely supported these gateways will form an important component of the global groupware infrastructure

TOWARDS A LONG TERM ARCHITECTURE

Over time, we see a gradual amalgamation of ideas from the Transaction Processing and workflow environments to form a more cohesive range of middleware, separating the principles of process and activity control (including security and integrity aspects) from the infrastructure to launch applications, organise data access, handle interactions with the users, etc. This infrastructure will operate across the distributed computing community within and between organisations.

This approach will be driven partly by the need to develop applications which are more responsive to the changing business patterns of the organisation (the typical drive towards business process re-engineering and workflow) and partly by the requirements to maintain many of the "mission-critical" engineering qualities traditionally associated with Transaction Processing applications. Evolution of today's base of Transaction Processing applications will take many years; the level of performance associated with process based systems today is not adequate to replace many of the traditional TP applications. However, over time this will become less of an issue as the normal cycle of hardware development continues to improve cost-performance.

Issues of data ownership and better support for data integrity and applications resilience will also have to be faced as data becomes more distributed, more user-centred and increasingly multi-media in nature. We are still in the early stages of document- and object-database technology and may expect to see improvements in the data integrity mechanisms available to office applications. Over time we expect to see more cohesion between structured databases and document databases enabling information to treated as more composite entities; recent developments in the area of object linking and embedding and incorporation of unstructured Binary Large Objects (BLOBs) within relational databases point towards this future direction.

Future "applications" will thus be a mixture of:

- process and activity control logic, defining the business process in terms of the IT and human activities, constraints on scheduling and process resilience and recovery requirements. This will include the ability to declare units of atomicity within the information processing associated with a particular business process, as well as the activity steps and associated information base.

- "traditional" programs developed to process and manipulate information at various stages of the business process where standard infrastructure services or packaged application tools are inappropriate or inadequate (functionality, performance, etc)

- client-server and office infrastructure to provide a range of standard application services—user dialogue support, message transfer between users, access to a range of structured and unstructured data repositories, etc.

These will be "developed" using a set of tools which support a more flexible and dynamic linkage between the business process world and the system development world. Issues such as the difficulty of imposing global co-ordination of process activities (and associated information states) within CSCW applications spanning distributed and increasingly autonomous organisations will have to be faced at the business design level. The IT infrastructure will provide a range of services for invoking different types of application, interacting with users, marshalling information for application or human use, maintaining information integrity at various levels, etc. The business system design will choose the appropriate set of services necessary for the particular business task(s).

A representation of the emerging runtime components and their relationships is shown in figure 6. This draws together functions from the Transaction Processing, workflow and office groupware models into an overall infrastructure framework.

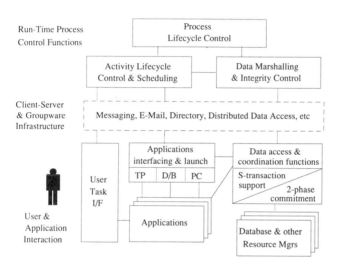

Figure 6   Infrastructure components

We have identified three aspects of the long term architecture for further consideration below:

- merging concepts from TP/Distributed Database and Workflow technologies in the area of process control and linkage with applications

- movement towards a more unified, task oriented, interface with the user, operating at a higher level of abstraction than today's relatively low level user interfaces.

- increasing exploitation of a general purpose directory to maintain the vast repositories of user and service related information.

Process control

Over time, we see a gradual amalgamation of ideas from the TP and workflow environments to form a more cohesive range of middleware, separating the principles of process and activity control (including security and integrity aspects) from the infrastructure to launch applications, establish paths for data access or transfer, handle interactions with the users, etc. This infrastructure will operate across the distributed computing community within and between organisations.

To some extent this will incorporate the best of both worlds:

1. greater adaptability and flexibility for linking in the use of standard applications within the distributed client-server infrastructure, whilst
2. maintaining control over the overall process definition and associated data integrity and recovery requirements.

Functional building blocks will support process control functions, coordination of data integrity across participating applications and interfaces to a range of application linking and launch mechanisms, supporting existing TP applications as well as office and standard groupware applications. Linkage of information to these applications may involve extraction and transfer of data to the application or establishing access connections from the application to data or document stores using the distributed infrastructure.

Components to control information access and preservation of consistency and integrity will offer a range of alternatives—global locking on a single copy of information, 2-phase commitment for distributed data accessed within a recoverable process activity block, or local autonomy of information access with support for compensating transactions to undo inconsistencies. The choice of appropriate mechanism will be part of the overall application design based on the characteristics of the business process.

Unified user interface

The previous section discussed integration from the server perspective; at the desktop, integration will require significant improvements in the nature of the user interface to cope with the wider range of concurrent tasks likely in an increasingly co-operative working environment. A high level task oriented interface has obvious attractions (cf the worklist handler concept within the workflow model) but will take time to become established for the wide variety of existing applications to which interfaces are required. Such an approach can map locally onto a windowing environment to provide visual separation of activities for the user.

We believe that this process can usefully start with the introduction of an integrated "business form" at the desktop, which is the primary source of local user interaction. Currently many different products exploit forms whose scope is local to the individual product—Transaction Processing dialogue design and control, word processing, database enquiry, shared groupware document based applications, etc. This detracts from a common user interface style and also acts as a significant constraint on information integration. The business form is structured in a conventional way using information "fields" which may be text, numeric, graphical, image, multi-media, etc. Information may be entered or captured locally or merged from existing applications or databases using appropriately defined connections, which may use a mix of message passing, procedure calls, electronic mail or even terminal emulation. Over time we would expect this approach to evolve towards a more sophisticated task oriented user interface, operating more closely with the user's own day to day task planning and activity scheduling systems at the desktop.

Directory

As noted previously we see an important role for directory technology within the long term architecture. For many organisations this will be the central component for the administration of large and diffuse workgroups. Functionally the X.500 model is very suitable although there are only a few usage schemas defined; electronic mail is the most advanced. The directory role within the long term architecture goes much further than maintenance of X.400 O/R Names and Addresses and it is questionable how rapidly, if at all, public standards will be defined for this wider range of functions we envisage. It is feasible to establish such a global directory (for example using private schemas within an X.500 framework) and import/export particular usage classes to subordinate directories associated with local groupware or other applications. Several vendors are now offering import/export interfaces to their local product directories to facilitate this style of operation; it is likely to be a long time before all infrastructure components can share dynamic access to a single, integrated directory. Flexibility and extensibility are crucial in the directory arena— management of user and service related information can become a major task in co-operative group working environments. We expect evolution towards an integrated directory to be an important consideration for most large organisations with extensive distributed IT resources and increasing usage of CSCW applications.

CONCLUSIONS

The architectural work done to date has concentrated primarily on structure, identifying the appropriate functional building blocks and points of interface between them, and the need to support particular quality concepts—performance, availability, integrity, potential-for-change, etc. This provides the overall direction for an architecture to support CSCW applications. The next stage is to identify the specific standard(s)—interfaces, protocols, formats, etc appropriate for each of the functional areas. The aim is to select open interfaces to facilitate the widest possible selection and integration of components from different suppliers and to meet the diversity of infrastructure appropriate to different organisations. Mention has been made throughout this paper of various standards activities—formal, informal and de facto market forces—which will shape the detail in various areas. This will not all happen immediately and is very much an evolving picture. Individual organisations will need to develop their own choices appropriate to the existing and intended infrastructure in use. Establishing the appropriate structure is an important first step.

REFERENCES

CCITT. 1988 & 1992. *X.500 series recommendations*, (also published as *ISO/IEC 9594 OSI—The Directory*)

ECMA. 1991. *TR/55 (NIST 500-201) Reference Model for Frameworks of Software Engineering Environments*

ISO/IEC. 1992. *JTC/110026 OSI—Distributed Transaction Processing*

Scott-Morton M. 1991. *The Corporation in the 1990s*, OUP

Veijalainen J et al. 1991. *The S-transaction model, Database Transaction Models for Advanced Applications (ed Elmagarmid)*, Morgan Kaufmann Publishers

The Workflow Coalition. 1993. Workflow Reference Model (Draft)

X.400 API Association. 1993. *Common Mail Calls Specification*

X/Open Group. 1991–94. *Distributed Transaction Processing Reference Model (and related CAE Specifications)*

X/Open Group. 1992. *XDS & XDOM Specifications*

Section II
Use of CSCW

4

"Workflow" Automation of the Desktop

Clive Aldred

ABSTRACT

This paper discusses the integration of CSCW tools with individual (or personal productivity) tools. It draws a clear distinction between two highly contentious terms: Groupware and Workflow, concluding by discussing the implications of rules based Workflow systems on the business and on the individual.

DEFINITION OF TERMS

Groupware tools are best illustrated by the product Lotus Notes. This is a software package that allows a group of people within a department to share common information, for example the names and addresses of suppliers within the purchasing department. It can also allow people to share documents created in personal productivity applications such as word processors. Groupware may be defined as software which allows common access to ideas, files, documents. Groupware can be identified

Computer Support for Co-operative Work. Edited by Kathy Spurr, Paul Layzell,
Leslie Jennison and Neil Richards
© 1994 John Wiley & Sons Ltd

by a facility for use as an information reservoir of individual ideas and information which can be shared to serve the needs of the group. In practice, within products like Lotus Notes, files created by many different software applications can be presented to users. This can be done in two ways:

- icons can be double clicked to launch specific files, running them with the application used to create it

- duplicates of documents can be directly copied from the originating application and then pasted into the relevant Notes database.

This latter technique may be used where the recipients do not have access to the same application used to create the original file. Databases created in this way can have information added or deleted from them provided access privileges have been assigned. When carried out across a network this updating occurs in "real time". However it is possible for people to work on their own local copies of data

Workflow tools on the other hand are best illustrated by Staffware. Staffware is a product that began life as an electronic mail system. Later the addressing mechanism was removed from the software and replaced by a rule set, which allowed the paths of mail messages to be predefined or procedurised. The person who created the first mail message was said to have initiated a *case*. Once mailed, cases change their content and appearance and may even trigger further cases as they communicate their content around a company's computer network.

During the last few years the product has been developed further so that several rules may be applied which control the actions initiated by the final destination of a case. Cases can contain fields which may draw their content from pre-existing databases containing "Legacy Data". Fields can also be used to trigger several other cases or execute external and remote applications. Mathematical controls and Boolean logic can be applied to trigger the cases.

The end result is a communications system which can control the flow of information (work) around a fully integrated and scaleable corporate network. Staffware is a Workflow application which allows tailored business processes to be remodelled in software and appear as electronic cases. Like the Groupware application Lotus Notes, cases may have attached to them other documents, images, or may launch personal productivity applications. Unlike Notes, Workflow products are tools that can be used to mimic the information flow of a business. They can control, and hence automate, the movement of information across the corporate network. In so doing they provide a method of controlling access, auditing, timing, deadlining and triggering the movement of corporate information.

STAGES OF OFFICE AUTOMATION

The majority of people would agree that computers are now an essential business tool. Once mastered, their use has been successfully applied to improve the storage and retrieval of written forms of communications, corporate wide.

Personal Productivity Tools

Word processors allow everyone to type documents. They have replaced typewriters and correction fluid and offered users a variety of new tools such as grammar checkers and spell checkers. These allow users to check their document for errors before printing.

Spreadsheets are the accountant's favourite tool. They allow people not only to calculate current expenditure and measure it against income, but also allow people to experiment by changing values within formule so that they can instantly see the effect of a VAT rate or interest rate change on their cash flow.

Databases provide a mechanism for recording stock items, customer lists, supplier list, prospective clients and so on. Their use has significantly reduced the amount of time take to mail-shot customers, or to isolate regular customers from one-off customers.

More recently electronic mail has allowed computer users to send files and messages from one person to another, or to a group of people. Hence e-mail provides an effective way of communication across multinational corporations. However the problem with this form of communication is that it relies on recipients using their electronic mail as well. It tends to be a passive system that breaks down if recipients do not access their mail on a regular basis.

Team Productivity Tools—Groupware

The definition of a group of people is; "a collection of individuals who are related together by sharing a common purpose or goal". It must then follow that the definition of Groupware is; "software that promotes activity across those individual computer users."

During 1989 it was recognised by Lotus that technology had failed to deliver a mechanism to allow the free exchange of information from one person to another and that the use of electronic mail systems alone restricted the free exchange of information between named groups of people. The amount of information produced within personal productivity tools was growing rapidly. As an example, a group of people may be working on the same project, using conventional personal productivity tools. Whilst information can be sent from one individual to another through electronic mail, problems quickly develop when a member of the team is temporarily out of the office. Access to those important files cannot easily be obtained.

Although the information is not confidential to any other member of the team, only one member of the team can access their contribution to it. No one is able to have a complete picture of the status of a project at any one moment. Using personal productivity tools alone there is no effective way of linking items that relate to the same project together.

Lotus Notes and other Groupware products help people work together in teams. Groupware products provide a shared area for the storage of related information that may be held centrally on a server and accessed over a local area network. Even members of teams who spend much of their time working remotely either at client sites or at home can share their ideas and information with other members of their team through a "Dial-In" "Replication" facility.

In practical terms there are a number of methods that can be used to place information into a Groupware application such as Lotus Notes. Two of the basic methods are file attachment and document placement. File attachment involves little more than the Lotus Notes application allowing external files, together with their attached applications, to be pasted into a Lotus Notes database. Other users can see that a file is attached to a document by the presence of a file icon. When they double click on this icon the related application is launched and the document file is opened.

The second method allows any user of a Windows application to "select all" within their application then copy and paste the document into a Notes database. In this way a full image of the original document is viewable and editable by other members of the group. They in turn may copy and paste the document into their own applications for amendment.

Using Groupware as the Corporate Knowledge Engine

A typical use of a Groupware tool such as Notes is the ability for a group of mobile workers to share common information or documents. Even though the workers may be isolated many hundreds of miles from each other they can each log into a central computer server, share information, and update the databases held locally on their own laptop PCs.

To illustrate this scenario we can imagine a group of ten senior consultants each working for many weeks away from their main office. Each may have many other clients to look after besides the one with which they are presently working. They will also need to keep in contact with their own secretaries at head office and be able to share ideas to help each other solve client problems.

Each consultant would simply need a locally installed copy of Lotus Notes on a laptop computer (figure 1). They would also need a fast modem and access to a hotel telephone line. Once the modem is connected to the PC and telephone line the consultants can replicate the information that they have entered into Notes through their own laptop. The replication process not only updates the office file server with their new information but automatically uploads new information from the office file server whenever it sees that this is not already available to the consultant on the laptop. In this way Groupware products may be used to support a team's effort to solve a common problem, even though the members of the team may be located throughout the world.

Figure 1 illustrates the use of Groupware applications. The diagram shows how Lotus Notes users can dial-in and replicate information held in their Notes databases.

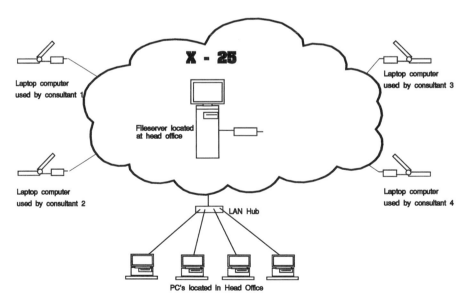

Figure 1

Corporate Productivity Tools—Workflow

It is not only important to improve the personal productivity of individuals within an organisation. Nor is it sufficient to provide teams of people working on the same project with a means of disseminating their ideas to one another. It is essential that all this effort is channelled and controlled in such a manner as to maximise the effort of all those involved in contributing to the survival of their business. Increasing the chance of corporate survival, securing future employment and the financial stability of those involved.

Staffware is a good example of a successful Workflow product. It has emerged from ten years of continual research and development. Staffware is a developer's suite of tools that allows electronic forms to be created. These forms can have attached to them other documents, images, or may launch Groupware or personal productivity applications. Usually the application is installed on a UNIX or Banyan Vines Server and a Windows v3.1 application is installed on the client's personal computer. Once installed it can be set up to access all the resources connected to the network on which the UNIX server resides.

WORKFLOW IN USE

To illustrate how Workflow packages work, this section contains screen captures from Staffware. A single simple HIRING procedure is executed by starting a new case which logs the application form of a potential new job candidate.

Here a new Staffware Case is created called HIRING and the case is given a specific name called a CASE DESCRIPTION (figure 2). Once the case description has been entered the HIRING procedure is started. This triggers the appearance of a blank job application form, into which must be entered details of the candidate. These details may be taken from the original Curriculum Vitae submitted by the applicant and viewable on screen by the click of a button. Figure 3 shows the form when completed with the candidate's details. Only when all the essential fields (outlined in RED) have been completed can the case be mailed off to the next person defined in the procedure. The envelope and letter icon appear at this stage. The form disappears from the screen when this icon is pressed.

Completion of the form may be speeded up by presenting the personnel administrator with selection boxes and pop down menus.

The original Curriculum Vitae would have arrived via the usual postal service and have been scanned into a document image processing package

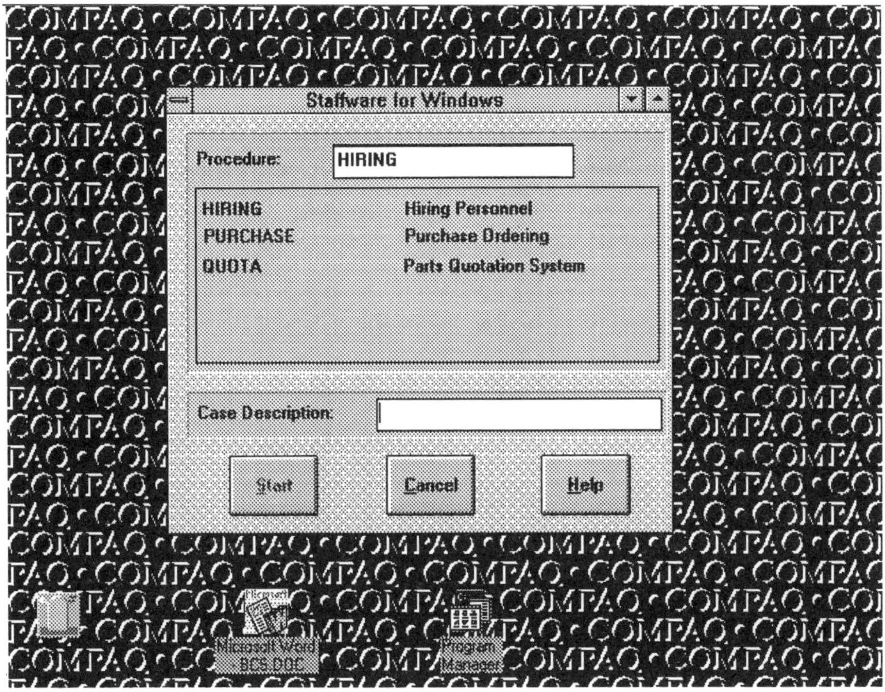

Figure 2

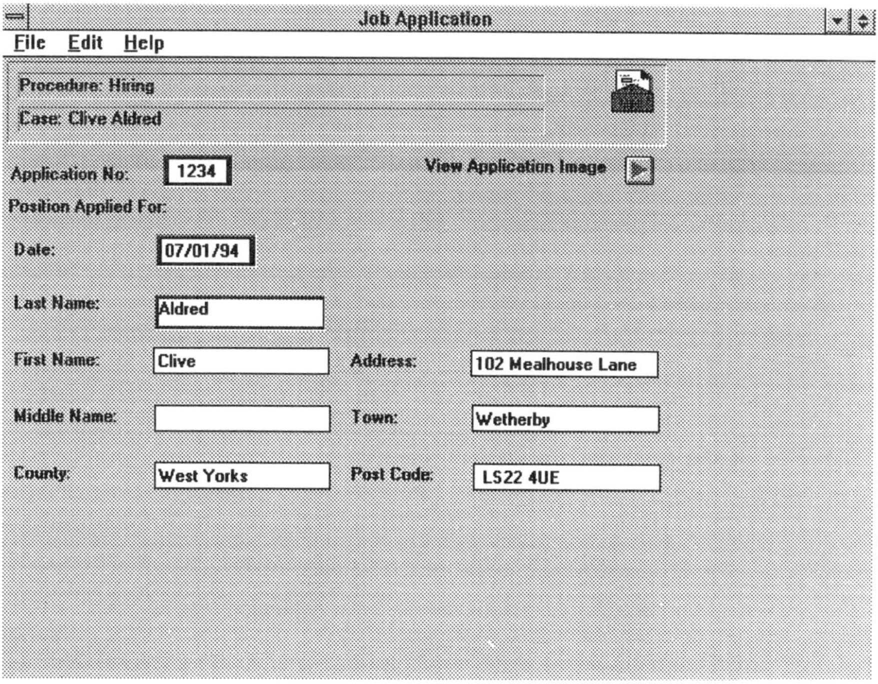

Figure 3

in the internal postroom, where it was indexed accordingly by application number.

Figure 4 demonstrates the use of buttons to launch external applications. Here clicking the "View Application Image" button reveals the original hand written application form, which may have been scanned in at the post room.

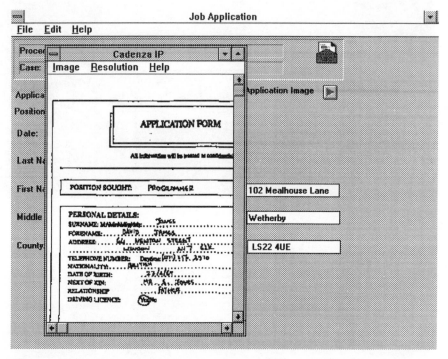

Figure 4

Forms may contain buttons which launch other applications: spreadsheets, word processors, databases etc. Files created in these documents then become attached to the form contents until the form is completed.

When the details required on the form have been entered, the form is mailed to the next person who needs to act on the information. In this example it would be the Personnel Manager, who would take the decision to interview or reject the candidate. The screen in figure 5 illustrates the appearance of the Personnel Manager's screen as he is notified that new work has arrived in the Work queue. This is represented by the minimised Staffware application icon, labelled "Workqueue Jon".

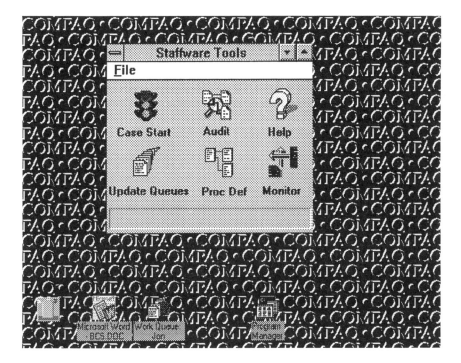

Figure 5

With only one icon available to them staff do not have the option to waste time launching other applications which may detract them from carrying out their work. Users of Staffware simply click on the work queue to select an item of work that must be completed. In our example the Personnel Manager "Jon" clicks on the Workqueue icon to reveal the screen shown in figure 6.

Initially the manager sees a list of work items: double clicking on one of the items in the list opens up that work item. Once open, the work item appears on screen an electronic form. Wherever possible these forms should appear to closely resemble their paper counterparts which they have replaced. In figure 7, notice that Jon sees a completely different form design from that originally filled in by the Personnel Administrator.

Jon has no need to waste valuable time entering data into the system. He simply has to make a decision, to either interview or reject the applicant. He does this by selecting YES or NO from the pop down field. He may also need to check the detail and appearance of the candidate's application form. He can do this by clicking on the button, which will allow the original application form to be viewed. In case he requires further information from

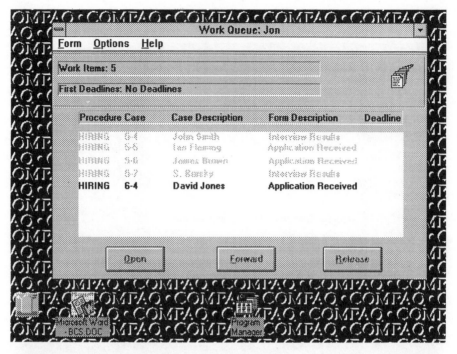

Figure 6

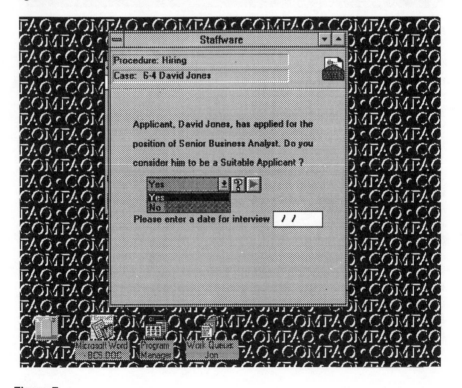

Figure 7

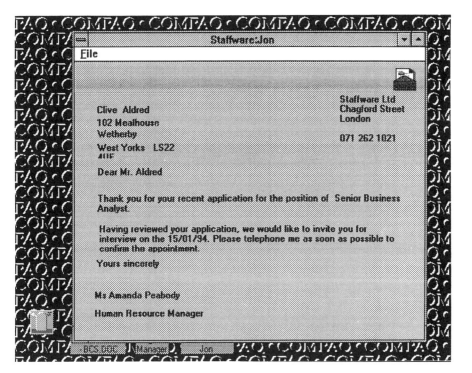

Figure 8

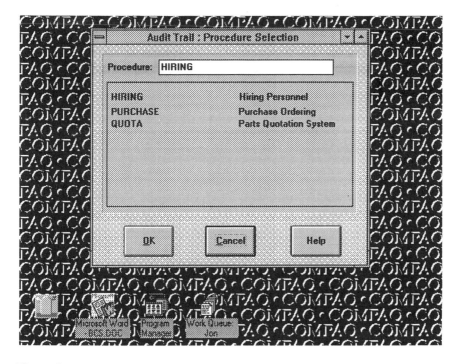

Figure 9

the Administrator the ? button allows him to query the applicant further via a message sent back to the Personnel Administrator.

Again, once the form has been completed with the relevant details the icon in the top right of the active window changes to an envelope icon. Double clicking on this icon closes the window and mails off the message and triggers the automated production of a letter to invite the candidate for interview. Staffware may be configured to print immediately or print all letters in a batch at a specified time. The printing can happen in the post room. Here the printed letters can be stuffed into envelopes and mailed.

In figure 8 the letter is being viewed by the Personnel Manager's secretary for final editing and customisation prior to being printed in the post room.

In the event that the candidate contacts the Personnel Manager to query the progress of his application, the Manager is able to view the Audit Trail which pinpoints the exact stage of progress that the application has reached. Figure 9 illustrates the appearance of the first Audit Trail Screen. This allows audit selection of the specific procedure required.

Double clicking the HIRING procedure reveals a detailed audit trail screen, figure 10. In this screen it is possible to view the activity and work-load of any management team. Here the activities of Ian McSwain's staff is about to be viewed, by a Senior Manager.

Double clicking on the text of his name will provide the detailed information shown in figure 11. Here, the activity of every member of Ian McSwain's staff involved in the HIRING Procedure is visible.

This can be used to provide valuable management information such as how long it has taken to process the application, or identify where blockages are appearing in the movement of cases within the HIRING Procedure.

CONCLUSION

Personal productivity tools (word processors, spreadsheets and databases) empower individuals. Groupware products empower teams of people to work co-operatively.

Workflow tools can be used to completely control these new businesses. It now becomes unnecessary for organisations to locate their staff physically within the same building. A business no longer needs to have a physical presence or to pay for expensive office sites. Control is maintained over remote workers via Workflow tools such as Staffware.

Workflow technology is best applied to the roles of people who are

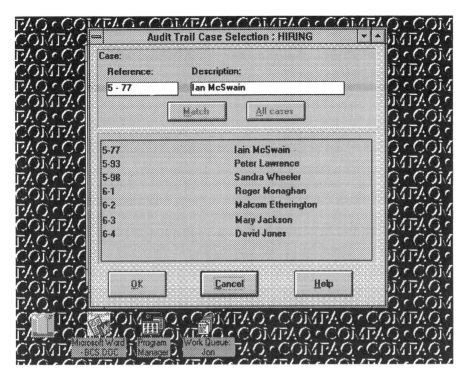

Figure 10

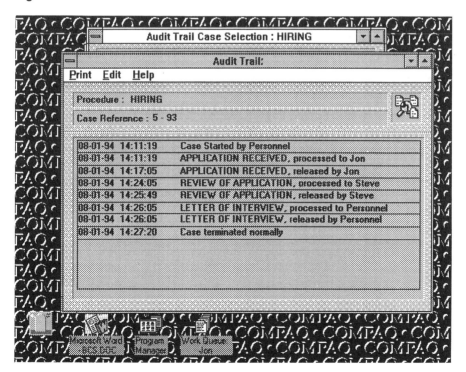

Figure 11

employed to carry out routine, repetitive tasks usually at a low level within organisations. These types of decisions have been categorised by H. A. Simon as programmed decisions. Programmed decisions such as inventory control decisions, purchase order approval and stock control maintenance are ideal for conversion into Workflow procedures. Workflow technology is thus best suited to automate the operational management processes.

Groupware applications are best applied to certain characteristic decisions. These types of decision are far more complex and are characterised by their uniqueness or novelty. They are difficult to predict and the decisions made to reach solutions to such problems are usually unknown. They are high risk problems that cannot be delegated to lower levels within the organisation. Examples of these types of decision are strategic planning, new product launches and so on. Groupware is best applied to help solve strategic management problems.

The two technologies overlap at the tactical management level (middle management) within their application to solve corporate problems. In practical terms this means that a Workflow procedure may trigger a Groupware application and vice versa, so that information is provided to help complete the Workflow procedure. Likewise a Groupware application may be used to trigger a Workflow case that is then delegated to the lower levels of management within the organisation. The two technologies are therefore complementary to each other.

BIBLIOGRAPHY

Belbin, R. M. (1981) **Management Teams**
Grudin, Jonathan (1991) **CSCW Introduction** Communications of the ACM December 1991.
Hastings, C. (1993) **The New Organisation** McGraw-Hill, Inc. New York
Humphries, J. (1992) **How to Manage People at Work** How to Books
Lucey, T. (1991) **Management Information Systems** DP Publications
Pearson, B. (1990) **Common Sense Business Strategy** Mercury
Quigley, J. V. (1993) **Vision—How Leaders Develop It, Share It and Sustain It.** McGraw-Hill, London

5

Groupware in the Making

Alan R. Fuller

ABSTRACT

This paper describes, with examples, the process of business problem definition looking into the underlying needs for information storage and information/data flow, showing how these needs place demands on the infrastructure of any potential groupware solution. The currently installed base of software (not necessarily groupware) is reviewed.

The scope of groupware solutions is investigated from the management perspective. Also the nature of the dialogue in one specific model of realtime conferencing is analysed. The paper shows how end-user needs analysis has had a profound effect on the design of a commercial, realtime groupware product.

Finally, field experiences of using realtime groupware are reviewed.

THE TRANSFER OF INFORMATION IN BUSINESS—A MULTIDIMENSIONAL PROBLEM

All business transactions involve the transfer of information. The transaction could be simple and personal, concerning the purchase of some consumer goods such as a packet of sweets. At the other end of the

Computer Support for Co-operative Work. Edited by Kathy Spurr, Paul Layzell, Leslie Jennison and Neil Richards
© 1994 John Wiley & Sons Ltd

spectrum, the transaction could be complex and financial involving the transfer of currency to bankers of a building consortium responsible for a national road building project involving a dozen subcontractors. Regardless of scale, each stage of a business transaction can be broken down into more elementary steps which rely individually on the transfer of information for their success.

The transaction usually has to take place between people even though there are many instances where computers take on the role of an intermediary. In information transfer there is always a sender and a receiver and the information transfer process becomes meaningless unless the receiver is able to comprehend the information being sent.

Even with computers as intermediaries, people are the ultimate recipients of information and the ease with which they can access information and act upon it is key to the successful transfer of information.

The majority of this paper concentrates on the needs of people making business decisions and how information is most effectively communicated.

To make business decisions people need information in different forms. Some information is best presented in the form of the written word; for example, contractual documents. Only the precision of the written word will suffice in many instances. Other information which is numerically based can be presented in tabular form. Where the numerical precision is important the exact values are essential but in other circumstances where, for example, the trend in a numerical sequence is important, a graphical representation is a far superior means of presentation. An extension to this means of presenting information is a still picture whose detail may range from a freehand sketch through precise engineering drawings to photographs. A further extension of this theme is the moving image. Again, there is a range of media which can utilised to present the information from the cartoon to broadcast quality television.

Much information isn't presented in a hard form such as paper. Indeed, many business transactions are conducted entirely by word of mouth—speech. This brings with it another dimension in information transfer—its two way or duplex nature. In the case of a face to face conversation, the two way nature of a conversation is obvious. Over long distances this is achieved through well known techniques such as the everyday telephone. However, there are more advanced forms of communication such as television. For example, although widely used in the form of video conferencing, two-way television is not as widespread as the telephone. Some of the important factors which affect this will be considered later in this paper.

One should also ask the question "How does the information get manipulated and presented?" The software application is often the key to both the presentation and communication of business information.

A number of generic items of software are used to manipulate information. Examples include: spreadsheets, databases, word processors, desktop publishing systems, computer aided design systems and business presentation systems

Spreadsheets are able to carry out complex calculations showing the numerical impact of variations in the relevant parameters. Databases are used not only to store textual information but they can be used to sort it and produce reports on it. Word processors have historically been used to replace typewriters whilst desktop publishing systems take word processor output and produce typeset material ready for printing. Computer aided design systems replace the chore of the draughtsman's pencil detailing changes to an architect's plans. Business presentation systems are the computer's answer to the preparation and presentation of business graphics.

Software packages in each of these disciplines have evolved over a fairly short time to a point where the technologies in the packages have merged. Databases can take input from spreadsheets. Spreadsheets can present their data in graphical form. Word processing systems can generate output which is comparable with the simple desktop publishing systems, and desktop publishing systems have taken on the role of total integrator combining the power of word processors and graphics packages. Business graphics packages take input from word processing systems and produce camera-ready artwork for slide production or direct presentation on a computer screen. The application areas have merged such that a number of the application areas have become almost indistinguishable.

Additionally, some of the packages have the ability of not only generating information in a very easy to use form but they are also capable of handling some of the information transfer needs. For example, many word processing systems also contain a file transfer function to transfer documents to other systems.

THE NEEDS OF THE BUSINESS—DERIVING THE FEATURES OF AN IDEAL SOLUTION

The preceding paragraphs have outlined business communication and information presentation. This paper now looks at the business needs and how the features of the ideal solution are derived. In analysing the business needs, it is pertinent to look at the needs from a number of different perspectives and a number of examples illustrate this.

(a) If you quickly need to have the correct spelling for a company contract, then asking for the spelling by telephone may well be the most effective way. If the person you are asking doesn't speak the same language as you then the spelling may not be correct because of differences in pronunciation of the same name in different countries. If there is a 12 hour time zone difference between you and the person you are asking then the convenience (or more pertinently, the inconvenience) of the telephone call may be substantial. Regardless, since even minor errors cannot be tolerated, handling the information in written form is probably the closest to the ideal solution.

(b) Consider the situation of a house builder preparing the foundations for a house who finds a water main which was not on the architect's plans. The main supply cannot be diverted but the builder doesn't have the authority to change the plans even though they know what needs to be done. The workforce is at a standstill until the matter can be dealt with both by the architect and planner who give authority to make structural alterations. In this instance, verbal communication rapidly identifies the solution but because of the possible legal consequences, written instructions may be obligatory for the necessary authority to deviate from the approved plans.

(c) Consider a further example of a manufacturer or supplier who has made a sale of goods. The goods are required urgently but the customer is a new customer and credit arrangements have not been established. The terms of the sale are "the goods to be despatched when the currency for the transaction has been cleared by the manufacturer's bank". All the manufacturer needs in order to despatch the goods is this simple confirmation which the bank can provide verbally, in written form or electronically—the ideal is probably in writing.

The above examples serve to show that there are a variety of needs which have to be met. These are summarised in general terms below:

- immediacy—information needs to be transferred in such a manner that there is only a short time span between the sending and receiving of information; it is often most inconvenient to communicate directly when there are wide differences in time zones.

- ease of use—it is often easier to make a telephone call rather than send a letter; it is often easier to send a facsimile rather than send a letter.

- speed—in the example of the house builder, an update to the plan may well be adequate providing it is underwritten by the architect/planner. A complete set of new plans would be ideal but this will take time to prepare and time to provide; speed is of the essence in this example.

- hard copy—in the example of the financial transaction, the transaction is most likely to be accomplished electronically and initial verbal confirmation is adequate. However, it is most likely that written confirmation will be needed later in the transaction. Verbal orders for goods are frequently "subject to written confirmation".

- cost—the cost of transferring information by one means may be much more than by another means.

The question which now arises is "how does one choose between the various options?"

ATTRIBUTES OF THE AVAILABLE TECHNOLOGY

The technology available to meet the business presentation and information transfer needs as illustrated by the above examples can be looked upon in the following way.

Firstly, there is the software application perspective.

At any one point in time, one, or a number of specific item(s) of application software will meet the information needs of a business. As time moves on, application software is further developed and consequently software will evolve. It is a matter for the company producing the software to ensure that it meets the needs of its chosen market. Both the needs of the market develop and the needs of a business may change. Consequently, an item of software which met the needs of a business at one point in time may or may not meet the needs of that same business at a point in time in the future.

This has led to the development of a number of specific software packages (in the generic application areas outlined above) which can be considered to meet the market needs of businesses today. This is illustrated in table 1.

(It is important to note that the author is not making any claim that any one of these packages is superior to any other—the market and the consumer decides this—and any package may be an ideal match to the needs of one customer whereas another may be the ideal match to the needs of another customer.)

A selection of technology for the business solution is made by matching the attributes of each technology against the business need.

Table 1   Examples of generic software applications

Spreadsheets	Lotus 1,2,3; Microsoft Excel
Databases	dBase; Paradox
Word Processors	Microsoft Word; WordPerfect
Desktop Publishing	Aldus Pagemaker; Ventura
CAD Systems	AutoCad; TurboCAD
Business Graphics	Harvard Graphics; Microsoft Power Point

Secondly, there is the information transfer perspective.

It has already been pointed out that a number of application packages have within them an element which is capable of carrying out some of the information transfer needs of a business. However, to give a better illustration of the diversity of the attributes of information transfer technology, three specific generic technologies will be reviewed. These are: (a) Bulk File Transfer, (b) Electronic Mail and (c) Facsimile.

The main attributes of these three technologies is as follows:

(a) Bulk File Transfer
    Large files transferred with no human interaction. File transfer tends to be computer to computer. Restart mechanisms are complex (i.e. restart part way through a file) because of large file sizes. Transfer tends to be point to point

(b) Electronic mail
    Files tend to be small to moderate in size. The transfer of information is person to person. Restart mechanisms are simple (i.e. resend the whole message in the event of failure). Transfer can be point to multipoint

(c) Facsimile
    Documents rather than files are sent. The transfer of documents is machine to machine and usually generate a hardcopy of the output. The size of documents is typically very small. Restart mechanisms are simple (i.e. resend the pages of a document which the receiver didn't correctly receive). The transfer tends to be point to point.

By reviewing the attributes of these three technologies, which are fairly simple to understand, it can readily be seen that each technology will have a different match to a business's need.

In much the same way as for software applications, both the needs of the market for information transfer develop and the needs of a business may change. Consequently, an item of technology which met the needs of a business at one point in time may or may not meet the needs of that same business at a future point in time.

Cost is frequently a very important factor in this decision making process.

SOLUTION DIVERSITY—REAL WORLD SOLUTIONS

There is an additional factor which increases the diversity of business solutions. This is in company mergers and takeovers. Even though one company may have implemented a policy of standardisation on a specific set of software packages to meet its business needs, diversity arises when that company merges with another company. When a merger occurs, some degree of rationalisation tends to takes place. The consequences of simply discarding one set of software applications in favour of another has to be taken very seriously. In the 1980's it is rumoured that a number of discussions regarding the merger of some prominent UK building societies broke down because it was felt that merging the IT infrastructures would be too costly to compensate for the benefits of the merger.

The result is a "plethora of diversity".

In simple words, a very wide range of excellent software exists which meets the needs of many business. Differences exist because of natural diversity. It is rather like Darwin's Origin of the Species applied to computer software—may the best one win!

This is the real world we live in. This is the world groupware has to contend with.

GROUPWARE—WHAT IS IT?

It could be argued that groupware as one specific item of software doesn't exist. Indeed, there is no simple, well-accepted definition of groupware. However, for the analysis in this paper, a suitable description of groupware is: "a set of something (frequently software applications) which have either been designed to work closely together or which can be coerced to do so". Since the component parts (software applications) in their own right carry out a set of functions for a business, getting them to work together means a smoother business operation. The benefits from using one application can be added to the benefits of using other applications and, additionally, there is the less tangible benefit of "working together".

This "working together" can be achieved in a number of ways. Sharing information between applications can be achieved by the use of a common filestore or a common file format. One application can read another application's files. Alternatively, quite separate mechanisms such as electronic mail, bulletin boards or server computer systems can be used to achieve the information interchange.

Taking this approach further, radically new applications have been designed which encompass all of these concepts in their design from a unified form-filling or menu system through to an integrated database management system, all of which is unified with an integrated electronic mail system.

Everyone of these solutions has a rightful place in business. One of the important question for any business is simply: "Can I afford to embark on a course of using new groupware applications?"

By using the business analysis process described in preceding paragraphs, the answer to this question for any specific business/company can be determined. Some of the factors involved can be characterised by considering two ends of a spectrum:

(a) The business is small, emerging and new. There are no established processes and therefore new standards can be set from the outset. Groupware solutions are probably a good solution. The need to invest in groupware may not be clear cut however since the number of people involved may be quite small and informal interactions are easier to manage.

(b) The business is large, complex and established. There have been attempts to standardise in the past but this has forced the business to be slow and unresponsive. There is already a huge investment in software systems, but more importantly in the training of the staff to use the systems. Any changes have to be implemented in a seamless fashion.

The solution for any real business is probably somewhere in between. But regardless, any investment a business makes has a high value—this is not necessarily just in the cost of the software systems used to meet the business needs. The value is often not well understood until the system fails in some way and then the value can be tangible—the business stops. This occurs if someone leaves a company after acquiring irreplaceable expertise. The company's wheels are well oiled. The time taken to train staff in the use of a company's systems is often taken for granted as part of their total training. On-the-job training is frequently not costed.

Consequently, there is a lot of resistance to using new systems unless the benefits far outweigh the potential problems. What we implement today we have to live with for many years.

GROUPWARE—A MANAGEMENT PERSPECTIVE

The preceding section has reviewed groupware from the perspective of the evolution of groupware applications. This section reviews groupware from a management perspective and from the degree of interactivity between the groupware players.

The scope of this discussion is shown in table 2.

Table 2   Management/interactivity groupware relationship

MANAGEMENT LEVEL	INTERACTIVITY		
	LOW	MEDIUM	HIGH
TOP	Executive Information Systems	Shared Insight	Group Decision Support
	Project/ Status	Discussion Conference	Workflow Monitoring
MIDDLE	Reports	Scheduling	Collaborative Writing
	Database Access	Resource Sharing	Meetings Phone Calls
OPERATIONAL		Messaging/ Mail	Time Critical Applications

This table summarises extensive research (Holtham, 1993) which shows that the type of interactions between people and systems in companies is related to the level of management within the company. The interactivity (low to high) is really a measure of the frequency with which people involved in the process need to communicate with each other. *Low* tends to imply offline processes; *High* tends to imply realtime process.

For the senior executives, information systems have been developed to present the detailed analysis of a company's financial and market position. This data can often be viewed in several dimensions so that the cause and effect nature of parameters can be assessed. The information is usually produced over a long time scale (perhaps months). Input to these systems is undoubtedly some from middle management project status reports and ad hoc access to database information.

In determining company policy, senior executives use systems which aid in gaining shared insight into the company's problems today and in the future so that strategies to solve the problems can be set out. Middle management use similar software tools to solve day to day problems— this is in the realms of discussion conferencing which is used to solve today's problems with today's scheduling systems. At an operational level, electronic mail and messaging systems are used to communicate the vital life blood information around a company.

Group Decision Support systems aid executives to execute company policy. The equivalent systems for middle management include workflow monitoring systems whilst working with colleagues on set pieces of work such as reports or proposals, collaborative writing tools are employed. At the operational level, meetings and phone calls are the order of the day. Order processing systems and warehousing systems are the equiv- alent software applications which meet the high interactivity needs of operational management.

Table 2 is not meant to be exhaustive nor exclusive but merely representative. For example, middle management use of executive information systems is not precluded and top management still make phonecalls!

What the table serves to illustrate is that just as there is a large scope for non-groupware applications, there is an equally large scope for group- ware applications. More importantly in the context of this paper, the matrix allows focus. The remainder of this paper focuses of the realtime needs for interaction between the various levels of management. This is shaded in the matrix.

REALTIME GROUPWARE—WHAT THE USER WANTS TO DO

The analysis of users' needs can be a complex task, particularly in a distributed information processing environment. However, some important insight into these needs can be obtained by inspecting the events which occur when one person asks a colleague for some advice, perhaps regarding the best approach to preparing a paper on groupware! A fictitious dialogue is used as an illustrative example.

Almost by definition, if one needs to interact with a colleague, this invariably requires some information flow from one person to another. Frequently, some of this information is held on a personal computer. Alternatively, a personal computer is used to access the information or present it. This assumption is made throughout the following paragraphs.

In this example of an interaction, the first phase involves some degree of **explanation**. This requires that the author of the paper explains to a colleague that he is writing a paper and he is seeking ideas. If the colleague is not close at hand then this discussion more than likely takes place over a telephone. If the author has some written material supporting the request then this too may be passed on to the colleague. At this early stage in the dialogue, the information flow is mainly one way from the initiator of the conversation to the recipient.

Depending on the nature of the paper, the author may already have a good idea about what sort of material to present. However, to fully understand what ideas may be appropriate, the colleague typically asks a number of questions—an interaction takes place and they enter the **discussion** phase. A real dialogue takes place when additional information is both sought and provided.

Many options may arise. Different approaches may emerge. Different styles may be appropriate. Soon the dialogue enters the third phase— the **evaluation** phase. As part of this process further discussion takes place regarding the criteria to be used in assessing the various options. The various options have to be agreed upon and some process has to be outlined to work out which options are relevant; which options are important; which options are to be discarded; and which options require further information before evaluation can take place.

Once the criteria have been discussed and agreed the process of determining the course of action takes place. This is the process of **decision making**. All the information which has passed between the two colleagues is now brought to bear on the problem. The criteria have been discussed and the process of applying the criteria takes place and the result is an outline of a paper on—groupware, for example!

A very important point to bear in mind is that once the decision making process is complete, the next stage is to **record** decisions.

Naturally, in the real world environment, these phases are only part of a larger set of phases involved in the preparation of a paper as in this example. Some preliminary phases such as a proposal to jointly work on such a paper might take place. Also, once the decision is made about the outline of the paper then further phases must exist to ensure that the process does not just stop—the paper has to be produced by some deadline and by some person—execution of the follow-on stages is necessary. However, it is pertinent to note that in this example, because the two colleagues are taking part in a discussion, the interaction is realtime. The process could have taken place over an electronic mail network but direct speech contact plays a vital role in transacting business today. Further, the surrounding phases of proposals and execution can take place without the need for direct realtime interaction. Indeed, they are probably best done not in realtime.

Further, it is pertinent to note that although the interaction described in the example involved only two people, the same paradigm can be extended to a number of colleagues working on the same task. Each and every stage then takes on an increasing degree of importance. The explanations have to be more thorough because there may be differing degrees of understanding. The discussions may need to be more formal because of the greater number of people involved. The evaluation process may be more protracted because of the diversity of views about what is important. Similarly, the decision making process may be protracted unless a good measure of agreement is obtained on the criteria to be employed in the decision making process.

Finally, the recording of the decision is probably all the more important if, as part of the decision making process, the work is to be shared amongst the participants. It is vital that everyone knows who is doing what and what is expected of them.

The paradigm is clearly not limited to the set of tasks described using the illustrative example. Almost any business task follows the stages outlined above.

From this analysis of the realtime needs of user interaction, the main processes involved are summarised in table 3.

Table 3   Main processes involved in realtime groupware interactions

Explanation
Discussion
Evaluation
Decision Making
Recording Results

The next section describes how the underlying user needs for realtime, computer-support for co-operative work can be met.

MEETING THE REALTIME USER NEEDS OF COMPUTER SUPPORT FOR CO-OPERATIVE WORK

When colleagues work together and have a need to discuss their work it is useful to consider that their cooperation (for the sake of clarity of description) follows the paradigm of a meeting.[1] Meetings can take place

---

[1] This is only one of a number of possible models of realtime conferencing; multiple simultaneous input during brainstorming is another.

with two or more people and one of these people usually takes on the role of a leader—the **chairperson**—whilst the others in the meeting take on the role of **participants**.

As the discussion in the paper evolves, the requirements which emerge will be *highlighted*.

The assumption made in the opening paragraph of the previous section was that the material being discussed is often held on a personal computer as much business information is today. Earlier sections of this paper have illustrated that the information being discussed is most likely to be available in a wide variety of forms because of the diversity of the software on personal computers. If the information is being discussed at all then some form of voice link must exist between the participants. Since the information exists in one personal computer, the simplest way for a colleague to see the same information is let the colleague see your personal computer screen. In other words, *"Whatever You See Is What I See* (WYSIWIS)". Rather than describing what is on your PC screen, your colleagues can see for themselves—the picture really is worth a thousand words. This requires that the PCs of all the participants in the meeting are linked in some way—*a network of PCs*.

Since the PC application showing the information on one PC (let us call it the chairperson's PC) is likely to be different from the PC application on your colleagues PC and yet your colleague ideally needs to see the same information, the effect is as though all participants have the same PC application—*live application sharing*. However, the cost of putting the same application suite on all PCs can be prohibitive and therefore an alternative means of live application sharing is desirable.

All modern PC applications are controlled using a mouse or keyboard and since all the participants in the meeting ideally have virtual access to the single application they need to *share the keyboard and mouse* of the chairperson who owns the application.

When explaining, discussing and evaluating options, the ability to point to specific items of information on the computer screen and to make annotations or sketches superimposed on the information provided as part of the meeting, just as one does on a paper-based *flipchart*, is essential to clarity of expression and aids the progress of discussion. Similarly, a clean flipchart or *whiteboard* is just as important in computer-based meetings as in real meetings.

Invariably messages are passed around meetings. Sometimes they are formally requested to canvas a view; at other times they occur secretly and informally between colleagues. *Messaging* is one way of determining if there is consensus.

As the meeting progresses, particularly when trying to determine what options are available, it is usual to put the various options on flipcharts around the meeting room for all to see. An electronic *conference* clipboard is a useful substitute in a computer-based meeting.

The main user requirements developed through the preceding discussion are repeated in table 4. Meeting these end user needs were the major design aims in the development of the Fujitsu DeskTop Conferencing product.

Table 4 Design aims

USER REQUIREMENTS	PHASES of DIALOGUE				
	Explain	Discuss	Evaluate	Decide	Record
WYSIWIS + voice	√	√	√	√	√
Live Application Sharing		√	√	√	√
Keyboard/Mouse Sharing				√	√
Flipchart Pens and Pointers	√	√	√	√	√
Flipchart Whiteboard		√	√		
Messaging/Chat				√	√
Conference Clipboard			√		√

Legend: √ means that the feature is required to support that specific phase of the dialogue.

There are a number of needs which have to be met which are orthogonal to the above discussion but clearly equally important. The meeting paradigm for the above discussion was used since it is a familiar concept. There are other important aspects of meetings which also need to be mirrored in computer-based meetings. One of the many worthy of note here is the role of the people in the meeting.

It has already been suggested that one person in the meeting (either formally or in an ad hoc manner) takes on the role of the chairperson whilst the remainder of the people in the meeting take on the role of participants. Throughout the progress of a meeting the person in charge of the meeting can change as the agenda is progressed. This is manifest in the *rotation of the chairperson* to one of the other participants.

The meeting as a whole can also take a different forms to some degree depending on the number of participants. If there are only two people in the meeting the meeting can be quite *informal*. When the number of people in the meeting increases there is a need for a greater degree of control over the progress of the meeting—the meeting becomes more *formal*.

FUJITSU'S DESKTOP CONFERENCING—TURNING AN APPLICATION INTO REALTIME GROUPWARE

Formal and informal sections occur within a meeting so there isn't a rigid demarcation as to when a meeting is formal and when a meeting is informal. The important aspect is really how control is exercised over any specific part of a meeting and that is how Fujitsu's DeskTop Conferencing handles this aspect—the control discipline can be changed.

When PCs are connected to a network they can become linked and the DeskTop Conferencing application transfers information amongst them. Up to 8 PCs can take part in a meeting which is called a conference. Almost 70% of the market in industrialised countries uses Novell Netware as the networking protocol and Fujitsu chose this for its first implementation. The vast majority of PCs in the business world are IBM compatible and run the Microsoft Windows 3 operating system and Fujitsu chose this as the platform for its DeskTop Conferencing application. The configuration is shown schematically in figure 1.

Each person involved in the conference has a telephone—it is the one already on their desk they've been using for years but now with the PC it becomes a multimedia device.

Whoever starts the conference takes on the role of the chairperson—they can say whether the meeting is to be formal or informal. It does not matter if they change their mind because changes can take effect once the conference has started. The fact that a conference exists is broadcast on the network—this allows others to "see" it and join when the chairperson rings them up and says "Help!" or "I've got the figures and we need to do more work on them". Other people who join the conference become participants and, just as in a normal meeting, they see and hear everything that's going on.

Anything that the chairperson gets on his PC screen is sent to other participants in the meeting—everyone sees his screen. The applications he is using can be very sophisticated and quite unique but it does not matter since everyone can see the output from them. What is more, as the chairperson switches from one application to another the participants follow his every move.

One of the participants knows much more about one of the applications than the chairperson does so he asks if he can take remote control. The chairman agrees (it was set up as a formal conference) and the participant enters data on the chairperson's PC without the chairperson doing anything. Full keyboard and mouse control is provided.

Another of the participants cannot understand exactly what is going on so the chairperson turns the flipchart on. This is like placing a sheet of

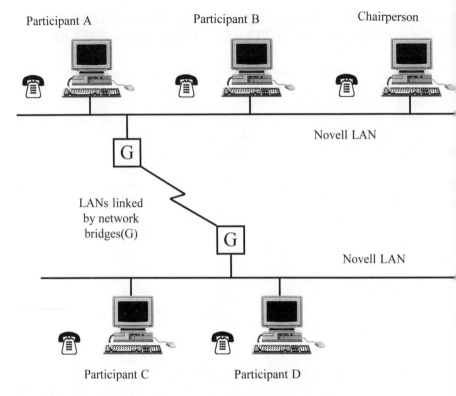

Figure 1   Personal computers in a conference on a LAN

acetate over everyone's PC screen. Everyone has a lightpen and the chairperson rings the data that has been entered by one of the participants. It does not show up very well in blue so a green pen trace is selected and now everything is clear—all the participants can now fully understand what is happening.

As the meeting progresses, a blank flipchart is brought up so that all the participants can bring their ideas to the meeting. These freehand drawings are saved for later use both as an aide memoir-as to what each person contributed and also to record what was agreed.

One of the participants has to leave the conference early but does not want to interrupt the flow of the conference so he sends a message to the chairperson.

This gives you a feel for the Fujitsu DeskTop Conferencing product. Since the product runs independently of the user application and runs seamlessly as a networking application it can conference any standard business application running under Microsoft Windows.

From the descriptions given it is probably clear that there can be substantial benefits in using computer-based conferencing but despite the benefits will computer-based conferencing be used to the full?

IS GROUPWARE THE BEST ANSWER?

Surveys show that between 30% and 40% of all PCs are networked and therefore the network infrastructure is generally available to support some form of groupware. It has been illustrated that there is a vast amount of computer software in businesses which is doing a satisfactory job. There is no need to change it but there is a need for it to be used more effectively. DeskTop Conferencing could be used to turn all existing applications into realtime groupware. It copes with the plethora of diversity which exists today and is likely to exist for the foreseeable future. People could become more proficient in using the software they have merely by asking advice when they need it. The overheads of getting this advice have historically been large since it has meant either sending someone on a training course or getting the company expert to show the inexperienced person how to go about some task. Company experts are usually thin on the ground; so getting any time with them is not so easy. With DeskTop Conferencing, the company expert is only a phone call away and rather than just telling you how to go about a task you can be given a tutorial online in real time. All of this can take place without either of you leaving your seat.

Large travel costs are replaced by much more manageable telephone calls. Stressful travel becomes a thing of the past so realtime groupware is the answer to everyone's dreams.

Groupware undoubtedly has a large appeal and without question there are application areas where groupware solutions are the ideal way forward. However, there are a number of areas where other important factors need to be taken into account.

CONCLUSIONS

Without making any judgement, the author would suggest the following points are worthy of further discussion:

- Many business applications are doing the job they were designed for and they meet the business needs of today save that every business wants to get more out of its workforce. There is a choice of (i) upgrading to a groupware version of an application or (ii) making the existing application work in a groupware environment by adding a product like DeskTop Conferencing at a fraction of the price.

- Groupware products are emerging on to a market which is immature. Some require a radical rethink of a company's business processes and how they are implemented. Can a business afford this? Can a business afford not to implement groupware?

- Collaborative working in the research arena has been with us for some time. The goal is often shared knowledge or insight. The process of producing a contract can be lengthy. It often starts with the first written draft from one lawyer and a set of written comments coming from a second lawyer. Then a series of iterations until there is total agreement. Can the legal profession afford not to implement groupware?

- Travel takes time. Time costs money. DeskTop Conferencing saves travel, and thereby saves time. If groupware gets implemented travel gets stopped. Who gets prevented from travelling?

- To some people video conferencing is groupware and vice versa. When you travel to a meeting you see people. You can see them with video conferencing and you cut out the expensive travel. If you have the option of looking at the person you are talking to or looking at the information you are discussing with them which option would you prefer?

Fujitsu has also found that there are many other factors which are important in the takeup of groupware solutions.

For example, the performance of groupware solutions can be an important factor. Fujitsu has found that unless the transmission times for screen transfers are comparable with the user's normal expectation of response times, the user becomes frustrated.

Further, even though the user is often very skilled in the use of certain PC applications, the same user is not prepared to become as skilful in using a groupware application. This led Fujitsu to make substantial developments in making DeskTop Conferencing really easy to use.

Finally, the range of the perceived value of groupware is exceedingly wide. One of the factors which gives groupware the highest value is when it is used over large geographic distances.

REFERENCE

Holtham, C. 1993. Unpublished material. City University Business School.

6

Small CSCW System Design

Dan Diaper

ABSTRACT

What is CSCW design and what is it so different from, if anything? A little personnel modelling of Computer Science, Software Engineering and IT professionals would expect to find at least two polar positions. At one extreme there must be those who would claim that designing a CSCW system is like designing any other software system. The other position, while rather more complex, would support a view that CSCW is different and the reasons would probably hinge on the demands of CSCW systems to support group working. This paper explores an alternative for designing some post-classic generation of CSCW systems.

DOCUMENT ANNOTATION

While the primary purpose of this paper is to address some aspects of CSCW design, it is necessary to choose a context, and for any detailed consideration of the design process what is required is a modest application domain that can be used to illustrate design aspects that may be more significant, and often less clear, in larger applications.

The area of 'Document Annotation' meets such requirements. There is a major application area within CSCW that is usually called 'Collaborative Writing' (Sharples, 1993). This application area can be further divided into

Computer Support for Co-operative Work. Edited by Kathy Spurr, Paul Layzell,
Leslie Jennison and Neil Richards
© 1994 John Wiley & Sons Ltd

'Collaborative Authoring' and 'Collaborative Editing'. Such a division is justified on the considerable difference in goals, styles, ways of working, etc. between writing (which involves the generation of new material), from editing (which is to do with the revision of material). The area of collaborative editing is itself complex, an example of which is the application domain of this paper, document annotation.

Within the field of collaborative writing, a document is generally very broadly defined, for example, as something that contains information that can be perceived by a person. Such a definition allows graphic or dynamic (e.g. video) objects, not restricted to paper, to be called documents. In contrast, a computer file, for example, is not itself a document because a person cannot directly apprehend the information it contains.

Taking the dictionary[2] definition of 'annotate' to mean 'furnish with notes', an annotation can be a note in any form or format. With a paper document annotations may range from a handwritten comment in the margin to a separate document which may be larger than its source.

Considering just primarily textual, paper documents the task of somehow annotating them is one that virtually all readers will be familiar with. For example, many organisations provide standard forms for document annotation as part of their QA and other business procedures. Such forms tend to have column headings concerning the location and the severity or importance of each annotation. Much document annotation in the commercial and academic worlds is less formal, of course, but the time, and hence cost, spent on this activity is very large.

While there are many reasons why people have to annotate paper documents, the example of refereeing submissions to an international journal is probably sufficient for this chapter's purposes. The germane issues of CSCW design discussed later are similar in many other applications within collaborative writing and CSCW in general.

Journal Submission Refereeing

In a year a typical, successful international journal will process some hundreds of reports from referees[3]. In many instances at least part of some of these reports need to be sent to authors when they are requested to revise their submission. There is therefore a frequent requirement that referees' reports be sufficiently 'formal' that they can be sent to authors

---

[2] Concise Oxford English Dictionary, 7th. Ed.

[3] e.g. the journal *Interacting with Computers* (Butterworth-Heinemann) processed about 150 referees' reports in 1993.

relatively easily. Given the size of the journals market there must be many thousands of people in the U.K. refereeing just journal papers every year.

In 1994 the most common means of transmitting documents, and referee's reports, is physical mail. Once submitted, a paper may frequently be forwarded to half a dozen people. International postal costs are quite high and not all countries perform with equal dispatch.

Fax is an entirely inappropriate alternative to physical post on the grounds that for large documents fax is too slow, too expensive, unreliable and also frequently of poor quality.

Given that in many technical areas virtually everyone in the field has access to electronic mail, then e-mail appears to be an attractive alternative to international postal services. Apart from its cost, speed and ease of transmission advantages, the attraction of e-mail is further enhanced because documents are transmitted to a person's own computer. Thus the document to be annotated (the submitted paper) is available on the same system that will be used to annotate the document (the referee's report). The global diversity and sophistication of document processing environments is such that documents must be transmitted as plain ASCII, although it seems to be current received wisdom that users are generally prepared to cope with ASCII documents. Furthermore, it is likely that document layout will be better if authors assume that their submission will be transmitted as an ASCII file, rather than starting with a marked-up document that has then had its format controllers removed.

At first it appears that the major problem for a scientific journal moving to the electronic submission and processing of papers is that of transmitting graphical information. Certainly the wide-bandwidth technology needed for photographic image processing is not yet sufficiently common internationally. Such images are relatively rare in most journals, not least because photographs are discouraged by publishers, as opposed to editors, on cost grounds.

Document Annotation on Paper

Diaper (1989) took video recordings of people annotating scientific documents destined for submission to journals or conferences. The purpose behind this paper was to illustrate the task analysis method TAKD (e.g. Diaper, 1989; Diaper and Johnson, 1989; Diaper, 1990) and the application domain was incidental then, but is central to this paper. While only a pilot study and recognising that further data collection would be highly desirable, the use of the TAKD method provides a very detailed description of how the people in the study annotated paper documents.

Before doing a task analysis it is critical to establish the *purpose* (the reason, rationale, goal, etc.) for the analysis. This is so because the observation, analysis and understanding of task performance is dependent on the subjective perspective of the analyst. The Diaper (1989) study had the purpose of analysing the annotation tasks so as to provide a requirements description for the design of a hypertext document annotation system. The general system idea was that an annotator could mark a section of a document as a hypertext node (a hot spot) and then create an annotation that would appear in a window when the hot spot was subsequently selected. The outcome of the analysis suggested that this apparently plausible idea would be much more complicated to design and implement than it at first appeared.

The study looked at three people, each annotating a document. There were 97 observed examples of annotation behaviour and the lowest level of the analysis indicated that there were 75 different types of annotation behaviour. These 75 types of behaviour could be categorised, using TAKD's 'generification' process, into four major classes that are relevant to the proposed hypertext system's design. These four major classes are described below:

Class 1: **Normal Annotations**
This class represented only 62% of the 97 annotation behaviours observed. They involved what the researchers had anticipated in that a small part of the document was marked, a comment written and related to the marked section.

These were the type of annotations that the proposed hypertext system was intended to support. One of the reasons this work did not go further was because of the remaining 38% of the observed behaviours.

Class 2 & 3: **General Annotations**
Nearly a quarter (23%) of the observed behaviours involved comments that were not specific to one particular part of the document. Some of these behaviours (13%) related the comment to at least one part of the document for illustrative purposes while 10% were comments that were so general they were not related to any specific part of the document.

One of our reluctances to continue with this work was that any system that was to do more than just list general comments effectively separate from the document would need very sophisticated many-to-one and many-to-many hypertext links structures, particularly in the case of meta-annotation (comments about comments); which was an expected requirement if the proposed hypertext system was to support collaborative writing as intended. From a theoretical point of view such hypertext structures, when represented in graph theoretic terms, are cyclic and the highly desirable properties of DAGs (Directed Acyclic Graphs) (e.g. Bench-Capon and Dunne, 1989) as document structures, would not have been available.

Class 4: **Non-annotations**
This style of annotation behaviour accounted for 15% of the observed

behaviours and involved marking a portion of the document, by underlining or circling and nothing else. In effect the marking served as the comment.

It was clear from this study that there would be considerable difficulty with designing a passive hypertext system that would effectively support natural, i.e. paper based, annotation behaviour. It was felt that for success it would be necessary for such a system's end users to modify how they undertake annotation tasks. As such, the proposed hypertext system would be a typical example of a 'large CSCW system' and would have constrained its users to a particular way of working.

Relevant to this paper is the summation of the above work that just annotation behaviour itself is varied and complex. An understanding of this leads to some of the design requirements discussed later in this paper concerning the style of software that might adequately support people in these tasks.

Document Annotation with Electronic Mail

Diaper (1993b) describes some of the problems with collaborative writing using just electronic mail, including and relevant to this paper, the differences in how to locate annotations on paper and via electronic mail. One overall, germane conclusion from this work is that there are considerable complexities to how a list of notes, i.e. the annotations, are located in the document. The conclusion is:

> '. . . that the electronic equivalent of marking a paper document version results in the production of the comments that are difficult to read and time consuming to produce. The commented version is also considerably longer. With paper documents one merely highlights a section of text and makes a comment on the paper, or numbers it for written comments produced on separate sheets. . . . the actual production of the comments took an order of magnitude longer than deciding on them. Furthermore, the process is not simply mechanical: there is a considerable problem solving element associated with the production of comments.'

SYSTEM STYLE

'System style' may be a rather grandiloquent phrase for the concept meant in this paper. The contrasting pair of styles described in the following two sub-sections are only points on a continuum and the mixed set of factors that constitute this continuum are merely one set from many. The contrast between large and small CSCW systems, even with the above provisos, need not be a straw-man, particularly since most CSCW systems can be classed as large CSCW systems and as such are nearer the non-preferred style with respect to the design options advocated in this paper.

Large CSCW Systems

A large CSCW system, at least and perhaps only for this paper's purpose, will share a number of, if not all, the properties of the general class of such systems. These systems need not be very large in software engineering terms, but the assumption is that the programs will be hardware and software platform specific to the extent that porting the programs to other platforms would require a major, new programming effort.

From an HCI perspective such systems enjoy some very severe restrictions. Many of the larger of these systems in effect assume that all their users will be associated, probably as employees, with the organisation(s) that owns the system. Thus the application of these systems is to 'in house' collaborative working. The functionality of such a CSCW system can be quite specific, tailored to the owning organisation's needs and it is often possible, if not wholly desirable, to enforce styles of working on the system's users, because they are employees. Given that many of the large CSCW systems listed by Greenberg (1991) were developed as R&D prototypes, then a not unreasonable analogy is to bespoke applications software such as large commercial databases.

It is unlikely that large CSCW systems will be successful unless the model of how people cooperatively work, on which the system is based, and which is usually extant declaratively or procedurally, i.e. at run time, is adequate. That these social and organisational psychological models are inadequate would be hardly controversial as a claim, but what cannot be controversial is that there are no large CSCW systems that contain the necessary multitude of models to cope with the rich diversity of people's working styles, habits and needs. That an entire book of readings (Easterbrook, 1993) can continually question our fundamental, applied psychological theories concerning the very nature of group working, that often it is conflict, not cooperation, that effectively drives groups, strongly suggests that the theories are not adequate and therefore neither will be large CSCW systems; or more accurately, these systems will not initially be successful.

Undoubtedly large CSCW systems, like bespoke applications software, can be made into successful IT products by using a post-installation prototyping approach that can modify, at least partially, the CSCW system, the users, say by training, and the organisation and/or its procedures. This approach is given the misnomer (Turski, 1981; Sommerville, 1989) of 'maintenance' in software engineering and is more accurately thought of as 'damage limitation' or 'repair' by many HCI practitioners.

The description of the application domain chosen to illustrate this paper shows that even an application as narrow as document annotation is one that is sufficiently complicated that any large systems approach is bound to be based on inadequate user and organisational models.

Small CSCW Systems

Brooke (1993) presents a rather different picture of the software industry to that described above for large, bespoke systems. He describes the 'generic product' approach to profit where 'one must sell as many units of product as possible' with the consequence that 'The typical product . . . is the "spreadsheet" rather than "the program for making an expense claim following the procedures of the Acme Tool Co, Ltd.".'

Brooke's proposed solution is the development of software that will support 'virtual applications'. These, he suggests, can be 'rapidly' built from the 'many small, interrelated applications' that Brooke says 'designers of CSCW systems should be striving to construct'.

While a plausible alternative, and the one that will be explored further in this paper, Brooke's proposals appear to shift responsibility from the designer towards, if not on to, the end user. I think that for success his approach will have to trade-off the perceived cost of building a virtual application from the anticipated benefits compared to doing the task in a more clumsy way without the virtual application. Cynically one might expect that for most users the benefits that they perceive are going to have to be very large, or the costs of building the virtual application absolutely trivial, if they are to make an adequate effort at building many virtual applications. Even amongst that small group of potential CSCW users who are familiar with customisable systems, most obviously UNIX workstation users and, for example, their personalised aliases and shell scripts, there are many of these expert users who use less efficient working methods than they might simply because they put little effort into maintaining, redesigning, etc. their personalised interface.

While the following proposal at first appears crude, it is in my opinion particularly apt with respect to CSCW systems:

The Pooh Proposal
Even if users know what they want to do, which often they don't, then it doesn't follow that they know how best to do what they want.

Many CSCW systems are fundamentally concerned with supporting the social and organisational infrastructure of group working, another way to say that users will be constrained, yet frequently neither the goals nor means of achieving them are clear to the users. In any of the decision making or supporting CSCW applications, for example, electronic conferencing, often neither the nature of the discussion or the outcome is known in advance. Furthermore there is the basic psychological problem of people accessing their expertise (e.g. Bainbridge, 1979; 1986; Diaper, 1989d). It is known from the expert system knowledge elicitation literature, for example, that expert performance may frequently be negatively correlated with the ability to be conscious of, i.e. be able to describe, the nature of the expertise. Furthermore, it is not implausible to suggest that some, if not most, of a person's social and management skills are of the 'riding a bicycle' sort that the person can do but not describe. From these suspicions it follows that even an expert electronic committee worker may not be able to specify the nature of a desirable virtual application.

As a further objection to shifting design emphasis towards the user, there is an ethical issue that needs raising with Brooke's proposals. One important role of the user interface is the safety of individuals, groups, organisations and so forth. Today the financial value of data to organisations is so high that its misuse, by error, ignorance or misdesign, rather than malice, is such that leaving such a responsibility to end users appears to me to be a dangerous strategy. There are already sufficient problems with the assignation of blame for failures (Pullinger, 1989) and there are legal, and hence financial, as well as ethical aspects to this issue. At least we should consider who might be held responsible for an expensive business failure caused by one or more less than ideal CSCW virtual applications. Answers to questions such as this one might very well determine the acceptance of Brooke's virtual applications approach amongst users and managers.

The above reservations about Broooke's virtual applications proposal in no way invalidates his position about large CSCW systems nor his general conclusion about the need for small systems. The alternative design style proposed in this paper supports his overall position for the need for small CSCW systems, or system components that can be configured. The difference, however, is that the software is simple, open, and can be used 'as is'.

The approach proposed in this paper is based on the only really successful CSCW system in the world, electronic mail. To understand the success of e-mail from the direct end user computing perspective, it is necessary to apprehend the fact that users need only possess a very simple program that allows them to send and receive mail. Most of any processing of things to and from e-mail can be carried out by the necessarily available systems and applications software in each user's own computer. Total platform independence has led to a global network (e.g. Harasim, 1993) that extends to even the more prosperous third world countries. If two or more people can solve their platform compatibility problems then very fancy things can be done using low bandwidth e-mail by each party having the appropriate software. But the beauty to every user of e-mail for sending messages is that one never has to ask what sort of computer other people have.

Unfortunately the 'fancy things' hinted at above has so far tended to mean each party possessing virtually the same large CSCW system and such systems are notoriously unportable. Thus e-mail used this way allows only a modest extension to the 'in house' bias that large CSCW system will have.

Perhaps an exception to the above view is software such as Lotus Notes which, at least for the PC market, is a move towards relatively simple software with a limited set of features that users can use 'as is'. One view of Lotus Notes is that it doesn't actually do very much. While this will appear a valid criticism to some, if it were true then one might still argue that 'not doing much' is the correct approach to CSCW system design.

The small CSCW system described in the next section follows Brooke's proposals for small software units but places little emphasis on their combinatorial reconfigurability. Each software unit is intended to provide a useful function to the end user. The expectation is that users will learn to do what they want with such software, exploiting its advantages and working around its limitations; just as people have done with e-mail.

DESIGN

There are two purposes to this section. First, it is necessary to at least show that the type of small CSCW system proposed is a plausible option in the absence of its implementation. Second, that even in a very modest application domain such as document annotation, the requirements and design considerations are complex but not impossible.

Requirements Specification

The general approach to requirements in the design used to illustrate the CSCW design issues is based on a User Centred Design approach and specifically one that is Task Orientated. The user requirements were generated by using a scenario (e.g. Carey, et al., 1991; Clarke, 1991; Young and Barnard, 1991) to simulate a general task structure.

User requirements

The scenario document annotation task from the point of the end user can be modelled, ignoring iteration, as three sub-tasks.

1. Document (and annotation) reception
2. Annotation
3. Transmission of document and annotations

These sub-tasks need expansion to at least their next lowest level of detail.

1. Document (and annotation) reception
    (a) Receive the document by e-mail
    (b) Check if document already formatted for annotations
    (c) Check if document contains annotations
    (d) Process document to format for existing annotations and/or for new ones.
    (e) Display and/or print processed document

2. Annotation
    (a) Select source part of document to make new annotation about
    (b) Make the annotation
    (c) Review/edit the annotation

3. Transmission of document and annotations
    (a) Process the document for transmission
    (b) Send the document by email

The annotation stage may require a number of different mechanisms for marking the source and making the annotation. These mechanisms should support the user in a natural way of working. At the least the source marking should be as easy as possible, which may require several different ways of doing such marking, say depending on the size of the source section. The annotation should be simply entered by typing and the software should deal with annotation format and its linking to the source. There needs to be a means of making general comments about the whole document, or large sections of it. There is a need for multiple sources being linked to one annotation and a mechanism for meta-annotation is desirable.

The annotation software should not change the document contents so that there always remains the option of reading the source document alone or with the annotations. It should be considered that the annotation software may be used by some people with collaborative editing software. Such software will probably be far more complex than the annotation software because of the dynamic variability, range of style, etc. that collaborative editing necessarily involves.

Whatever design solutions are offered, the end user should be able to use their own machine and most of their own software, most importantly their own, preferred editor (Bornat and Thimbleby, 1989) and usual e-mail software.

System requirements

First the software must be portable as complete platform independence is required because the journal refereeing application is international and not all involved are equally well equipped. This inevitably leads to a need for open software and editable source code. Platform independence will be enhanced if the software is available in several different languages so that the probability is small of someone with a computer without a compiler or interpreter for one of the languages. This has consequences for the possible size of the programs (i.e. they must be small).

The programs must be able to run independent of the user's other applications software which will inevitably require that the programs are able to read and write to backing store.

It cannot be assumed that a user will have access to any I/O devices except a keyboard and VDU. Thus while the software should be written so that more sophisticated interfaces, GUIs, etc., can access the programs it is safest that a very low user interface standard, say VT100, is assumed.

The requirement that the contents of the source document are not changed places a constraint on the system that there must be two representations, the document and the document plus annotations. There are likely to be several version management problems caused by this user requirement.

Concept Design

At the heart of the design problem is how a user can mark the source of an annotation in a document. Most hypertext systems use some version of mouse click and drag to designate a 'hot spot'. The user I/O technology constraint means that a keyboard method is required. Not being able to change the document precludes using an embedded restricted character set in the document itself. There are also related problems of how such annotation sources are displayed.

Starting with the model of how people annotate a paper document (Diaper, 1989), the end product is a document with brief annotations in the margin and markers to more extensive notes elsewhere. In the case of journal refereeing one of the most time consuming parts of the task is listing annotations with an address to part of the document that is unambiguous (Diaper, 1993b), if the annotated document is not to be sent to the submission's authors[4].

Current, personal experience with electronic mail suggests that there are some people who still send mail with line lengths greater than 80 characters. There remains in the world a sufficiency of computers to which this is an inconvenience. It is also the case that the ASCII output of many text processors and some word processors possess a variable line length determined by the author's carriage returns during input and editing; these are ignored of course when processed for output.

The design option pursued here, and there are other alternatives that may well be better, is that a new document to be annotated will have one change made to it, it will fit the lines to an 80 column format. Since this is to be done then the design will exploit the process by restricting text to about 60 characters and reserving the final character positions for annotations. Ideally this format should be universally adopted as there will clearly be additional problems for those who have to receive and deal with annotated documents that have different line splitting conventions (Diaper, 1993b).

Annotations will be automatically numbered and either displayed in the margin or referenced to the annotation list.

Annotations will be created in the user's own editor. A portion of text is marked and this involves creating a new line. The annotation is simply typed in across 80 columns. The annotation marking will allow a post editor, document processing program to format the document and its annotations.

The 'document processor' will take as its input an annotated document file, as described immediately above, and generate as its output the document, without annotations and appended to the end, to remove some version management problems, an encoded form of the annotations.

The user can now use the 'document formatter', i.e. the same program

---

[4] *Interacting with Computers* suggests that annotated submissions can be returned to authors although few referees opt to do this.

that adjusted the line lengths, to see the annotated form of the document. The document formatter remains a relatively simple program and the document and appended, encoded annotations can be transmitted by e-mail. Provided the same annotation encoding convention is used by everyone then these two programs, the processor and formatter, would appear to meet the minimum requirements.

Different versions, or output options, of the document formatter would allow the generation of different styles of annotation. For example, list all annotations together versus using the margin plus a list for long annotations (see below).

The following sub-section illustrates how a part of a document may be annotated as a brief way to show by simulation the overall design. The specifics of the design, such as the choice of control characters and the encoding algorithm that locates annotations in the source document, would need to be the subject of a level of design that is not relevant here, but would be essential before any implementation could be attempted.

Design Simulation

The following paragraph is part of a larger document that has been received by the end user who is going to referee it using the annotation software.

```
Given the above it is reasonable to ask why it is worth returning to
the foundations of HCI's theoretical interface design efforts.  Direct
Manipulation (DM) and WIMP interfaces have been designed with some, if
not complete, success by basing design on prior experience.
There is a cultural inertia dimension to interface design
such that users can be very satisfied with an interface design
that is similar to their previous computer experience.  Thus icons, for
example, may be
chosen for their visual appearance based on what experienced users
are already familiar with such that experimental testing of icon
design is unnecessary, in contrast to Bewley et al.'s (1983)
work on the STAR icon set.
```

Figure 1   Part of the original source document.

Running this through the document processor produces an output file that appears like this:

```
                                                    :
    Given the above it is reasonable to ask why it is   :
    worth returning to the foundations of HCI's         :
    theoretical interface design efforts.  Direct       :
    Manipulation (DM) and WIMP interfaces have been     :
    designed with some, if not complete, success by     :
    basing design on prior experience. There is a       :
    cultural inertia dimension to interface design      :
    such that users can be very satisfied with an       :
    interface design that is similar to their previous  :
    computer experience.  Thus icons, for example, may  :
    be chosen for their visual appearance based on      :
    what experienced users are already familiar with    :
    such that experimental testing of icon design is    :
    unnecessary, in contrast to Bewley et al.'s (1983)   :
    work on the STAR icon set.                          :
                                                    :
```

Figure 2   Document after initial processing.

The user can now make annotations on this file in their own editor. They might produce a file similar to figure 3.

Creating these annotations is very easy for the user. In the simulation above one merely creates a new line (one key-stroke), uses the space bar and then minus to underline (the number of underlines is not critical). There is also a convention for longer sources where three full stops are used. The annotation is simply typed in by the user.

Several features are not illustrated, including embedding annotations, annotation from different people, and so forth. While these will be desirable, if not essential, in other CSCW writing applications, they may not be necessary for a single referee's report.

The problem with the result is that it is a visual mess. What is easy for the user is not easy on the reader of the annotated document. The document formatter program produces an output file from one formatted as above. This file contains the source document and the encoded annotations. To generate the encoded annotations the program uses the property that lines containing annotations do not have a colon control character in the appropriate column and start with the marking convention (in this case minus or minus and full stop). The annotation is simply the string that follows until a document line is reached (identified by its colon). The actual data type specification is not relevant to this paper but is a fairly straightforward piece of software design.

```
                                         :
Given the above it is reasonable to ask why it is  :
worth returning to the foundations of HCI's        :
theoretical interface design efforts.  Direct      :
Manipulation (DM) and WIMP interfaces have been    :
                ---- spell out acronym
designed with some, if not complete, success by    :
basing design on prior experience.  There is a     :
cultural inertia dimension to interface design      :
such that users can be very satisfied with an       :
interface design that is similar to their previous :
computer experience.  Thus icons, for example, may :
                -- insert references to Carroll?
be chosen for their visual appearance based on      :
what experienced users are already familiar with    :
such that experimental testing of icon design is    :
        ----...
unnecessary, in contrast to Bewley et al.'s (1983)  :
    ...---  I do not think that this conclusions follows from the
evidence so far presented.  At least a representative sample
of the published literature should be surveyed.
work on the STAR icon set.                          :
                                         :
```

Figure 3   Annotations made in an editor.

The document processor takes an annotated document file from the document formatter and generates a neatly annotated document similar to figure 4.

In this version the document processor locates annotations by starting them on the target line and allowing them to extend to lower lines if they do not interfere with other annotations; where this happens the annotation is placed in the notes section generated either before or after the document. Annotations are automatically numbered for reference purposes and the location within the line indicated with an appropriately truncated string.

For the referees' reports application the file generated by this document processor would probably be satisfactory. The advantage of providing the output in the document formatter's format is that other collaborative editing software could combine annotations from different users. The two-program structure anticipates such applications and is one reason why the two programs are not combined in the design offered.

```
                                          :
Given the above it is reasonable to ask why it is   :
worth returning to the foundations of HCI's        :
theoretical interface design efforts.  Direct      :
Manipulation (DM) and WIMP interfaces have been    : A14 'WIMP' spell out
designed with some, if not complete, success by    : acronym
basing design on prior experience.  There is a     :
cultural inertia dimension to interface design     :
such that users can be very satisfied with an      :
interface design that is similar to their previous :
computer experience.  Thus icons, for example, may : A15 '. ' insert
be chosen for their visual appearance based on     : references to Carroll?
what experienced users are already familiar with   :
such that experimental testing of icon design is   : A16 'exper..unnecessary
rork on the STAR icon set.                          :
                                          :
```

```
Notes
-----

A16 'experimental testing of ... unnecessary,'
I do not think that this conclusions follows from the evidence so
far presented.  At least a representative sample of the published
literature should be surveyed.
```

Figure 4   The annotated document.

CONCLUSIONS

Document annotation is just one small application within the broad CSCW area of collaborative writing. The design illustrated in this paper shows that, even for a narrow application within just document annotation for journal refereeing, there are a wealth of complex design issues. Furthermore, while perhaps sufficient for this paper's purposes, we can be confident that the design offered is far from optimal and even at the concept design level it is undoubtedly incomplete. On the other hand, it is a fairly typical and straightforward piece of software design once the concept design is established; that is, it's no harder, or easier, than designing any piece of software well.

One aspect that makes the software design easy, and hence the approach attractive, is that there is no implementation of a groupware component in the software. The software can be used on a stand-alone basis if someone wished to annotate their own documents[5]. It can be used as the groupware in CSCW applications but how it is used will be up to the particular end users. Looking at a range of CSCW uses of the basic software we might anticipate a range of applications by building user definable slots into the ADT of the encoded annotations so that annotations could, like e-mail, have a variety of uses. Thus annotating the minutes of a meeting may use the software among the group in a different way from a group collaboratively writing, or reviewing a document as part of a formal QA procedure.

At the heart of this small CSCW system approach is a restriction that needs to be coped with. The format of the encoded annotations, if you like the formatting language or the ADT of an encoded annotation, has to be agreed by all users. The consequence of this is that this format needs to be 'right' before any general release because once in the public domain the software will be difficult to upgrade as problems are inevitable if different versions of the format are used.

This paper suggests that the focus of human considerations needs changing slightly in the small CSCW systems approach. The purpose of the non-computing side of CSCW should be to address the issues concerning user functionality. The contrast is with the large CSCW systems that constrain how users interact with each other, often by explicitly implementing software to control group interaction.

Perhaps underneath the whole small CSCW system approach advocated in this paper there is a belief that we are not able to design systems that contain many computers and people trying to work together. If one accepts that we are unable to do adequate social psychological, small group engineering without generating far too many unforeseen consequences, then it also follows that we will be unlikely to be able to implement an adequate, appropriately flexible model of group working in software. Overall this leads to the view that as CSCW system designers we will do a better job if we concentrate on designing useful, simple tools that people can choose to use as they like in the rich, exotic diversity of their social working lives.

REFERENCES

Bainbridge, L. (1979) *Verbal Reports as Evidence of the Process Operator's Knowledge*, International Journal of Man-Machine Studies, 11, 431–436.

---

[5] There may be a student application here where teaching materials are available on-line.

Bainbridge, L. (1986) *Asking Questions and Accessing Knowledge*. Future Computing Systems, 1, 2, 143–150.

Beer, M. and Diaper, D. (1991) *Reading and Writing Documents using Headed Record Expertext*. in *Proceedings of the Fourth Annual Conference on Computers and the Writing Process*. (Ed. Sharples, M.). University of Sussex. Reprinted in: AISB Newsletter, (1991), 77, 22–28.

Bench-Capon, T. and Dunne, P. (1989) *Some Computational Properties of a Model for Electronic Documents* Electronic Publishing, 2, 231–256.

Benyon, D. (1992) *The Role of Task Analysis in Systems Design*. Interacting with Computers, 4, 1, 102–123.

Benyon, D. (1992b) *Task Analysis and System Design: The Discipline of Data*. Interacting with Computers, 4, 2, 246–259.

Brooke, J. (1993) *User Interfaces for CSCW Systems*. in Diaper, D. and Sanger, C. (Eds.) *CSCW in Practice: An Introduction and Case Studies*. 23–30. Springer-Verlag.

Bornat, R. and Thimbleby, H. (1989) *The Life and Times of DED, Text Display Editor*. in Long, J. and Whitefield, A, (Eds.) *Cognitive Ergonomics and Human-Computer Interaction*. 225–255. Cambridge University Press.

Diaper, D. (1989) *Task Analysis for Knowledge Descriptions (TAKD): The Method and an Example*. in *Task Analysis for Human-Computer Interaction*. (Ed. Diaper, D.), 108–159. Ellis Horwood.

Diaper, D. (1989b) *Task Observation for Human-Computer Interaction*. in *Task Analysis for Human-Computer Interaction*. (Ed.) Diaper, D., 210–237. Ellis Horwood.

Diaper, D. (1989c) *The Discipline of Human-Computer Interaction*. Interacting with Computers, 1, 1, 3–5.

Diaper, D. (1989d) *Designing Expert Systems: From Dan to Beersheba*. in *Knowledge Elicitation: Principles, Techniques and Applications*. (Ed. Diaper, D), 15–46. Ellis Horwood: England.

Diaper, D. and Johnson, P. (1989) *Task Analysis for Knowledge Descriptions: Theory and Application in Training*. in *Cognitive Ergonomics and Human-Computer Interaction*. (Eds.) Long, J. and Whitefield. A., 191–224. Cambridge University Press: Cambridge.

Diaper, D. (1990) *Analysing Focused Interview Data with Task Analysis for Knowledge Descriptions (TAKD)*. in *Human-Computer Interaction: Interact'90*. (Eds.) Diaper, D., Gilmore, D., Cockton, G. and Shackel, B., 277–282. North-Holland.

Diaper, D. and Beer, M. (1990) *Headed Record Expertext and Document Applications*. in *Hypertext Update*., 63–69. UNICOM Seminars.

Diaper, D. and Addison, M. (1991) *User Modelling: The Task Oriented Modelling (TOM) Approach to the Designer's Model*. in *People and Computers VI* (Eds.) Diaper, D. and Hammond, N., pp. 387–402, Cambridge University Press.

Diaper, D. and Beer, M. (1991) *Developing User Interfaces for Headed Record Expertext*. in *Proceedings of the UKUUG (United Kingdom UNIX system User Group) Conference: Interfacing Unix to The User*. (Ed. Beer, M.). University of Liverpool.

Diaper, D. and Addison, M. (1992a) *HCI: The search for Solutions*. in Monk, A.F., Diaper, D. and Harrison, M.D. (Eds.) *People and Computer VII*., 493–5. Cambridge University Press.

Diaper, D. and Addison, M. (1992b) *Task Analysis & Systems Analysis for Software Engineering*. Interacting with Computers, 4, 1, 124–139.

Diaper, D. (1993a) *CSCW: Psychology, Sociology . . . and Computing*. Computer Bulletin, February, 22–25.

Diaper, D. (1993b) *Small Scale Collaborative Writing using Electronic Mail*. in Diaper,

D. and Sanger, C. (Eds.) *CSCW in Practice: An Introduction and Case Studies*. 69–92. Springer-Verlag.

Dillon, A., Sweeney, M. and Maguire, M. (1993) *A Survey of Usability Engineering Within the European IT Industry—Current Practice and Needs*. in *People and Computers VIII*. (Eds. Alty, J.L., Diaper, D. and Guest, S.), 81–94. Cambridge University Press.

Easterbrook, S. (Ed.) (1993) *CSCW: Cooperation or Conflict?* Springer-Verlag.

Gilbert, G.N. (1993) *CSCW For Real: Reflections on Experience*. in Diaper, D. and Sanger, C. (Eds.) *CSCW in Practice: An Introduction and Case Studies*. 31–38. Springer-Verlag.

Greenberg, S. (1991) *Computer-supported Cooperative Work and Groupware*. Academic Press.

Hughes, J.A., Somerville, I., Bentley, R. and Randall, D. (1993) *Designing with Ethnography: making work visible*. Interacting with Computers, 4, 1, 239–253.

Long, J. (1986) *People and Computers: Designing for Usability* in Harrison, M. and Monk, A. (Eds.) *People and Computers: Designing for Usability*, 3–23. Cambridge University Press.

Long, J. and Dowell, J. (1989) *Conceptions of the Discipline of HCI: Craft, Applied Science, and Engineering* in Sutcliffe, A. and Macaulay, L. (Eds.) *People and Computers V*, 9–34. Cambridge University Press.

Norman, D. (1986) *Cognitive Engineering* in Norman, D. and Draper, S. (Eds.) *User Centered System Design: New Perspectives on Human-Computer Interaction*, 31–61. Lawrence Erlbaum.

Pullinger, D.J. (1989) *Moral Judgements in Designing Better Systems*. Interacting with Computers, 1, 1, 93–104.

Sharples, M. (1993a) *Adding a Little Structure to Collaborative Writing*. in Diaper, D. and Sanger, C. (Eds.) *CSCW in Practice: An Introduction and Case Studies*. Springer-Verlag.

Sharples, M. (Ed.) (1993b) *Collaborative Writing*. Springer-Verlag.

Sommerville, I. (1989) *Software Engineering* (Third Edition). Addison Wesley.

Turski, W. (1981) *Software Stability*. Proceedings of *6th. ACM Conference on System Architecture*, London.

Young, R. and Barnard, P. (1991) *Signature and Paradigm Tasks: New Wrinkles on the Scenarios Methodology*. in *People and Computers VI*. (Eds.) Diaper, D. and Hammond, N., 91–102. Cambridge University Press.

Section III

Human and Organisational Issues

7

Concurrent Engineering and CSCW: The Human Factor

C. E. Siemieniuch, M. A. Sinclair

ABSTRACT

One of the main aims of the European automotive industry is to improve its competitive position by accelerating design to production timescales through the concept of concurrent engineering. Applications, based on the premise of high speed, low cost public switched communication networks, will facilitate cooperative working and therefore help to improve the quality and reduce the costs of the design process. This paper presents the results of research into the role for real time, multi-media CSCW tools in this area, concentrating on issues of integrating such systems into organisational environments. We begin with a brief introduction to the CAR project, on which this research is largely based, followed by a short resume of the benefits and dangers of concurrent engineering. The remainder of the paper discusses the likely impact of real time CSCW tools under four main headings: changes to the overall design process, human computer interaction, organisational structure and roles and implementation.

Computer Support for Co-operative Work. Edited by Kathy Spurr, Paul Layzell, Leslie Jennison and Neil Richards
(c) 1994 John Wiley & Sons Ltd

INTRODUCTION

Concurrent engineering has been defined as an attempt to optimise the design of the product and manufacturing process to achieve reduced lead times and improved quality and cost by the integration of design and manufacturing activities, and by maximising parallelism in working practices (Broughton, 1990). The DTI has defined Computer-Supported Co-operative Work (CSCW) as the generic term covering the application of information technology in support of [such] co-operative work groups (Anon 1992). They go on to say that there is a requirement to develop tools to transform the efficiency of computer-assisted group working in order to promote levels of efficiency not attainable in current organisations. In many quarters, Concurrent Engineering philosophies and CSCW technology are being offered as a panacea to solve many current and foreseeable business problems by decreasing time to market for new products, enhancing product quality and manufacturability, improving customer service levels, increasing efficiency and productivity etc. Heady stuff indeed!

The aim of this paper is to discuss some of the implications of introducing concurrent engineering and real time, interactive, IT-based CSCW tools into organisations, with particular reference to end user and organisational issues. Most of the findings reported in the paper emerged from a four year RACE funded project, entitled *CAD/CAM in the Automotive Industry in RACE (CAR)*, whose aim was to investigate the potential for real time interactive applications within the design-to-manufacture process in the automotive industry in Europe. It is not the purpose of this paper to minimise the importance and potential of the technology itself, but rather to discuss issues of specifying, using and implementing these philosophies and tools.

The CAR Project

CAR (CAD/CAM in the Automotive Industry in RACE) was a four year project supported by the European RACE initiative (Research into Advanced Communications in Europe) focusing on the identification of new opportunities in the domain of CAD/CAM applications for the European automotive industry. The overall aim of this project was to improve the effectiveness of the European automotive industry by accelerating design-to-production timescales through the concept of concurrent engineering or co-operative working via applications based on low cost, high speed, public switched communication links; it also set out to identify any requirements for public network services that might emerge. It was a fundamental requirement of the project that any new applications developed should reflect the needs of the user companies involved.

Typically companies working in the automotive industry have widely distributed design and manufacturing sites and close contacts with equally widely distributed clients, suppliers and subcontractors. At many sites heavy use is made of sophisticated CAD modelling systems and a range of other complex CAD/CAM tools. A certain amount of electronic transfer of data is carried out but capacities and speeds of current systems severely limit the usefulness of this means of communication. Current technology available to the automotive industry allows sequential integration of design and manufacturing activities, but concurrent engineering is carried out only at the risk of prejudicing work elsewhere. Hence the overall integrity of the design is endangered, and design mismatches can occur, leading to costly and time consuming remedial work. There is also an increasing emphasis on a requirement for much closer working with suppliers and subcontractors, but little technological support exists for such activity.

Therefore, because the industry has a wide distribution of its various activities, there is an important requirement for distributed computing enabling interaction between all the parties involved (often in different locations) from the initial design to the manufacture of the component concerned (i.e. sales, finance, maintenance and in particular between design, engineering and production personnel).

Collaborators in the project included three internationally prominent user companies in the automotive industry and a national telecommunications organisation; also included were well-known organisations providing expertise in computing, video/telecommunications technologies and graphics and leading academic institutions, specialising in the computer science and human factors domain respectively.

Concurrent Engineering Context

The concurrent engineering concept implies the almost-simultaneous design of a product, its development, and preparation for regular volume production. Many authors have shown that, although there are great advantages from this strategy, it is also risky; e.g. Jurgen (1990) points out that development costs are about 10 times as much as research costs and production costs are about 100 times as much. Consequently, because in the concurrent engineering paradigm there is a rapid commitment of resources to any project; a mistake can be expensive if it is not caught

very early. And if time is lost as a result of these mistakes, the effects can
be severe; a survey has indicated that a product which is late to market
by six months in a product life of five years can lose one third of its total
recoverable profit. But if there is a 50% overspend in product development,
the loss of profit is less than 4% (Nichols, 1990). In support of this, it has
been reported in the press that in Europe Ford lost $1.5 billion in profit in
recovering its market share, by being one year behind General Motors in
introducing a new model (Holberton, 1991).

Figure 1, based on data taken from Clark and Fujimoto (1987a), illustrates
the reductions in product development time that concurrent engineering
can produce in the automotive industry (about one third), and in a later
paper (Clark and Fujimoto, 1987b), they state: '. . .the US and the Europeans
use about twice as many engineering hours to complete a project of the
same size class, with the same number of body types, selling for the same
price, as the Japanese'.

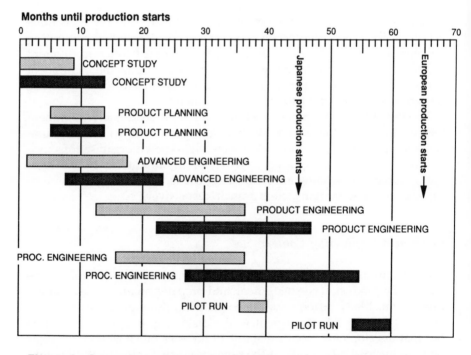

Figure 1 Comparison of average automobile product development times in
European (dark bars) and Japanese companies (light). Based on data from Clark
and Fujimoto (1987a)

Most definitions (Broughton, 1990; Eversheim, 1990; Hartley and Mortimer, 1990) emphasise the importance of co-ordinating and integrating design engineering activities which have hitherto been sequential in what has evocatively been called an automotive industry where design teams may be spread across sites in different countries. This problem of geographical distance can be serious; some figures from Harkness (1986) indicate that, for meetings in the United States in which travel is involved, the median time required for a single meeting is 3 hours; an average of 6 people attend, of which 3 travel; and the travel time involved is about 5 hours (nearly 30% of the total time).

However, it should be understood that it is the people involved who occupy the central role in concurrent engineering, and that CSCW tools, whether or not they are integrated into design systems, will be subordinate to them. Therefore it follows that these tools and systems must be usable if co-operative working is to result in reduced lead times.

REQUIREMENT SPECIFICATION FOR CSCW TOOLS

One of the main principles underlying the CAR project was that of user centred design. Accordingly the project's first emphasis was to provide an in-depth user requirements specification to be iteratively translated into a functional specification for the design and implementation of a demonstration of the components of the CAR system within the project. Running alongside this was an investigation of the user company's current technical base and any emerging technology which might influence or assist in the design of the CAR demonstrator. It is fair to say that all the work carried out in the project was geared towards satisfying the collective needs of the project user organisations. Furthermore these needs were also validated by two other major European automotive manufacturers outside the project and therefore can be said to represent the requirements of approximately 50% of the industry in Europe. A description of the methodology used, rationale and findings are given in Powrie and Siemieniuch (1990), but to set the context for the reader a resume of the main findings are given below.

Due to resource constraints within the project it was decided to define a minimum set of user requirements for the CAR system that would be acceptable to the user companies involved. The minimum set of user requirements was agreed with users and can be encapsulated in three main statements:

- The CAR system should demonstrate communication between three workstations across Europe. This presupposes a low cost, high bandwidth network being readily available.

- The CAR system should demonstrate both synchronous interworking and asynchronous interworking. This type of interaction should occur between like with like workstations, like with unlike workstations and like/unlike with a low cost workstation.

- The CAR system should demonstrate communication of each (and any combination) of the following objects: text, audio, video (both full motion and snapshot), CAD/CAM files, graphics pictures and images (scanned).

The final CAR system comprised 3 main components: a multimedia messaging tool, a co-operative design conferencing system (incorporating interactive graphics, multimedia conferencing, image catalogue and image compression) and packetised full motion video transfer.

ORGANISATIONAL REQUIREMENTS FOR IT SYSTEMS TO SUPPORT CSCW

The discussion above indicates that a successful implementation of CSCW systems, based on high speed, low cost communication links, would enable companies to gain substantial benefits by facilitating moves towards a concurrent engineering environment. Such a move will only be successful, however, if considerable attention is given to the process of integrating such a system into the host organisation's culture and working practices. Thus, one of the main goals of the evaluation of the CAR system concentrated on obtaining subjective opinion from end users as to how they felt the availability and use of applications, as encapsulated in the CAR system demonstrator, might impact on current working practices, the way they interacted with colleagues (both inside and outside their organisation), their ability to solve design problems, their roles/responsibilities within the design process, and any implications for skills or training. User responses have been grouped into four main categories for ease of reference for the reader:

- Changes to the Overall Design Process (tasks and working practices)
- Human Computer Interaction issues (the end user)
- Organisational Structures and Roles (the organisation)
- Implementation and Training requirements.

Changes to the Overall Design Process

It is clear that the use of future CSCW applications, as developed in the CAR project, will impact on the nature of the design process and the quality of the design itself. When asked how use of the CAR system might change the way the design-to-manufacture process was carried out in their company, virtually all the responses were positive. Several users felt it would speed up the design process for a variety of reasons: information could be made available more quickly where members of a project team were dispersed across different sites (thus permitting discussion and agreement on ideas and proposals at a much earlier stage in the design process); design problems could be solved more rapidly, particularly if suppliers and/or clients have instant access to the same information and do not have to rely on faxed drawings or tape transfer of data; fewer design mistakes would occur as a result of clearer communication channels. Many subjects felt use of the CAR system would help improve task efficiency and quality of output and that communication between product development and manufacturing would improve whilst reducing the time and costs involved in arranging many off-site meetings.

However, some possible negative effects of this style of working on quality of design output were also noted. It was felt that a culture which places supreme value on speed of design decision-making may in fact foster under-design. Rather than considering the merits of a number of possible approaches to a particular design problem, designers may end up putting forward their very first feasible proposal for comment by colleagues, relying on the review procedure to pick out potential flaws.

Similarly, the greatly increased quantity of readily available feedback on proposed designs was seen as both a benefit and a cost in terms of the performance of the design task by the designer. A more complete dataset is clearly conducive to the making of more informed design decisions, and thus contributes to a more satisfying task. However, this effect could be reversed should the designer reach the stage of becoming overwhelmed by information. Other comments focused on the possibility of increased frustration being caused by the non-availability of communication links and interestingly on the concern that the large potential increase in information flows could reduce a designer's ability to think creatively and therefore limit the scope for innovative solutions.

All of the respondents were unanimous in stating that security policies, particularly with regard to accessing files, were very important (e.g. in one company some users are not connected to e-mail to prevent unauthorised access to files). However, apart from some general comments about restricting access to files and file paths to authorised users, very few concrete suggestions for changes to existing security policies were made. However it is clear that any mechanisms will need to be fast reacting in order to cope with, for example, the granting of temporary access rights for a marketing specialist to a small part of the design data.

The need for a much more rigorous management of design evolution and version control within the product development cycle was also identified. Any review process in place would have to be efficient enough to ensure not only that the master set of design data is kept up to date, but that individuals using subsets of that data are aware of its current status and who in the project team is working on related data. One important area which emerged as likely to speed up this process is the provision of electronic signing off procedures to avoid the necessity for eight signatures to be found for 800 drawings to sign off one stage in the design of a component—an occurrence not unknown in the automotive industry! Such a system would have to consider all the legal implications and have all the implicit authority of the paper version. The whole issue of recording and flagging design decisions for traceability and control, links to new or existing management information and version control systems will have important implications for many areas of organisational policy e.g. fault traceabiity and legal accountability.

Human Computer Interaction Issues

The means by which end-users carry out specific tasks and the nature of their overall role in the organisation are both certain to change with the impact of CSCW applications. The question of how to achieve a balance between increasing speed and levels of communication and allowing individuals to work without interruption where necessary, is a difficult one and can only be properly resolved once on-site trials in real working situations have begun. Metaphors for communicating the effect of a closed office door or the lunch break, for example, will be important. Design of the user interface in general will need a great deal of care. In particular, the user must retain a feeling of control, and the facilities available must not be overwhelming in their range and variation. Human information processing capacity is limited. There is little extant research on the cognitive load imposed by communicating via multi-media real time communications, and fundamental work needs to be done here.

Concurrent engineering requires that the old, functionally-based department structures, where the development of products was carried out sequentially, be replaced by product-based teams that combine people from all aspects of the product life cycle (including researchers, designers, engineers, suppliers representatives, etc.). When considering the provision of appropriate tools to facilitate interaction within this type of new project team a number of issues arise:

- The design styles of individuals and organisations differ markedly (Dillon and Sweeney, 1989) and individuals must be able to tailor applications to suit their needs—organisations will need to match new tools with working practices and policies and these two requirements can sometimes be in conflict (Sinclair *et al.*, 1989).

- At present, it may be enough for companies merely to group people together to achieve a considerable improvement in concurrency of design, but this process is limited and further steps will be necessary. Design engineering knowledge will need some restructuring (Siemieniuch and Sinclair, 1993), and the old design culture in which generations of people have operated will have to change. In particular, communication skills, and an understanding of other team-members technical domains will be required.

- The trend to require suppliers to take full responsibility for their products, including their design, is likely to spread and increase the exposure of individual members of one organisation's design team to members of a supplier's project team. This exposure increases the responsibility on the individual and the security risks for the organisation and highlights the requirement for appropriate support and help systems for individual end-users.

One particular area highlighted during the user trials that requires further investigation is the area of human protocols for multimedia interactive communication. Will different control software be required to support individuals in co-operative v negotiative situations? What is the real requirement for face to face video in on-line, real-time conferencing environments? How to eliminate the "Hollywood Syndrome" (unnatural behaviour on video)? etc.

It is not clear whether existing verbal and non-verbal control protocols currently used in face-to-face meetings will be sufficient in a multi-media working environment or whether special software and hardware controls will be needed. For example is it necessary for a conferencing system to provide a computer mediated method of passing control in an interactive graphics session or will established human protocols of turn taking be sufficient to permit efficient interaction? For point-to-point conferencing the answer is not clear since subjects in experimental work carried out at Loughborough to date have been unfailingly polite (Joyner *et al.*, 1991). It would appear that if these systems are used by experts in order to solve a defined problem at a technical level, then no additional control software may be necessary. However it is not clear that conferences with less well defined or even conflicting goals will be conducted with the same degree of harmony and politeness. Current software techniques for turn taking (e.g. voice switched) have been shown to be less than satisfactory and it will be necessary to develop new skills in chairing meetings of this sort if misunderstandings are to be avoided.

Another point worth mentioning in this section is whether the use of face-to-face video will add enough in terms of improved effectiveness and efficiency to justify its current high cost in terms of bandwidth and money. Video as a communication medium seems to be most useful to the end user as a means of transmitting images of text and solid objects and of less use for face to face contact, other than establishing a social context within which to work. However, as technology improves and costs reduce, the role of face to face video will undoubtedly evolve. One interesting aspect emerging from the experiments was the increased use of video for face to face contact when conferences were held between mixed language groups. This point should not be underestimated since in the real world it is quite likely that, during a conference situation within a multi-national organisation, conferees will possess a range of mother tongues.

Organisational Structure and Roles

The advent of usable, efficient means for co-operative working across and between organisations promises to revolutionise the structure of organisations. Given the right technology and communication links, it will become feasible to uncouple the organisation intellectually, as well as geographically (Drucker, 1989; Porter, 1990). It is also clear that organisational level structures and procedures will need to become more flexible to make best use of newly enhanced communications links. Rigid hierarchical structures will need to open up to accommodate communication links which are more lateral and less vertical or pyramidal, which in turn will involve a planned devolution of responsibility and accountability down through project teams so as not to impede the potential streamlining of design to production timescales. The degree of restructuring is more clearly identifiable at the level of the work group or project team, but it is important that organisations also realise the wider potential for change.

Most users did not feel that the introduction of the CAR system would substantially change the roles and responsibilities of those individuals involved in the design to manufacture process in the short term. Responses, however, highlighted potential problems in clearly identifying and delineating responsibilities throughout the design process and the need to consider and overcome natural resistance to any organisational change.

All of these points indicate the probability of some redefinition of design tasks and hence users roles in the design process. The general effect at the role level is likely to be that jobs will become more fluid and interactive. For example the project manager's role will expand to force him/her also to have to monitor a higher proportion of communications at a horizontal level within the organisation without the routing of such communications through him/her as intermediary, otherwise there is a very real danger of middle management level losing touch with what is going on in their project teams. As for individual team members, more devolved change control procedures necessary to streamline the design decision-making process may mean more responsibility and autonomy for individual designers, process engineers etc. However, as already stated, there is a real danger that it may be difficult to fix the boundaries of role authority and influence as roles change during the design process and that this may lead to a problem of overlap and duplication of roles leading to conflicting decisions being taken.

Another underlying theme was the belief that the CAR system would lead to improved relationships and trust with clients and suppliers due to the potential for more frequent, interactive problem solving and decision making. Knock-on effects identified by the users included the need to restructure information systems to facilitate data sharing without prejudicing security, a need to select and classify suppliers and clients according to their requirements for data access, and potential savings in resources spent visiting clients. Negative aspects were the dangers of becoming too exposed to other companies, the cost of the hardware and software for small companies, and compatibility of systems.

More specifically supplier organisations are likely to want to respond earlier in the design cycle. Both the technical system and organisational structures and procedures may need to cope with an order of magnitude growth in external communications; while suppliers' links with competing clients will require secure partitioning of data and its communication. Such tight coupling between organisations will lead to the standardisation of methods, equipment and components, and possibly to the functioning of supplier organisations as virtual satellites of their larger clients.

Finally, and at least as important as the aspects mentioned above, there are very significant cultural and language differences to be taken into account when considering collaborative working between organisations on an international basis. As Kanoi (1991) has stated, based on his experience in the Sony Corporation:

> The most difficult issues confronting production control today concern the globalisation of factory locations. . . . This need has grown from a number of factors including fluctuations in market demand, increasing logistics costs, and risks due to unstable exchange rates. . . . Against the backdrop of internationalisation,. . .the communication gap between people of different nations, different lifestyles and ways of thinking—this whole question has become the key issue.

For Europe, this is a crucial issue as it will always be characterised by a diversity of regions, cultures and languages and, notwithstanding treaties and single markets, these differences will remain. In manufacturing, they lead to different organisational philosophies and different ways of doing things. Because these arise from cultural norms, they will be persistent and will require considerable training before changes become accepted.

The significance of this is that new tools must recognise that they will be used in different organisational cultures. What the software developers frequently fail to recognise is that the design of interfaces between the tool and its environment, including its human users, inevitably and always involves assumptions about the organisations culture as it is expressed in its procedures, and the knowledge, skills, authority, and roles of the users. It is particularly undesirable that tools should be predicated on one particular culture (that of the tool developers) which then require considerable, specific training and possible restructuring of jobs in certain other cultures, because they just do not fit the norms of that culture.

Implementation Issues

In order to facilitate the introduction of concurrent engineering and CSCW tools it is important that new designs should use old, well-understood components where possible as this minimises both the R&D resource requirement and the design requirement. It will also be important that the design history and field performance information for each component must be made available to whoever needs it, as early as possible, and in a digestible form (Hartley and Mortimer 1990). This issue is not a simple one e.g. it is reported that for one of their newest engine families, Cummins offers 86 different flywheels, 49 flywheel housing options and 17 types of starter motors with 12 possible mountings—all of which could be assembled in approximately 1200 combinations to satisfy customer applications. . .the catalogue has more than 100,000 parts. This also places a premium on generic design specifications, and generic engineering solutions to these to ensure the re-usability of components.

As was stated earlier, concurrent engineering requires the old, functionally-based department structure, where the development of products was carried out sequentially, be replaced by product-based teams that combine people from all aspects of the product life cycle. One particularly important training issue arises here—the development of multi-skilled team members, such as a Component Engineer who is responsible for ensuring the design, manufacturability, testing and sourcing of a component of a product, and who will evidently need many skills beyond those of a mechanical engineer. It also seems likely that all members of a multi-functional and multi-skilled design team will require, as a minimum, some understanding of all the competencies and skills that will need to be applied by the team as a whole to fulfil their goals. The difficulty is in understanding what *content* and *depth of content* each individual will need in order to fulfil their role within the team. Identifying and understanding these competence requirements will provide valuable information relating to identification of appropriate roles and hence training and recruiting requirements.

None of users felt the effort required to learn a CAR-type system would prevent its uptake within their company and several commented on the user friendly nature of the application. The comment was made that older engineers may exhibit initial reluctance to use the system but that proper training should overcome this.

Cost was mentioned as being a critical factor in the availability of the system, but the general consensus of opinion seemed to be that one terminal should be available per small department or team (i.e. between 10 and 18 people). The crucial point seemed to be that the system should be readily available to all members of project teams according to their needs but that component engineering and associated design (e.g. drawing office areas) may have the greatest need. Further analysis is certainly required within an organisation to determine need.

CONCLUSIONS

From the selection of issues discussed briefly above, it is clear that for CSCW systems to realise their potential, both the design of the systems themselves and their implementation within organisations must pay full regard to achieving a closer match between organisational features at all levels from the task and the end-user to the organisation as a whole. But this should not mean that the organisation must change to meet the demands of a rigidly designed technical system, rather that both the system must be designed around organisational needs and that the organisation must be flexible and creative in exploiting this exciting technology to the full. Above all, this process should be an iterative and continuing one: the organisation's external environment will inevitably change with time, giving rise to new priorities, goals and procedures, while within the organisation users will adapt to new facilities and invent uses undreamed of by systems designers.

In summary therefore, it is clear that there is a very real need for multi-media CSCW tools that will allow individual users to interact within and between organisations in real time, exchanging ideas and data. The apparent potential for these tools is only limited by cost, technology and the developer's imagination. However, developers should remember that, after a decade of unfulfilled promises and large sums sunk into technological solutions that have repeatedly failed to deliver, the automotive industry in particular is wary of taking further giant leaps forward into the unknown and, thankfully, is more inclined to view new developments in this area with some scepticism. The cash-strapped, recession-weary real world of industry want and need stepwise progression in the area of collaborative systems for many reasons—one of the most important being that they realise that advent of CSCW will require a fundamental shift in organisational culture and working practices and that this cannot be achieved overnight. For the majority of organisations human beings still represent their most important resource—a resource that requires the provision of appropriate and usable tools to function efficiently. If the problem holders themselves do not take the opportunity to input to the design of these new applications or the time to provide the right context and training for them, then CSCW will become another sad tale of investment in technology that is still looking for a problem to solve!

REFERENCES

Anon 1992. Advanced Technology Programme, Computer Supported Cooperative Work. The CSCW Technical Workplan, Department of Trade and Industry, UK.
Broughton T. 1990. Simultaneous engineering in aero gas turbine design and manufacture. In *in Proceedings of 1st Int. Conf. on Simultaneous Engineerting*. London 4–5 December 1990, Status Meetings Ltd, pp. 25–26.
Clark K. B. and Fujimoto T. 1987a. Overlapping problem solving in product development. Harvard Business School Working Paper 87–048.
Clark K. B. and Fujimoto T. 1987b. Product development in the world auto industry: strategy, organisation and performance. Paper presented to the Brookings Institute Microeconomics Conference, Dec.3, pp. 22–28.

Dillon A. and Sweeney M. 1988. The application of cognitive psychology to CAD. In: Jones D. M. and Winder R. (Eds) *People and computers IV*. CUP, Cambridge.

Drucker P. F. 1989. *The New Realities*. Heinemann, Oxford

Eversheim W. 1990. Trends and experience in applying simultaneous engineerign in German. In *Proceedings of 1st International Conference on Simultaneous Engineerting*. London 4–5 December, Status Meetings Ltd, pp. 5–23.

Harkness R. 1986. Videoconferencing. In: Bartee T. (Ed.) *Digital communications*. Indianapolis, IN: Sams.

Hartley J. and Mortimer J. 1990. *Industrial Engineering[E1*. Industrial Newsleters Ltd, Dunstable, UK.

Holberton S. 1991. R&D deserves a strategic position. *Financial Times*. 12th February.

Joyner S.M., Parker C.G. and Cooper K.A 1991. An investigation into control protocols and use of video in a multimedia task environment. In *Proceedings of the Ergonomics Society Annual Conference*. 16–19 April, UK, pp. 169–174.

Jurgen R. K. 1990. R&D isn't what it used to be. *IEEE Spectrum*. 27: pp. 34–39.

Nichols K. 1990. Getting engineering changes under control. In *Engineering Design*. Quote from McKinsey & Co. report. 1(1), 5–16.

Kanoi N. 1991. Manufacturing modernisation—Sony's approach. In *Proceedings of First International Manufacturing Lecture*. Institute of Manufacturing Engineers 21 November.

Porter M. E. 1990. The competitive advantage of nations. In *Harvard Business Review*. 90 (2), 73–90.

Powrie S. E. and Siemieniuch C. E. 1990. An investigation of User Requirements for Broadband Communications in the Automotive Industry. In: Diaper D., Gilmore D., Cockton G. and Shackel B. (Eds.) *Human-Computer Interaction: Interact 90*. Elsevier.

Siemieniuch C. E. and Sinclair M. A. 1993. Implications of Concurrent Engineering for Organisational Knowledge and Structure—A European, Ergonomics Perspective. *Journal of Design and Manufacturing*. 3, 189–200.

Sinclair M. A., Siemieniuch C. E. and John P. J. 1989. A user-centered approach to define high-level requirements for next-generation CAD systems for mechanical engineering. *IEEE Trans. Engineering and Mangement, special issue: Social Impacts of Computer-Aided Design Systems*. 34 (4), 262–279.

8

The Effective Use of Groupware in the Corporate Business Environment

Jack Cutts

ABSTRACT

There is a great deal of interest being shown within the corporate business community on the move to some form of Computer-Supported Co-operative Working (CSCW). This has mainly been fuelled by the computing press extolling the benefits which could be accrued by such a paradigm shift. The author will argue that this move will only be successful if the implementation is not treated as a stand alone process. The critical success factors of the shift should be how well the systems are integrated within the business and subsequently how they are aligned to the overall business objectives of the organisation. If these steps are followed the benefits should be forthcoming.

The author's view is supported by evidence based on his experience in integrating such systems and gives detailed information on the pitfalls and issues involved. To assist future practitioners in this area a check list is discussed which details a pragmatic process which if followed will assist the successful implementation of groupware products.

Computer Support for Co-operative Work. Edited by Kathy Spurr, Paul Layzell,
Leslie Jennison and Neil Richards
© 1994 John Wiley & Sons Ltd

INTRODUCTION

Implementing a groupware product into a corporate environment can be fraught with danger. However, if this is done effectively the organisation will accrue significant benefits. In the following sections there is information which has been gathered in the implementation of Groupware products, and particular Lotus Notes, into such an environment. A significant amount of which concentrates on the first implementation at CMS. The aim of this paper is to try to point prospective implementers on the right path.

CMS

CMS is a division of British Steel plc which was established in 1968 to serve the information needs of the steel industry. It moved to its present location, a purpose built computer centre in Rotherham, in 1975. CMS currently supplies a wide range of IT services to its parent company and a significant number of other organisations in manufacturing, financial services, distribution and the public sector.

CMS employs 300 people at its headquarters in Rotherham and a further 40 located at data centres across the UK.

COMPUTER-SUPPORTED CO-OPERATIVE WORKING

Since 1984 when Cashman and Greif (Grudin,1991) first coined the term computer-supported co-operative work (CSCW) IT professionals and academics alike have been struggling to define exactly what it means. Is it the same as groupware or workgroup computing or is it different? Salesmen will provide as many definitions as they have products to sell. I must therefore apologise because this paper does not attempt to give you a definition. As a user, I do not feel it is important to label a product as belonging to one family or another. This will limit the growth and development of such products. I do feel however that the overriding priority of any prospect implementer is how the product can be used to support the primary business objectives of the organisation.

THE MOVE TO CSCW

'Would you tell me, please, which way I ought to go from here?'
'That depends a good deal on where you want to get to' said the Cat
'I don't much care where' said Alice
'Then it doesn't matter which way you go' (Carroll,1988)

When you are considering a move to any product there are a number of factors to consider. The most salient one being, "Why do you want to do the project?"

With a product such as Lotus Notes the reasons for the project will be slightly different to the majority of mainstream developments.

Within CMS the main processes range from the development and maintenance of bespoke software systems to the facilities management of a customer's entire IT function. It was therefore imperative that the groupware solution that was chosen was the most flexible system available.

Lotus Notes was chosen because of its ability to allow CMS' staff to share information wherever they are located and what ever time they are working and regardless of which of the major technical platforms they are working from.

This enabled the main commercial process of bidding for new business to be substantially improved.

The following sections detail some of the main driving forces behind the move to groupware. A number are specific to CMS: however they will still be applicable to any business contemplating the move.

Competitive Advantage

A number of companies have gained a significant competitive advantage by moving to Groupware products. This did not come about by accident. It was as a result of a well thought through process. The rise in the fortunes of Price Waterhouse is well documented. This was attributed to the use of groupware to solve a significant business problem. Lotus Notes has enabled Price Waterhouse to get information to clients in a significantly shorter time period. This has significantly enhanced their reputation in the market.

Within CMS the mission of the business is 'Outstanding Customer Satisfaction' This needed to be illustrated in actions as well as words. The implementation of Lotus Notes was a key component in leveraging the keys skills of the organisation on behalf of the customer. Allowing the customer access to CMS' key skilled personnel has made available a greater knowledge pool than ever before. This enables the customer to improve the decision making in regards to the IT environment of their own business.

Legacy Systems

Within most organisations there will be a number of systems which have been around for a long time. These tend to have been amended frequently from their original conception and re-engineering would be prohibitively expensive. These are the so-called legacy systems.

Within CMS we have utilised the Application Program Interfaces (API's) available for Lotus Notes and, in conjunction with in-house written software, built front ends to these systems. This has significantly prolonged the life of the systems and at the same time provided a Graphical User Interface (GUI) which makes the systems easy to use. This technology has enabled the hard and soft data to be merged and displayed within one system. This has significantly increased the benefits of these systems to the business.

Cross Platform Information Access

In the majority of cases large companies will grow by acquisition as well as organically. When this happens the result will be a number of disparate systems and platforms within the organisation. The resultant IT strategy will be either to integrate or standardise. Both of these have inherent strengths and weaknesses which should be weighed up for the specific business. In a number of cases, however, Lotus Notes can be used as the 'glue' which can integrate these systems, which as a result will enable expensive re-engineering of the business systems to be delayed until the financial picture of the business is stronger. In the first few months following an acquisition the need for relevant and up to date information is paramount. The use of Lotus Notes could enable this information to be available across the whole organisation with the minimum of development work. The investment in Lotus Notes could be financed entirely by the benefits accrued from the early availability of the information.

Integration of Electronic Mail Systems

Effective communications within an organisation is crucial. It is likely that different functional areas will be operating on different platforms. It is essential that these people can talk to each other. The problems arise when the functional areas are geographically dispersed. British Steel like many companies has a number of distinct mail systems spread around the world and needs to ensure that there are seamless communications from user to user. The availability of gateways and the ability to use the product across a number of platforms have ensured that Lotus Notes is considered as a solution in this area.

In addition, CMS uses electronic mail as one of the methods of getting closer to its customers this helps to differentiate itself from its competitors. A system which incorporates electronic mail must at the minimum match the functionality and ease of use of the system which was already in place; if not the business may suffer.

Knowledge Based Staff

In the 1990s the companies which make the most significant use of their staff will be the most successful. One of the problems is that when the staff are on holiday, off sick or working on another project their skills are not available to the company. What is needed therefore is a Corporate Memory. This would entail every member of staff entering the knowledge they possess into a number of corporate databases. These databases would then be available to any other member of staff which needs the information. Although this may take time to complete, a majority of staff have their own information stored in one form or another and gradually they have been transfering this information to Lotus Notes. The flexibility of the data imports within Lotus Notes has greatly assisted in this process.

Paper Intensive

If you think your business is highly computerised and you are the model of efficiency collect one more metric. How many sheets of A4 paper does your business use per annum? This information usually has two effects. Firstly, every time somebody in the organisation uses the photocopier you go and see which knitting pattern or pools coupon they are copying and secondly, there is meeting between the IT Manager or Director with his management team on how can we move to a paperless office. Groupware will never replace the need for paper in all instances, but it will however reduce the need for the multitude of filing cabinets needed to store the paperwork and vastly reduce the number of copies which are taken of each document. The cost of office space in most major cities is expensive.

The reduction in space needed for paper storage could pay for this system in the first year.

Flattening of the Organisation

There is currently a move towards the reduction in management layers within an organisation. Implementing a system such as groupware brings together people of all levels and locations of the business. The free and open availability of information reduces the need for control and cross functional coordination. This new feeling of empowerment will in turn release the overall creativity of all concerned to the benefit of the customer.

Downsizing the organisation

In the past few decades computerisation has had a profound effect of staff numbers within organisations. These have until recently focused on the traditional blue collar areas. In the next few years there will be a significant reduction in the number of white collar jobs in most sectors. The effective use of technology will enable this to happen. The synergetic effect of using groupware products will enable less people to do the same amount of work.

Everybody Else Is!!!

This is as a direct result of the old adage of the past decades that 'nobody has ever been sacked for buying xxx'. If everybody else is doing something then it must be right, the so called 'Lemming Syndrome'. Within the business environment there are leaders and there are followers. Even if you do not wish to be at the 'bleeding edge' of technology before you make the decision to implement groupware you really need to ensure you know where the path will take you or you may find that the people shaping your destiny have read the quote from Alice in Wonderland as well!!!

THE PROCESS OF IMPLEMENTATION

There are a number of distinct areas which should be considered when implementing groupware products, these are listed below in the following sections. However there is one area which has more significance, that of the Project Sponsor. Disregard this at your peril!

Project Sponsorship

There are very few software systems on the market which if implemented successfully have the capability to radically reshape the organisation. To this end having a sponsor with enough influence over the business is crucial. During the implementation phase there will be a significant number of the organisation which will have doubts about the benefits of groupware. Unless the sponsor is in a position to counteract these comments the project will be in jeopardy. The use of groupware products should be seen as a strategic direction and supported from the highest levels of the organisation

The Use of Consultants

When planning a business venture one of the most important skills to have is experience. The problem arises when you are attempting to do something for the first time. This is where the use of consultancy can be beneficial. Consultants if used effectively will enable the project to succeed. However, if the wrong consultants are employed the opposite may happen. It is imperative therefore that you know exactly what you require from the consultant before he is appointed. The following sections detail what issues you should be aware of when choosing a consultant.

Management empathy

The implementation of groupware products will be a stressful time. It is imperative that you will be able to work with the consultants you choose. The success of the project will depend on all members of the team working together effectively. If you have any doubts about the consultant in question have him replaced.

Business knowledge

Experience in similar businesses as your own is important. If the consultant understands the type of pressures your business works under it may change the direction in which he guides you. However, if you work in a specialised area it may be difficult to find such a person. It may then be appropriate for the consultant to spend a period of time talking to the users and management to familiarise himself with the working environment.

Product experience

It has been known in the past for consultants to exaggerate the level of skills they possess. If you are paying standard consultancy rates you should expect that the people you are buying should have the right skill level. You should ask for a detailed list of experience in the field before agreeing to a specific consultant.

At times however it may be prudent to agree to a reduction in the rates you are paying for the use of your organisation as a reference site. This is a risky venture and may not result in the most effective system being implemented.

Integration skills

No groupware implementation should be seen in isolation. At some time during the project life cycle integration with other systems will be required. Skills in the area of integration are few and far between. One possible answer may be to have a number of consultants working together. This may cause problems in where the responsibilities of one consultant starts and where another ends. Using all consultants from one supplier may be the most pragmatic solution to the lack of availability of an hybrid consultant. In this way it would be the responsibility of the supplier to ensure that all aspects of the system fit together.

Support

As the groupware product skills within your organization grow the requirement for top class support will become more important. After a short period of time your own internal skills have exceeded the ones being supplied by the consultancy. If this is the case access to the product supplier is paramount. During initial discussions with prospective suppliers of consultancy, investigate how they intend to support your business long term. A company with a working relationship with the original suppliers is the most appropriate one to choose.

The Project Team

If you are to successfully implement this project you will need the right team. Choosing this team is also one of the most difficult areas. The project will tend to cross a number of functions within the organisation; the choice of the leader is therefore crucial. The ideal candidate should be seen as a strong leader and have some experience of the functional areas involved.

Picking the right team to support the leader will be a difficult task. The products tend to lend themselves more to the prototyping way of working than to any other methodology. To this end the type of people you use will be different to most projects. In every business you will find members of staff who do not seem to fit into the normal routine. Depending on who you are talking to, these people are seen as the mavericks or the innovators. These are the people who can think laterally as well as logically. Successful groupware project teams usually contain a number of these people. The management skill is in ensuring that they are all aiming towards the same goal.

A Level Playing Field

This is also an appropriate time to look at the total LAN and PC infrastructure within the organisation. The exponential growth of personal computing within the last decade has resulted in a number of problems: software piracy, the lack of standards and the robustness of the system.

In a recent MORI survey (1990) they estimated that 2.4 million users may have been breaking copyright law. The penalties for adhering to this law may include imprisonment for the manager responsible.

Very few businesses can guarantee that every personal computer within their organisation has the company 'standard' configuration. To implement Lotus Notes effectively there are a number of pre-requisites which will need to be in place. An appropriate minimum configuration needs to be devised and implemented. A suitable entry level standard for a LAN connected PC would be:

- 386 processor
- 12MB disk space
- VGA screen
- Windows 3.1
- 4MB memory
- LAN connected

The proliferation of Local Area Networks within the corporate business environment has resulted in business critical systems being run on infrastructures which were not designed for the purpose. The traditional values associated with mainframes such as reliability, data storage, security and capacity planning need to be replicated down onto the LAN. In many instances, distinct and stand alone LANs have been installed in different functional areas throughout the business. Recently there has been pressure from the users to share resources across these LANs. This has resulted in many systems being 'bolted together' on a best endeavours basis. It is hard to believe that if an organisation could start again its LAN infrastructure would look the same as it is today. The redesign of the LANs within CMS resulted in the number of servers reducing from 11 to 4 and at the same time the number of users increased from 70 to 260. All this was achieved with a significant reduction in the administrative overheads of supporting the network.

Electronic Mail

Ensuring seamless communications across the British Steel mail network was a significant problem area. The resulting network as shown in figure 1 below shows how this was achieved.

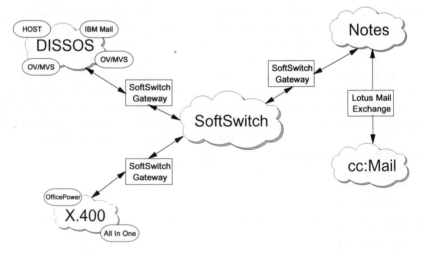

Figure 1   The British Steel plc Electronic Mail System

There are number of significant issues involved in this configuration.

When mail is sent from a Lotus Notes User to another Lotus Notes user the message stays within the Lotus Notes environment and does not cross the gateways. This significantly reduces the risk of overloading this critical part of the system.

The Lotus Notes Address book is synchronised on a daily basis with the Enterprise Address Book (EAB) stored in Officevision 2 on the IBM mainframe. This is achieved by a suite of bespoke programs both on the mainframe and Lotus Notes servers.

An automatic system has been written and installed which on a regular basis polls every connected system within the mail network. If there is not a reply within a set period of time an automatic note is sent to each of the system administrators.

Multiple Platforms and Networks

Very few businesses will have the luxury of a standard computing platform for every one of its staff. Within the organisation there will be Windows, OS/2 and probably the odd Apple Macintosh. When you are choosing a product you should take this into account. The configuration shown in figure 2 is a representation of a working solution implemented within CMS.

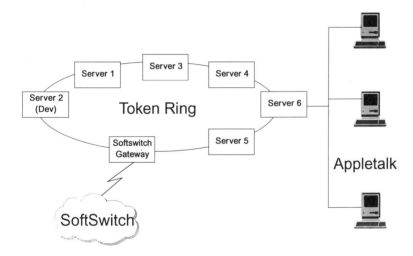

Figure 2   A working multi-platform implementation.

The configuration is as follows.

All servers are IBM PS/2 model 95 with a minimum of 1GB of disk space. There is 16MB of memory and each machine is running OS/2 V2.1.

All servers contain a Token Ring card and are connected to a 4MB/s backbone segment of the network.

One server contains an additional Ethernet card to bridge to the Apple network. This server runs the OS/2 Appletalk drivers.

The back up security server doubles up as the Soft Switch gateway.

This configuration however, has its limitations. The Apple users have only got access to the server to which they are connected via Ethernet. However this would be rectified if the LANs were moved to a new operating system.

Design Standards

At the start of the development phase ensure that all members of the team are working to the same design standards. With a product such as Lotus Notes there will be a tendency by the team members to exploit all of the design features of the product. Although the standards will evolve as more users get involved, it will be substantially easy to change in the future if all the developments are consistent.

When setting standards be aware of the use of the type of screens the users will be using. This could be VGA, XVGA or an Apple screen. It is difficult to choose fonts which will be appropriate for all of these.

Capacity Planning

This is split into two areas, the number of users per server and the amount of storage space required. If the system is to be used on a regular basis a maximum of 75 users per server is recommended. If this is exceeded there will be a corresponding degradation in the level of service provided. The issue of data storage is more difficult. An accurate estimate cannot be made until an analysis of the proposed system takes place. However, CMS after a few years of operation used approximately 5MB of disk space per user.

There are a number of ways in which data storage may be reduced: this may result in the system not being used to its full potential.

Backup Security

This was one of the areas in which there has been very little work in the market place. At the time of implementation the only recommendation

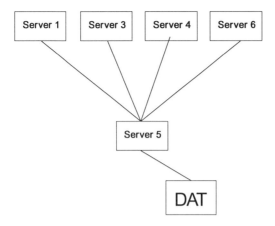

Figure 3   System backups

was to take the servers down before doing a back up. This resulted in down time for the users and an increased administrative workload.

The system which was implemented at CMS is shown in figure 3.

The data recovery was deemed as critical to the project. On a regular basis (dependent on the assigned priority of the information) all databases are replicated to a central server. During the night this data is spooled to a DAT tape for archiving. On a monthly basis one of these daily tapes is taken offsite for disaster recovery purposes.

The resultant system enables data to be recovered from one of three sources: the off site tape, the daily backup or the replicated copy on the backup server. This covers all probable areas of concern.

BUSINESS/ORGANISATIONAL BENEFITS

There will be significant changes within the organisation as a result of implementing groupware products. The following sections give information on how the introduction of Lotus Notes has significantly improved the working practices of CMS.

Communications

The amount of information flowing electronically within the business has increased four fold. This is based on the number of messages being sent and does not take into account the increased functionality now available. A substantial slice of the traffic is now taken up with the rich text aspect of Lotus Notes; this includes font, colour, and the use of bit map pictures. One of the most visible uses of this technology within the organisation has been the passing of charted information. This enables recipients to quickly assimilate the information transmitted without having to chart the information themselves. This has greatly increased the speed in which certain decisions are made.

Consensus Management

The introduction of electronic discussion forums has helped to ensure that the decision making process within CMS is more effective. No one person within an organisation will have all the information necessary to make a decision. In the past within CMS it was difficult to get views of all of the salient parties before decisions were made. This occasionally resulted in inappropriate decisions being made. The introduction of Lotus Notes has enabled discussion forums to be set up on a wide range of issues, varying from the CMS strategic direction to formulation of the social programme for the year. These forums enable relevant personnel to be aware of the decisions which are about to be made. This new awareness has resulted in a substantial increase in the views being attained and subsequently improved the quality of the decisions being made.

Effectiveness of Meetings

Since the introduction of Lotus Notes the number of ad-hoc meetings held within the business has reduced significantly. Using the discussion forums enables the meetings to be a decision making forum and not a 'talking shop'. This has resulted in more time being made available for customer related topics. The minutes, agendas and actions for meetings are stored and tracked through Lotus Notes which has resulted in a reduction in the storage space required and the speedier availability of information.

Teamworking

The benefits of teamworking are plain to see. Since the introduction there has been a significant shift in the way staff from different functions work with each other on a day to day basis. However, the problems arise when the teams who need to work together are dispersed throughout the company. Lotus Notes has enabled CMS to be more flexible in its approach to team forming. In a recent project the Project Manager was based in Humberside, the development team in South Wales, the Technical Support team in South Yorkshire and the Account Manager in London. All members of the team had access to the same information at the same time.

Reorganisation

The availability of information and the new teamworking ethos has enabled CMS to reshape its organisation. The days of IT staff working away in their ivory towers are gone. Today one of the most important skills IT professionals need is an understanding of the business they are supporting. Lotus Notes has enabled technical experts to share their specialised knowledge across customer based teams.

This method of working enables the customer teams to develop specific business skills for their customer and at the same time continue to develop their own technical skills.

Knowledge Sharing

Francis Bacon once said that 'Knowledge itself is power'. Within the IT community this has been regarded as the one of the main driving forces. Getting IT staff to share their skills has always been a difficult task. In the last year however, there seems to have been a major shift in this area. A number of specialist databases have been set up which are the repositories for information on a wide range of specialist areas. These have included Client/Server, OS/2, Windows, Rapid Application Development (RAD) and object orientation. The resident experts in these fields have shared their expertise with the whole organisation. The benefit to them is that they can use some of the time they were spending working in these areas to learn new skills. CMS and the individual both benefit from this arrangement. Additionally, the technical experts will have time to contribute to a wider spectrum of debates in which they may be interested.

Core Processes

A number of the core processes within CMS have been implemented onto Lotus Notes. These have included aspects of workflow computing. One of the most significant has been that of the project lifecycle. All aspects of this cycle now use Lotus Notes, from the original project initiation right through to the system documentation.

The use of Lotus Notes has enabled CMS to look at its core processes with a view to improving them. Significant benefits have been gained by redesigning the resource forecasting process using Lotus Notes. This has increased staff utilisation markedly.

CMS has used the routing capabilities of Lotus Notes to automate the paper forms which circulate the business. These include the request and authorisation of purchases. This new system has reduced the amount of paper being used and at the same time improved the turnaround speed of documents.

Catalyst for Change

The decision to invest in Lotus Notes was the catalyst which enabled a number of significant changes to be made, some of which were not related to the implementation. The move to some form of CSCW is seen as a significant change in the business attitude. This encourages many members of staff to make improvements in their own specific areas. These improvements have proved to have significant benefits to the organisation as a whole.

PITFALLS

With all implementations there will be pitfalls, and Lotus Notes is no exception. There is a perception within some parts of the industry that Lotus Notes is the panacea to all of the ills of the world. If you go into the project thinking this you will be disappointed. There is a great tendency to bend the product to fit all situations. If you attempt to do this the users of the system will get a false view of the capabilities of the product and will be disillusioned.

It is important that you analyse the processes you wish to computerise before you implement. The whole project may be in jeopardy if the first system you release is the computerisation of a bad process.

It is important that the momentum of the project is maintained. Users may lose interest in the project if they are not constantly treated to new experiences. A phased introduction of systems will enable the users to build up confidence with the systems and at the same time continue to keep their interest.

AN IMPLEMENTATION CHECKLIST

Information gained from initial projects has now been used to improve the effectiveness of subsequent projects. The method used is in the form of a checklist. If you are confident of every one of the items on this list then the chances of success are greatly increased. The sections above contain more information about the individual items.

- Ensure you have the right level of management support
- Understand why you are doing the project
- What are the criteria for success
- Ensure the budget is adequate
- Choose the right processes
- Choose the right consultants
- Choose the right team
- Set design standards early
- Ensure the infrastructure is adequate
- Phase the implementation
- Document as you go along.

CONCLUSIONS

The information above is a detailed analysis of the issues involved in the implementation of CSCW in the corporate business environment. The benefits to the business can be substantial if the project is well thought through and implemented effectively. The checklist will point to the areas in which special attention needs to be given.

Although this paper has concentrated on the implementation of Lotus Notes, the comments will equally apply to other groupware products. This is because the most significant issues are the people issues and not that of technology.

ACKNOWLEDGEMENTS

I would like to thank the Lotus Notes Implementation team at CMS, without their support the project would have not been the success it was.

REFERENCES

Carroll L. 1988. Alice's Adventure in Wonderland. In *The Complete Works of Lewis Carroll* 6: p.64. Penguin, Harmonsworth
MORI. 1990. In *FAST Corporate Membership Policy Manual*. 5: . FAST, Maidenhead
Grudin J. 1991. Introduction to CSCW. *Communications of the ACM*, Vol: 34 No. 12 Dec 1991 p. 30-34

Section IV

Future Issues in CSCW

9

The Impact of Distributed Multimedia Systems on Computer Support for Co-operative Work

Neil Williams, Gordon S. Blair, Geoff Coulson, Nigel Davies, Tom Rodden

ABSTRACT

Recent advances in distributed multimedia technologies are likely to have a significant impact on the co-operative work practices of organisations. However, at present there is little practical experience with distributed multimedia systems. This paper examines the potential for multimedia systems within a particular end user organisation. A pilot multimedia information system is described which has been designed to support a specific co-operative working scenario identified within the organisation. The paper concludes that multimedia can have a significant impact on co-operative working. However, considerable attention must be given to the required system support for such applications. The development of integrated multimedia information systems is seen as particularly important. Without this, the full potential of multimedia and co-operative working cannot be fully realised.

Computer Support for Co-operative Work. Edited by Kathy Spurr, Paul Layzell, Leslie Jennison and Neil Richards
© 1994 John Wiley & Sons Ltd

INTRODUCTION

Co-operative working involves a number of people working together to achieve a common goal. The distribution of organisations, however, often requires that personnel are forced to work with colleagues who are situated remotely. The geographic distance between personnel constrains the degree to which they can collaborate. Communications technologies are important in helping to overcome these constraints and achieve the desired level of remote co-operation. Until recently, however, communications technologies have failed to provide the required level of support for remote user interaction. For example, technology constraints have restricted computer support for co-operative working (CSCW) to a limited set of media types. The majority of applications have been restricted to text and graphics communication, but have not been able to exploit media types such as audio and video. Those systems developed to provide co-operative working in conjunction with audio and video have been forced to use non-digital networks for these more demanding forms of media. Such systems present the user with a non-integrated information system.

However, advances in networking technology and the availability of multimedia workstations have led to the emergence of *distributed multimedia systems*. Such systems are able to support a full range of media including text, graphics, image, audio and video in an integrated manner. Multimedia applications can now be developed which fully support remote co-operative working and provide a viable alternative to actual co-location. To exploit the potential offered by multimedia, however, the role of collaborative applications within organisations must be understood. Questions need to be answered as to the types of application which will develop and the way in which they will be used. Furthermore, an understanding must be achieved regarding the nature of the support systems for these applications. This paper addresses the issues of CSCW applications by considering a potential application and its support environment.

WHAT IS CSCW?

The term Computer-Supported Co-operative Work was initially coined by Irene Grief and Paul Cashman in 1984 in the call for papers of a conference. Since that time, the field has grown to become one of the most prominent research areas of the 1990s. The exact meaning of the term CSCW has undergone considerable debate (Bannon and Schmidt, 1991) (Robinson, 1991). Most authors however agree on the following principles:

(i) work is a *co-operative* activity, generally involving *groups* of people interacting to achieve common goals, and

(ii) the designers of supporting computer systems must address this co-operative nature of work.

It could be argued that the above statements are obvious. However, it is clear when reviewing the current state of the art in computer technology that the co-operative nature of work has been largely ignored. For example, existing word processors provide excellent environments to help an author to produce highly professional documents and yet fail to consider the fact that most document production is collaborative.

The term *groupware* has emerged to signify software systems which address the co-operative nature of work. In the words of Lynch *et al.* (1990):

> Groupware is distinguished from normal software by the basic assumption it makes: groupware makes the user aware that he is part of a group, while most other software seeks to hide and protect users from each other...Groupware...is software that accentuates the multiple user environment, co-ordinating and orchestrating things so that users can 'see' each other, yet do not conflict with each other.

Good discussions on groupware can be found in (Ellis *et al.*, 1991) and (Baekar, 1993).

MULTIMEDIA AND CO-OPERATIVE WORKING

Two main types of groupware application exist to support remote co-operative working. Firstly, there are those applications intended to support *asynchronous* exchange of information between users. Secondly, there are a number of applications which support synchronous, real-time interaction between groups of users. Often these two types of application are combined so that more comprehensive co-operative systems can be developed. The two styles of application are described in more detail below. In each case, the potential role of multimedia is highlighted. This is then followed by the description of a hybrid environment featuring both styles of co-operation.

Asynchronous Co-operation

Applications which support the asynchronous exchange of information are often referred to as *message systems* (Malone and Lai, 1988) (Rodden and

Sommerville, 1989). Such systems are referred to as asynchronous because there is no need to wait for a recipient to be available. They normally provide users with the ability to build messages and send these messages to other users. The message size can vary considerably from short notes to messages which contain many pages of information. This variation in size means that message systems are well suited to a range of different user needs. For example, messages can be used as Post-it notes and memos as well as for the exchange of papers and technical reports.

Although widely accepted and used, a limitation of current systems is their restriction on media types. Many existing systems provide only textual messages and do not give the user the full benefits of mixed media information. However, a number of multimedia message systems (Postel et al., 1988) are now becoming available. Such systems allow voice annotations or video clips to be included in mail messages.

Synchronous Co-operation

Synchronous interaction requires the presence of all co-operating users. With this form of co-operation, users typically interact through a *shared information space*. This provides multiple users with synchronous access to the same data and can greatly speed up processes which require the involvement of remote users. Joint access to information reduces many of the overheads of travel and pre-arranged visits. In addition, periods of interaction between remote users can become more frequent and shorter in duration. This style of collaboration gives a close match to that of users who are actually in the same building or office.

There are many examples of synchronous systems including multi-user document editors (Fish et al., 1988) (Hahn et al., 1989) and (virtual) shared whiteboards (Stefik et al., 1987) (Lu and Mantei, 1991). The concept of shared whiteboards has proved to be particularly useful for informal brainstorming between groups of users. Note, however, that many of the systems developed to date are based around a limited set of media types: the shared information space may consist of only text and graphics data. The emerging distributed multimedia technologies, however, allow the information space to contain a wider variety of information, e.g. audio, video and animation in addition to the more traditional text, graphics and image. Similarly, it becomes possible to provide *audio-visual communication* between members of the group. Such developments have led to an interest in multimedia desktop conferencing (Crowley et al., 1990) (Ahuja et al., 1988).

A Hybrid Multimedia Environment

As mentioned above, it is also possible to provide hybrid environments supporting both synchronous and asynchronous modes of co-operation. When combined with multimedia information, such groupware environments clearly have the potential to dramatically impact the working methods of distributed organisations. In such a hybrid environment, users can share *and* exchange a full range of information types via a single integrated system. In such systems, desktop audio-visual conferencing tools may also be provided to enable the user to user communication needed for remote colleagues to work together. Without this direct communication, tools for remote co-operation will be difficult to use. Figure 1 illustrates such a hybrid environment.

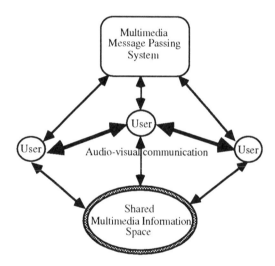

Figure 1   A hybrid environment for co-operative working

AN END USER STUDY

Motivation for the Study

The exploitation of the new technologies for co-operative multimedia systems can only be achieved if real end user needs are satisfied. Application developers must fully understand the types of application which will evolve and the ways in which they will be used. However, a major flaw in achieving this understanding has been a lack of communication between the application developers, the expected future users of multimedia applications and the technologists developing support systems. As a result there has been very little in the way of requirements analysis for co-operative applications and little experience of the real potential of the emerging technologies.

Collaboration between end users and technologists is important to gain experience of the types of application which will develop. For this reason, technologists at Lancaster University have formed a collaboration with a large end user organisation. The objective of this work is to help the end users appreciate the potential of the emerging technologies and help Lancaster to understand how these technologies can be applied in specific user domains. The target organisation is a large chemical company which is widely distributed with both expertise and equipment dispersed across a number of different sites. Furthermore, the organisation's scientific and technical nature means that it handles large quantities of information which includes a full variety of media types. Thus, the effective communication of information between sites is a major concern and the potential offered by distributed multimedia computing is of interest. However, technical applications are a challenging area for multimedia technology and make considerable demands on system resources. Support systems therefore need to provide the level of service required by such applications.

Methods Used

Various personnel were interviewed in order to understand the types of information created within the department and the interchange of this information. The interviews were purposely kept informal to allow the discussion of a wide range of issues ranging from complaints about current procedures to informative guesses regarding future computer usage. It is felt that a formal interview technique with pre-formulated questions would not have been applicable in this study since the objective was to obtain a general understanding of the area, not an in-depth analysis of specific operational procedure. It was desirable that the study had the flexibility to generate a broad outlook on the behaviour of the company from which a number of possible application areas might be identified.

Note that recent work in CSCW has highlighted the role of sociologists, in general, and ethnographers, in particular, in studying work practices in organisations. Although this approach was not used in the studies reported in this paper, we recognise the importance of this work.

General Results

Discussions with the end user organisation have identified a number of applications as having the potential to improve their existing information systems (Williams and Blair, 1994). Many of these are based on the same theme, i.e. the provision of access to remote information sources (monitoring equipment, cameras, etc.) and the storage of this information. Applications must also support co-operative access to information, thus allowing group discussion to take place regarding the information content. In summary, applications are needed which enable users to create and distribute mixed media information freely within the organisation. This may involve messaging systems for asynchronous communication or real-time interactive applications for the synchronous sharing of information.

A further issue identified during discussions with the organisation is the importance of *integration*. Integration is required to enable the full range of information sources (hardware devices, databases, etc.) to be accessible throughout the organisation. However, such a level of integration becomes particularly important to achieve given the level of heterogeneity found in the computer systems of large organisations. More specifically, two levels of integration are identified:

(i) systems integration in a heterogeneous distributed environment, and

(ii) multimedia integration across the range of media types.

In other words, technologies are required which allow applications to be accessed, independently of their location, implementation or the information types produced.

A Specific Applications Scenario

The area of microscopy was identified for more detailed study. Electron and optical microscopes produce a variety of information including photographic images, video, and X-ray spectra. Additional processing of this information may take place to produce analytical information regarding microscope output (e.g. photographs may be passed through an image processing system). A typical microscope session involves an operator browsing a sample using the video output of the microscope. If a particularly interesting image is located, a high resolution photograph may be taken. Hence, the browsing process produces both video output and a series of images which together provide a general overview and understanding of the sample.

It is usual for the sample under examination to be of interest to a particular person who has specific requirements regarding the analysis results. In order to achieve the desired results therefore many analyses require the presence of both a microscope operator and the sample owner. The sample owner guides the operator during the analysis period by identifying areas of specific interest, levels of magnification required etc. In fact, in many cases it is necessary to have several individuals involved in the analysis, each with differing expertise with respect to the sample. For example, when assessing a possible new type of fibre, expertise is required in strength testing, durability testing, mass production viability and commercial potential.

In practice, however, it is often difficult to achieve this level of co-operation due to the problems of arranging convenient meeting times, and because expertise within the organisation is dispersed across a number of sites. Experimental results, therefore, need to be recorded and sent to the relevant people for assessment. The recording of an analysis may either be a sequence of photographs (when particular images are required) or a video (when a general understanding of the sample is to be obtained). Currently the latter case is catered for by recording the video output of the microscope to a video tape. Whilst being recorded, the video tape can be annotated with an audio commentary describing the sample position, magnification, etc. This form of information exchange, however, can be slow and time consuming. Users must rely on postal services, fax messages and telephone conversations for their communication needs.

Microscopy is therefore an activity within the organisation which produces multimedia information and often requires several users to co-operate by sharing and exchanging information. The computing technology currently in use however does not support this range of media types. With the emergence of distributed multimedia technology, though, it becomes feasible to integrate the output of a microscope into a digital system. Once this is achieved the benefits of a fully automated information system are obtainable. For example, it becomes possible for a microscope to be controlled remotely, the video output of the microscope being transmitted to the controller's workstation through a distributed system. Microscope operators can therefore utilise a range of equipment at various sites without needing to spend time travelling. This fact is especially significant when it is realised that microscopes are expensive and may be tailored towards specific types of sample.

The real benefit of distributed multimedia systems however is the impact on user co-operation. The microscope's video output can be displayed simultaneously at a number of workstations when a group of people wish to discuss an experiment in a conference. Furthermore, the microscope output can be stored digitally for incorporation into mixed media documents. These documents can then be used as a means of communicating analysis results via messaging systems such as electronic mail. Figure 2 illustrates a possible information system suitable for the microscopy application area.

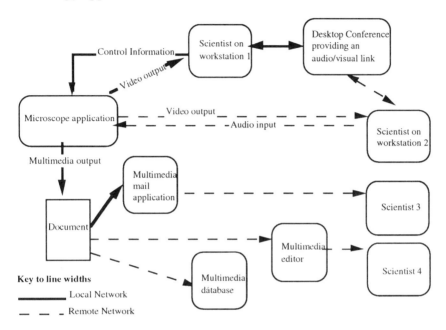

Figure 2   A possible microscope system

APPLYING THE RESULTS

The study described in the previous section has been extremely useful in helping Lancaster to understand the needs of end users with respect to distributed multimedia systems. This improved level of understanding has been influential in the development of Lancaster's distributed multimedia application support platform (Coulson *et al.*, 1992). This platform has also been evaluated by a pilot groupware application to support electron microscopy. The platform and pilot application are discussed in more depth below.

A Support Platform for Co-operative Multimedia Applications

Overall architecture

Utilising the experience gained from collaboration with the end user organisation and from the experience of distributed multimedia systems, Lancaster has developed a system architecture considered suitable for supporting a range of distributed multimedia applications. The Lancaster architecture is shown in figure 3.

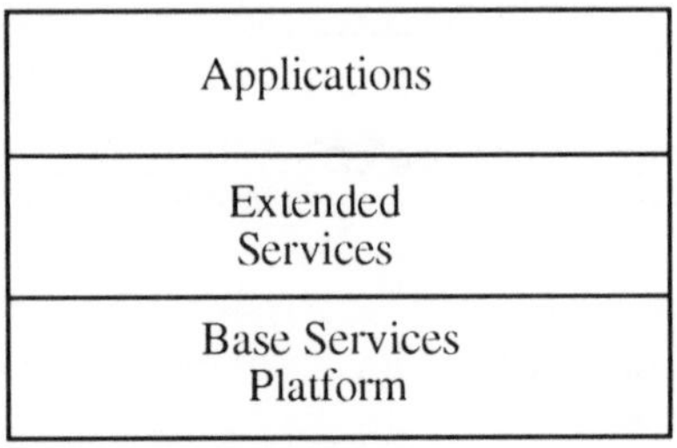

```
┌─────────────────────────────┐
│                             │
│         Applications        │
│                             │
├─────────────────────────────┤
│          Extended           │
│          Services           │
├─────────────────────────────┤
│        Base Services        │
│          Platform           │
└─────────────────────────────┘
```

Figure 3   The Lancaster architecture

The base services platform provides a range of mechanisms to access services (including multimedia services) in a heterogeneous environment. The extended services build on this base and provide facilities such as multimedia documents. Finally, applications within the architecture are those tools which are specific to a particular domain such as medical imaging systems or interactive training systems. By factoring out generic base services and extended services, it is possible to simplify applications since much of their required functionality is provided by the support environment. Integration can also be achieved as all applications share the same support services thus standardising on many aspects of the system. The base services platform and the extended services are examined in turn below.

The base services platform

The Lancaster system is based directly on work from the open systems community and in particular from the International Standards Organisation (ISO) initiative on Open Distributed Processing. It is now recognised by ISO that existing standards for Open Systems Interconnection standards (OSI) are primarily concerned with communication *between* end systems. In a distributed processing system, it is also important to consider standards *within* end systems, thus allowing the full functionality of a distributed system to be described. In recognition of this, ISO have established a new work program to define a Reference Model for Open Distributed Processing (RM/ODP). It is important to stress however that this is a difficult task, complicated by issues such as the existence of legacy systems.

Work on refining a Reference Model for Open Distributed Processing is supported by a number of collaborative projects. Most significantly, the ESPRIT funded Integrated Systems Architecture project (ISA) is addressing distributed systems architectures and standards for a range of application domains. This work is derived from the Alvey sponsored Advanced Networked Systems Architecture project (ANSA) (APM, 1989). This work has produced a distributed systems platform known as ANSAware. This provides system integration by allowing services to be accessed in an open manner in a heterogeneous distributed environment. ANSAware, however, does not provide multimedia integration; in particular, there is no support in the architecture for media types such as audio and video. Lancaster have therefore added these services to the basic ANSAware platform. A brief description of ANSAware is provided below followed by a description of the Lancaster extensions.

ANSAware ANSAware provides a distributed system platform within which all interacting entities are treated uniformly as *objects*, i.e. encapsulations of state and operations defined on that state. This allows applications to interact with services in a uniform manner, irrespective of their implementation and location. Services may be distributed, in which case communication between services is (normally) via remote procedure call. Objects are accessed through *interfaces* which define named *operations* together with constraints on the object. Interfaces are first class entities in their own right, and references to them may be freely passed around the system. Objects are made available for access by *exporting* an interface to a *trader*. The trader therefore acts as a database of services available in the system. Each entry in the trader describes an interface in terms of an abstract data type signature for the object and a set of attributes associated with the object. A client wishing to interact with a service interface must *import* the interface by specifying a set of requirements in terms of operations and attribute values. This specification will be matched against the available services in the trader and a suitable candidate selected. Once an interface has been selected, the system can arrange a *binding* to the appropriate implementation of that object and thus allow operations to be invoked. Figure 4 shows the process of trading and binding.

In ANSAware, export statements contain the following three parameters:

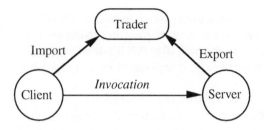

Figure 4   Trading and binding

(i) *Type parameter*—this gives the name of the abstract data type interface being registered with the trader.

(ii) *Context parameter*—the trader maintains a hierarchical naming scheme; the context is therefore equivalent to a file system path (if no specific path is required then the root node (/) must be specified).

(iii) *Constraint property*—this is a general property that must be satisfied in order for matching to take place.

The following is an example of an ANSAware export statement registering a printer service with the trader.

   ! {eh} <-traderRef$export (" printer ", " / ", "Name Laser1")

The corresponding import statement by a client would look like the following.

   ! {i} <-traderRef$import ("printer", " / ", "Name == Laser1")

The ' / ' refers to the context (in this case the root), and the 'Name' statement is the constraint property specifying the constraint on the name of the interface. Notice that an import statement expresses a constraint *predicate* as opposed to a simple list of properties. The constraint predicate specified by the import must be satisfied by the exported constraint property in order for a match to occur.

ANSAware adds some limited flexibility of querying at the type level by making use of subtyping information as seen above. In addition to the flexibility provided by subtyping the trader may also be searched given type, context and constraint parameters. This is done on an all or one basis. Instances of given types satisfying given constraints may also be deleted from the trader.

It is also possible to *federate* traders to create large name spaces. Federation is the interworking of (potentially distributed) different traders and is a term taken directly from the database community. In ANSA there are two ways in which traders may be federated. The context tree of one trader may be bound to the context tree of another trader at a given context. Again the reverse is possible and traders may be 'defederated' by unbinding the context trees. Another method is to use *proxy exports*. A trader, A say, may make a proxy export of one of its services to a different trader B. This simply registers the *existence* of the service in B. The service is not strictly registered in B and when a client scans through trader B looking for the service it will be given a pointer indicating that the service is really registered in trader A. Again proxy offers may be deleted by using the federation manager.

The collected interfaces to the object represent the *type* of that object, representing the external behaviour of the object. Each object type is implemented by one or more templates which describe the internal behaviour of the object in terms of data structures and algorithms. In addition, new objects can be created from templates by *factory* objects, i.e. objects which respond to a new operation by creating a new instance of a type using a particular template.

Extensions to ANSAware for Multimedia Computing In order to support multimedia, a number of extensions must be made to this basic architecture. More specifically, the extensions made to the architecture are intended to support *continuous media* types such as audio, video and animation (Anderson, 1990). The approach taken at Lancaster is to introduce a number of additional object types which abstract over the details of multimedia manipulation. These extensions are described briefly below.

(i) *Streams*—these are abstractions over multimedia protocols. They represent unidirectional m:n connections between a set of media sources and a set of media sinks. In order to model the variety found in multimedia systems, a stream can be requested with a particular *quality of service*. This is modelled as a number of properties of the stream (i.e. throughput, latency, jitter and error characteristics). The architecture also supports *synchronisation* across two or more streams (Coulson and Blair, 1994a). This is used when it is necessary to maintain a temporal relationships between a number of transmissions, e.g. to achieve lip sync between a voice and a video stream.

(ii) *Multimedia devices and chains*—continuous media devices such as cameras, microphones and video windows are all represented as objects. Each device presents two interface to the system, i.e. a *device-dependent* interface and a *device-independent* interface. The device-dependent interface varies from device to device. For example, a camera will support operations such as focus, tilt, etc. In contrast, the device-independent interface is generic across all types of device. This interface is based on the concept of a *chain* (a generalisation of the rope concept employed in the Etherphone project (Terry and Swinehart, 1988)). A chain is an abstraction over a continuous media source or sink and has operations to control the production and consumption of continuous media data. The chain provides the necessary control to manage a continuous media transmission. Each chain also supports the concept of an *endpoint* which is a connection point for a stream. As with streams, endpoints can be created to support a particular *quality of service*. Note that it is possible for a device to support multiple chains/endpoints, thus modelling simultaneous connections to a single device.

(iii) *Groups*—related objects can be collected together in a *group*. Groups are themselves objects with two interfaces. The first interface allows operations to be invoked on all members of the group in a single action (*group invocation*). The second interface is a *management interface* which includes operations to join or leave the group, and to return the current membership of the group. This interface also allows policies to be set for constraining membership of the group, for event ordering on group invocation, etc. Groups play an important role in the Lancaster architecture. For example, a stream expects a group of source endpoints and a group of sink endpoints as parameters.

A number of other extensions have also been made to the ANSA architecture, including *persistence* and *migration* of multimedia objects (Davies *et al.*, 1992) and a *video window* service based on X-Windows. Full details of the Lancaster architecture can be found in (Coulson *et al.*, 1992).

The extended services

Multimedia Documents A facility is provided to support the creation and subsequent manipulation of multimedia documents. When initially created a document is empty, i.e. it has no media components. The application must then create these components and associate them with the document. In addition, the document may also be given structuring information regarding the inter-relationships between these media. Structuring information is actually stored in a separate object known as a *presentation* (see below).

Within the current system a basic document service is available which simply maintains a list of components and a handle to an associated presentation. Although simple, documents allow information to be stored, passed between applications, and played back. The Zenith project (Kemp *et al.*, 1992) at Lancaster is addressing the problems of complex objects and their management within a distributed system. This project has developed models and ideas for complex objects which will apply to documents. As such the documents in use at present are seen as a placeholder for the development of the ideas generated within the Zenith project. Similarly, other forms of document based on standards such as the Office Document Architecture (ODA) (Brown, 1989) could also be used.

Presentations A presentation object is responsible for maintaining knowledge regarding a document's structure. Applications which require structured documents can create a presentation and notify a document of its existence. The application can then take its knowledge of the document's required structure and create a script describing this structure in terms of the synchronisation required between the media types. This script is then passed to the presentation object.

The presentation object is responsible for parsing the given script and playing out the document's components accordingly. The script indicates how the support system is to be configured for the document playout and when particular media components are to be started or stopped. For example, an audio component may to be started on the second frame of video and stopped at the tenth. The presentation monitors system generated events to achieve this synchronisation.

A simple script is currently in use which allows for experimentation with document playout. As with the documents themselves, the presentation object and its script are seen as place holders for future development. Real-time synchronisation languages such as Esterel (Berry and Gonthier, 1988) are being considered to provide the script in the future. Similarly, the presentation object will take input from the Zenith project regarding the methods of structuring objects and the constraints to be imposed on this structuring.

The Pilot Groupware Application

The pilot groupware application is a hybrid environment supporting both synchronous and asynchronous modes of co-operation as discussed below.

Supporting synchronous co-operation

The microscope groupware application provides multiple users with simultaneous access to microscope devices located on a network. Access to these devices is identical irrespective of their location. The application queries the system for available devices and lists them by name for the user. The list will vary according to the state of the system, but will consist of all the currently accessible microscopes. From the list of available devices, a user can select a microscope from which the output is to be displayed. A video window is then created on the user's workstation and the video output from the device is placed into this window. Whilst viewing the microscope output a user also has control over the device. In the demonstration system this control allows users to adjust the size and colour of the video image, but could be extended to provide control over other microscope operations. Multiple devices can be simultaneously accessed from the application thus allowing the user to compare different samples.

The co-operative working environment is enhanced by a desktop conferencing tool. This tool allows users to communicate through an audio channel whilst also showing a video picture of the conference participants (see figure 5). In general, however, the video connection only serves to enhance the conference, and can be switched off to reduce the information overload on the conference participants. In contrast, the audio channel is frequently used to avoid conflict in accessing the shared information. When using the conferencing service, a shared white board is also available. The white board is a useful aid for helping users collaborate through the use of diagrams, etc. In a technical environment this additional support for user co-operation is vital. At present, no integration is provided between the white board drawing facilities and the microscope output. For example, it is not possible to draw over the video image. This level of integration would be required in a live system and could easily be provided since the video output display drivers are based on X-Windows and use standard X-Windows image manipulation procedures. Similarly, there is no integration between the desktop conferencing tool and the microscope tool; for example, they maintain separate lists of group membership.

Supporting asynchronous co-operation

Whilst using the microscope application, any user can select a record mode which instructs the application to create a multimedia document. The video output from the microscope device complete with an optional voice annotation is then stored in this document. The voice annotation

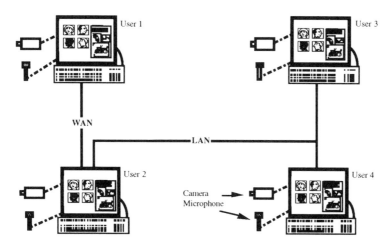

Figure 5   The desktop conferencing tool

can be provided by any number of the current application users. Once created, the document contains the various media components and a script describing the document structure. This structure is specified in terms of when to start and stop individual components when the document is played back. After creation, documents can be communicated to system users asynchronously. Two services are being developed to provide this type of information sharing. First, there is a document editor which enables users to view and edit available documents. Second, a mail service which gives users the ability to send multimedia messages.

The multimedia editor allows the structure and content of documents to be changed. It is not intended to provide a fully functional editing service, but to demonstrate the potential for flow of information throughout an organisation. The user interfaces to multimedia editors and their required editing facilities are not an issue for this particular implementation. Such work has been covered by other research projects (Bessiere *et al.*, 1991).

The mail service also utilises the availability of documents within the system. The mail service provides users with a tool to send documents to other users. As with the document editor, the mail service is intended to display the potential for a number of distinct co-operating applications to provide an integrated information system. The mail tool, therefore, does not attempt to solve the many issues associated with multimedia mail (Huitema, 1989), for example, issues concerning the size and structuring of mail messages. Instead the mail service passes documents by reference to other users. A single copy of each media component is held in the system.

PROJECT STATUS AND FUTURE WORK

The platform and associated groupware application described in this paper have been fully implemented on top of an experimental multimedia workstation/ high speed network environment built at Lancaster (Blair *et al.*, 1993). This environment, based on transputer technology, offers the basic real-time communication and processing support required by multimedia applications. Multimedia workstations are composed of a standard workstation with an added multimedia network interface (MNI) unit. The MNI connects directly to the workstation, and supports a complete set of multimedia devices (i.e. display, camera, speaker and microphone), and a high-speed network connection. It manages all continuous media sources and sinks at its host workstation. Figure 6 illustrates the transputer configuration of which the MNI unit is built. Connection to the workstation is via a single transputer link as illustrated.

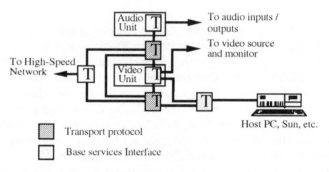

Figure 6   The Multimedia Network Interface unit

While the transputer environment has been successful in managing continuous media data, it is now recognised that there is a need for some applications to be able to process such data. This requires an approach where continuous media data can be read and manipulated in the same way as traditional media types such as text and graphics. This however requires tailored operating system support in order to meet the real-time requirements of such media types.

Ongoing research at Lancaster is examining the area of operating system support for continuous media data. More specifically, the SUMO Project (Support for Multimedia in Open Distributed Processing) is designing and implementing communications and scheduling components designed to handle continuous media data (Coulson *et al.*, 1994b). This work is based around the Chorus micro-kernel (Bricker *et al.*, 1991). Research is also focusing on the problems of requirements capture in CSCW. As mentioned above, recent research in CSCW is challenging the existing methods of requirements capture and systems analysis. In particular, many CSCW researchers believe that existing methods fail to recognise the social processes involved in group activities. They therefore believe that new techniques are required which recognise the *sociality* of work practices. Most of this research is multi-disciplinary in nature, involving sociologists, psychologists and computer scientists (Comic, 1993).

CONCLUSIONS

The major conclusion of the paper is that the combination of distributed multimedia computing and CSCW can have a significant impact on the work practices of an organisation, particularly where co-operating users are geographically dispersed. The paper highlights an example scenario of groups of experts co-operating (possibly remotely) on electron micro-scopy experiments. A groupware application to support this activity is also described. However, if this potential is to be realised, it is important that computer systems provide the necessary support for such group-ware applications. A distributed systems platform, based on ANSAware is described. This platform provides integrated access to a range of services, including multimedia services, in a heterogeneous environment. The authors believe that such technologies have an important role to play in enabling a range of groupware applications to be developed within an organisation.

REFERENCES

Ahuja S.R., Ensor J.R., and Horn D.N. (1988) 'The Rapport Multimedia Conferencing System', *Proceedings of COIS88 Conference on Office Information Systems*, Palo Alto, California, March 23-25.

Anderson, D.P., Tzou, S.Y., Wahbe, R., Govindan R. and Andrews, M. (1990) 'Support for Continuous Media in the DASH System', *Proceedings of the 10th International Conference on Distributed Computing Systems*, Paris, May.

APM Ltd. (1989) 'The ANSA Reference Manual Release 01.00', Available from APM Ltd., Poseidon House, Castle Park, Cambridge, CB3 0RD, UK.

Baeker, R. (1993) 'Readings in Groupware and Computer Supported Co-operative Work, Morgan Kaufmann, San Mateo CA.

Bannon, L. and Schmidt, K. (1991) 'CSCW: Four Characters in Search of Context' in J.M. Bowers and S.D. Benford (eds): Studies in Computer Supported Co-operative Work. Theory, Practice and Design, North-Holland, Amsterdam.

Bentley, R., Hughes, J., Randall, D., Rodden T., Sawyer, P., Sommerville, I. and Shapiro, D. (1992) 'Ethnographically Informed Systems Design for Air Traffic Control', Proceeding of CSCW'92, Toronto, November 1992.

Berry, G. and Gonthier, G. (1988) 'The Esterel Synchronisation Programming Language: Design, Semantics, Implementation', Report Number 842, INRIA, France.

Bessiere C., Leonhardt J.L., Zeiliger R. (1991) 'Multimedia Authoring Tools: Atelier ORGUE', Computer Networks and ISDN Systems, Vol. 23.

Blair, G.S., Campbell, A., Coulson, G., Garcia, F., Hutchison, D., Scott, A., and Shepherd, W.D. (1993) 'A Network Interface Unit to Support Continuous Media', IEEE Journal of Selected Areas in Communications (JSAC), Vol. 11, No. 3.

Bricker, A., Gien, M., Guillemont, M., Lipkis, J., Orr, D., and Rozier, M. (1991) 'Architectural Issues in Micro-Kernel based Operating Systems: The Chorus Experience', Computer Communications, Vol. 14, No. 6, pp 347-357.

Brown, H. (1989) 'Standards for Structured Documents', The Computer Journal, Vol. 32, No. 6, pp 505-514.

Comic Project, 'Informing CSCW System Requirements', Comic Esprit Basic Research Action, Deliverable 2.1, ISBN 0-901800-29-5, Lancaster University, October 1993.

Coulson, G., and Blair, G.S. (1994a) 'Meeting the Real-Time Synchronisation Requirements of Multimedia in Open Distributed Processing', To appear in the Distributed Systems Engineering Journal.

Coulson, G., Blair, G.S., and Robin, P. (1994b) 'Micro-Kernel Support for Continuous Media in Distributed Systems', To appear in Computer Networks and ISDN Systems, Special Issue on Multimedia.

Coulson, G., G.S. Blair, N. Davies, and N. Williams. (1992) 'Extensions to ANSA for Multimedia Computing', Computer Networks and ISDN Systems, 25, pp 305-323.

Crowley, T., Baker, E., Forsdick, H., Milazzo, P. and Tomlinson, R. (1990) 'MMConf: An Infrastructure for Building Shared Applications', Proceedings of the Conference on Computer Supported Co-operative Work (CSCW'90), Los Angeles, CA, October 7-10 1990, ACM Press.

Davies, N., Blair, G.S., and Mariani, J.A. (1992) 'Supporting Persistent Relocatable Objects in the ANSA Architecture', Internal Report MPG-92-04, Computing Department, Lancaster University, Bailrigg, Lancaster LA1 4YR, UK.

Ellis, C.A., Gibbs, S.J. and Rein, G.L. (1991) 'Groupware: Some Issues and Experiences', Communications of the ACM, Vol. 34, No. 1, pp 38-58.

Fish R.S., Kraut R.E., Leland M.D., and Cohen M. (1988) 'Quilt: A Collaborative Tool for Co-operative Writing', Proceedings of COIS88 Conference on Office Information Systems, Palo Alto, California, March 23-25.

Hahn U., Jarke M., Kreplin K. et al. (1989) 'CoAuthor: A Hypermedia Group Authoring Environment', Proceedings of EC-CSCW the 1st European Conference on CSCW, Gatwick Hilton, September 13th-15th.

Hopkin, V.D. (1991) 'The Impact of Automation on Air Traffic Control Systems', in J.A. Wise, V.D. Hopkin and M.L. Smith (eds.), Automation and Systems Issues in Air Traffic Control, Berlin, Springer Verlag.

Hughes, J.A., Randall, D. and Shapiro, D. (1992) 'Faltering from Ethnography to Design', Proceeding of CSCW'92, Toronto, November 1992.

Huitema, C. (1989) 'The Challenge of Multimedia Mail', Computer Networks and ISDN Systems, Vol. 17, pp 324-327.

Kemp, Z., Oxborrow, E., Davy, D., Linington, P., Thearle, R., Blair, G.S., Dark, P.,

Davies, N., Mariani, J.A., and Snape, C. (1992) 'The Zenith System for Object Management in Distributed Multimedia Design Environments', *Information and Software Technology*, Vol. 34, No. 7, pp 427-436.

Lu, I.M., and Mantei M. (1991) 'Idea Management in a Shared Drawing Tool', *Proceedings of the 2nd European Conference on Computer Supported Co-operative Work*, Amsterdam, Holland, September 1991.

Lynch, K.J., Snyder, J.M., Vogel, D.R. and McHenry, W.K. (1990) 'The Arizona Analyst Information System: Supporting Collaborative Research on International Technological Trends', in Gibbs, S. and Verrijn-Stuart, A.A. (eds): Multi-User Interfaces and Applications, North-Holland, Amsterdam, pp 159-174.

Malone T. W., and Lai K. (1988) 'Object Lens: A Spreadsheet for Co-operative Work', *Proceedings of CSCWi88*, Portland, Oregon, September.

Postel J.B., Finn G.G., Katz A.R., and Reynolds J.K., (1988) 'An Experimental Multimedia Mail System', *ACM Transactions on Office Information Systems*, Vol. 6, No. 1, pp 63-81.

Robinson, M. (1991) 'Computer Supported Co-operative Work: Cases and Concepts' *Proceedings of Groupware'91*, Software Engineering Research Centre, Postbus 424, 3500 AK Utrecht, Nederland, pp 59-74.

Rodden T., and Sommerville, I. (1989) 'Building Conversations using Mailtrays' *Proceeding of 1st European Conference on CSCW (EC-CSCW)*, Gatwick Hilton September 13th-15th, 1989.

Stefik M., Foster G., et al. (1987) 'Beyond the Chalkboard : Computer Support for Collaboration and Problem Solving in Meetings', *Communications of the ACM*, Vol. 30, No. 1, January 1987

Suchman, L. (1987) Plans and Situated Action: The Problem of Human Machine Communication, Cambridge University Press.

Terry, D.B., and D.C. Swinehart (1988) 'Managing Stored Voice in the Etherphone System' *ACM Transactions on Computer Systems*, Vol. 6 No. 1, February.

Williams, N., and Blair, G.S. (1994) 'Distributed Multimedia Computing: An End User Perspective', *Proceedings of the Second Biennial Conference on Engineering Systems Design and Analysis*, London, July.

10

Co-operative Requirements Capture: Prototype Evaluation

Linda Macaulay, Greg O'Hare, Paul Dongha, Steve Viller[1]

ABSTRACT

The purpose of the paper is to present the results from an evaluation of groupware which was developed to support a multidisciplinary team engaged in a co-operative requirements capture activity.

The prototype groupware was developed as part of a collaborative project called Cooperative Requirements Capture (CRC). CRC is concerned with providing computer support for a multidisciplinary group who are engaged in the early stages of requirements capture for a proposed computer system. Such a group would normally hold a series of face to face meetings in order to reach agreement on a set of requirements. The diversity of interests and motivations within the group could potentially lead to conflict and disagreement. In a face to face setting a facilitator would normally be employed in order to ensure participation and to assist the group in reaching such agreement.

The CRC project has developed prototype computer support which has the following overall aims:

Computer Support for Co-operative Work. Edited by Kathy Spurr, Paul Layzell, Leslie Jennison and Neil Richards
© 1994 John Wiley & Sons Ltd
[1] Steve Viller is now at the Computing Department, Lancaster University.

(1) To enable the group to operate effectively but with less time spent in face to face meetings.

(2) To assist the group in the process of reaching agreement.

(3) To provide feedback on communication between group members from the system to the facilitator.

(4) To provide support for synchronous and asynchronous distributed working of group members.

(5) To be easily used by people from a variety of backgrounds.

(6) To maintain the sense of 'group' developed during face to face meetings.

A number of evaluations of the CRC prototype have taken place involving representative groups of users from collaborating organisations. The paper will present the findings of these evaluations and discuss the potential for future development.

THE CRC PROJECT OVERVIEW

The main aim of the CRC project is to develop prototype tools which can be used to support a multidisciplinary team in the process of capturing requirements for computer based systems.

The members of the multidisciplinary team will all have a stake in the decision taken concerning the proposed system. Four major categories of stakeholders have been identified:

(a) Those who are responsible for its design and development, for example, the project manager, software designers, communications experts, technical authors.

(b) Those with a financial interest, responsible for its sale, for example, the business analyst or in some situations the marketeer, or those responsible for its purchase.

(c) Those responsible for its introduction and maintenance within an organisation, for example, training and user support staff, installation and maintenance engineers and user managers.

(d) Those who have an interest in its use, for example, user managers and all classes of users, i.e. primary (frequent hands-on users), secondary (occasional users or those who use the system through an intermediary) and tertiary (those affected by the introduction of the system).

Some of the stakeholders identified above, particularly in categories (a) and (c), have a direct responsibility for the design and development of the various system components and hence have a major interest in being involved in the requirements capture process. Those in category (b) have a financial responsibility for the success of the computer system and therefore may also need to be involved. The stakeholders in category (d) will be the recipients of the resulting computer system. They also have a major contribution to make in terms of specific task knowledge and the ability to assess the likely effects of the new system.

It is argued within the Cooperative Requirements Capture Project that requirements capture should be a collaborative and cooperative activity allowing the views, insights and needs of the representative stakeholders to be actively incorporated as part of the requirements capture process (Macaulay, 1993a). However, whilst it is argued that requirements capture would be enriched by cooperation between representative stakeholders it is by no means clear that interaction between people with such a diversity of motives would result in anything but chaos. By definition, the representative stakeholders all have different 'stakes' in the resulting system and each 'team member' will want to discuss those issues which are of interest to them . Thus, simply identifying the stakeholders is not sufficient.

Two further components are needed: firstly a mechanism for focussing the discussion of the 'team' and encouraging sharing of views and concerns; and secondly a structure is needed which will enable the team to address all the important issues and produce all the outputs needed by the commissioning organisation within resources allocated. Within the CRC project the first component is provided through use of a meetings facilitator and the second component provided through use of a user centred requirements capture method based on User Skills Task Match, USTM (Macaulay et al., 1990).

Following the analysis of the target user population it was decided to develop a prototype system which was capable of supporting the stakeholders, the facilitator and the requirements capture method.

REVIEW OF RELATED CSCW SYSTEMS

The work carried out at UMIST on developing the CRC prototype can be compared with other CSCW research projects and systems in terms of:

- *Application area.* What is the system supposed to support? Is it limited to a particular area, or could it be used in a number of application domains?

- *Support for the social/group process.* What does the system do to support the social process for a group of users?

University of Lancaster, UK

Their current work centres around projects undertaken to examine and support air traffic controllers in the UK. Their major contributions have been to the discussion on the use of ethnographers in the design process (Sommerville, *et al.*, 1992; Bentley *et al.*, 1992a; Hughes *et al.*, 1992), and to the development of computer support for Command & Control Systems (Bentley *et al.* 1992b).

Application area

The system they have developed is to support UK Air Traffic Control (ATC), but they believe that the architecture they have used is applicable to command and control systems in general. These systems are typified by users cooperatively controlling external processes using a shared information space. In this case, the information space is a reactive data base system—one where the information is continually updated either from external sensors or concurrent inputs from different users (Bentley *et al.* 1992a, p123).

Support for the social/group process

There are two aspects to the support provided for cooperation in the Lancaster system. Firstly, there is the cooperation via the shared data base, which is supported through the use of User Display Agents and their selection, presentation, and composition criteria. Secondly, there are the aspects of the interface design that were informed by the observations of the air traffic controllers at work by the ethnographers. These studies provided insights into the informal coordination that takes place between the controllers, which the developers believe would have been overlooked had they been following a more traditional systems design approach.

MCC, USA

The Software Technology Program at the Microelectronics and Computer Technology Corporation (MCC) has been responsible for some significant CSCW research. They started with studying meetings and meeting improvement in Project Nick (Cook *et al.*, 1987), and have proceeded to study real-time groupware, in particular, producing the GROVE group outline editor (Ellis *et al.*, 1990, 1991a). They have also examined groupware toolkits (Gibbs, 1989), and post-session group process feedback (Rein, 1991b).

Application area

Their primary area of concern is real-time groupware. The work done by MCC is focussed on the support for design teams in large systems design projects. Project Nick examined meetings support, and GROVE is a group outline editor for use by co-located and distributed teams working synchronously.

Support for social/group process

One aspect of the research started off in Project Nick, and carried through to more recent work, was the provision of an 'affective subchannel'. In Project Nick, this allowed team members to select and enter phrases such as 'this is interesting' or 'I'm bored' into the channel, and these were picked up by the facilitator. In (Cook *et al.*, 1987), it was stated that this type of information could be summarised in a 'mood meter' for the group, to provide an 'average' view of the group's current feelings in the meeting. This line of work was reflected later in (Rein, 1991b) where such a meter was implemented, based upon Bales SYMLOG notation (Bales and Cohen, 1979). The data for the meter, however, was provided by *post hoc* analysis of a video recording of the group session (the participants were co-located), by four group analysis experts. They could only speculate as to the utility of such a device if one were available in 'real-time'.

University of Calgary, Canada

The department of Computer Science at the University of Calgary has produced various research into, and implementations of, synchronous CSCW. Greenberg (1991a) examined synchronous, collaboration transparent use of single-user applications by multiple users, with the use of a group viewing system that allows choice of turn-taking protocol. GroupSketch is a stand-alone real-time freehand drawing application that runs on Sun workstations. GroupKit provides support, in toolkit form, for the development of real-time 'work surfaces', with numerous activities supported (Greenberg 1992a; Roseman and Greenberg 1992). The rest of this section will concentrate on GroupKit.

Application area

A toolkit for developing synchronous CSCW, or groupware, applications. The developers have implemented paint programs, editors, brainstorming tools, and structuring tools, all for synchronous use by a distributed group.

Support for the social/group process

The developers have worked from the standpoint that software should not embody any notion of social process. They believe that negotiation about collaborative working with a shared object, or set of objects, is best left to the users themselves. So, for example, in GroupSketch, it is possible for any number of users to draw in the same region at the same time, and one user can follow another user's pencil with their own eraser, 'rubbing out' the other user's work as it is being done. Obviously, this type of behaviour would not be tolerated for long, and the users would resolve the problem amongst themselves. As indicated by demonstrations of the software (Roseman and Greenberg, 1992), the developers believe that group-maintenance activity will take place over the audio channel, with support from the gestural and annotative overlays.

NTT Human Interface Labs, Japan

Also looking at support for synchronous collaboration, Hiroshi Ishii at NTT Human Interface Labs has concentrated on providing rich communication channels to support 'seamless' CSCW, bridging the gap between CSCW shared workspaces, and what he terms 'interpersonal space'. He has built a number of prototype systems to support (predominantly) diads working on design tasks. TeamWorkStation (Ishii and Arita, 1991a; Ishii and Miyake (1991b) is based on a personal computer, and ClearBoard (Ishii *et al.*, 1992) is a dedicated drawing board hardware and software.

Application area

TeamWorkStation is intended to create an open shared workspace for a small group of users, typically two members, but possibly more. It does this by integrating the computers and the desktops of the collaborators. In doing so, it provides synchronous support for a distributed group, the members of which could be collaborating on any task. ClearBoard is more specifically targeted at a pair of collaborators, who are working together on a drawing board. Once again, the users are working synchronously whilst distributed geographically.

Support for social/group process

Like Greenberg, Ishii does not get involved with 'hard-wiring' social protocols into the system, relying instead on the users to use existing protocols, and to develop new ones, to regulate their interaction via the shared workspace. The rich channel of communication available enables the users to make use of techniques they would employ in a face to face situation, thus negating the need to learn a vast new repertoire of interaction techniques.

The inclusion of the video link, and the way that it has been implemented, allows Ishii to address a number of social issues that are of use with the type of task being supported. Because each user sees an image of the other user(s), in the context of the piece of work they are collaborating on, they are made aware of which part of the work their partner is looking at (gaze awareness). They are also able to talk directly to each other (eye contact), and because the work and face image are superimposed, this switching of attention is possible without a great deal of head movement.

MIT Center for Coordination Science, USA

Oval (Malone *et al.*, 1992; CCS 1992) is a direct descendant of the Information Lens (Malone *et al.*, 1987, 1989) and Object Lens (Lai *et al.*, 1988) systems developed at the Center for Coordination Science, a part of the Sloan School of Management at MIT. They are all systems to support physically and temporally distributed cooperation.

Application area

Tom Malone and his various collaborators at MIT have been involved for some time in research that is aimed at supporting the coordination of users work within an organisation. The Information Lens (Malone *et al.*, 1989) is a system that allows the filtering of e-mail for a group of users such that messages are not delivered to users that do not want to see them, and users are sent messages of interest to them, even if they are not specified as a recipient. Object Lens (Lai *et al.*, 1988) generalised the Information Lens concepts, and allowed non-expert computer users to create their own CSCW applications using simple building blocks. Oval (Malone *et al.*, 1992), an acronym for Objects, Views, Agents, Links, takes these concepts further into a 'radically tailorable tool for cooperative work', which will be the focus of the remainder of this section.

Support for the social/group process

Oval does not provide any specific support for the social processes involved with cooperative work. It can be envisaged, however, that some aspects such as awareness of other group members and their activities could be implemented with agents.

University of Arizona

The systems produced at the University of Arizona's Department of Management Information Systems originated with the Arizona Planning Lab, or PLEXSYS. This is now known as GroupSystems, or under its guise as an IBM product, TeamFocus. They are Real-time Electronic Meeting Systems (EMS), supporting brainstorming, description, & prioritisation of ideas in 'anonymous' face to face sessions. (Dennis *et al.*, 1988b; Dennis *et al.*, 1990; Grohowski *et al.*, 1990; Nunamaker *et al.*, 1991b; Valacich *et al.*, 1991a).

Application area

The University of Arizona team coined the term Electronic Meeting Systems to describe the work that they were doing (Dennis *et al.*, 1988b). In collaboration with IBM, they have implemented a number of meeting room facilities, complete with hardware and software at each seat, in order to support various sizes of meeting. The facilities are primarily used for 'same-time, same-place' meetings, with up to 48 team members supported, but other modes of work are possible.

Support for the social/group process

GroupSystems is one of the few CSCW/groupware systems that makes explicit references to the role of a human facilitator. In fact, the developers advocate the use of a facilitator in most, if not all, sessions. The primary reason for the inclusion of a facilitator, however, is to provide technical support to the group in their use of the GroupSystems tools, and social facilitation has to take a somewhat lesser role. Nevertheless, they do provide support for facilitation tasks such as agenda management, and recognise that pre- and post-meeting activities are equally important as during-meeting support.

THE CRC PROTOTYPE

The remainder of this paper deals with the CRC Prototype, its design and implementation, results from user evaluations and finally a discussion on what has been learned concerning support for the social process within requirements capture.

The CRC prototype supports a multidisciplinary, possibly geographically distributed team to undertake a requirements capture task in a cooperative manner. There may be aspects of the requirements task which are performed synchronously, that is, all members of the team agree to hold a 'meeting', while other aspects of the task will be asynchronous, with members monitoring and actively participating in the requirements evolution, as and when they can.

The prototype supports a representative subset of the whole of a requirements capture method, more specifically it supports object analysis. (See (Macaulay, 1993) for a fuller description of the object analysis.) The users of the CRC prototype are able to hold a synchronous 'brainstorming' session in which they generate a single pool of ideas for objects associated with the particular problem domain within which the requirements capture process is situated. The CRC prototype represents a generic tool in that it is not customised for any particular domain. The support offered is not based on any semantic understanding of the objects that are being brainstormed. The users are then able to discuss, evaluate, change and agree on these objects either synchronously or asynchronously, resulting in an accepted set of objects. We had initially intended that the prototype would support cooperative development of object structures, like those of whole-part or generalisation-specialisation structures. Whilst initial efforts to do this proved fruitful and offered considerable insight into how this support may be provided, it nevertheless became clear that we required further investigation as to how a group would undertake this task in a non computer supported environment.

The prototype goes considerably beyond merely supporting communication between team members. A key feature of our approach to requirements capture is the recognition that not only does the requirements capture task need to be managed but additionally the social process taking place between the team members needs to be managed (Westley and Waters, 1988). We believe that the effective management of both these processes is pivotal to any CSCW system and for this reason the CRC prototype explicitly provides support in both these 'dimensions'.

We have examined the role of a human facilitator in managing face to face meetings and have adopted the view that the tasks of the facilitator should also be supported by the prototype. In brief, the tasks of the facilitator are to set and manage the agenda, to monitor the progress of the group and to strive to maintain the social cohesion of the group. Maintenance of social cohesion necessitates the ability to monitor the group dynamics with a view to recognising potential problems, intervening if appropriate and suggesting strategies for the group to pursue when undertaking specific tasks. (See (Viller, 1991) for further details of the role of the facilitator.)

The primary objective of the CRC prototype, therefore, was to develop an integrated set of software tools that support a group in the solution of a common problem. To this end, key user operations were identified as follows:

- An ability to exchange both private and group messages.
- An ability to work within a private workspace.
- An ability to observe the efforts and contributions of other group members in a public shared workspace.
- An ability to recognise the receipt of messages.
- An ability to enter into some synchronous private communication with another group member.

A further set of operations specific to the facilitator were identified. These involved the provision of software support for the effective management of the social process. This demands:

- An ability to witness and view the behaviour and activities of the group.
- An ability to intervene in the group task.
- An ability to see individual members activities in a dynamic manner.

Implicitly, the software needed to support further capabilities:

- The recording and saving of messages in a persistent message base for subsequent interrogation.
- The ability to print various views of this message base for subsequent inspection by facilitators and managers alike.
- The ability to set and control a task agenda.

THE CRC PROTOTYPE FROM A USERS POINT OF VIEW

The CRC Cooperative Working Platform provides support for two types of user: the stake-holder and the facilitator. It supports the following user tasks:

(1) Producing a list of objects.
(2) Analysing the list of objects (i.e. discussing, withdrawing/adding items on the object list).
(3) Facilitating social interaction between team members.

Tasks (i) and (ii) use social interaction techniques of brainstorming to produce the object list, and discussion for evaluating the list (figure 1).

Brainstorming

Brainstorming was identified as a suitable technique for allowing CRC team members to contribute suggestions in order to build up a single list of system objects. The characteristics of brainstorming are the rapid generation of a single pool of ideas by individual group members, with evaluation and criticism being discouraged at this stage. Therefore the interface for brainstorming needs to permit the members of a distributed team with a means of inputting a suggested object at their terminal, and sending it to update a common area, which is seen by all team members.

Discussion and Analysis

To enable group members to agree on the list of objects produced by brainstorming, it was decided to provide computer support for discussion between members, allowing them to send messages to each other in a similar way to a mail tool. After the brainstorming session is over, members may propose amendments to the object list in the form of a message sent to the other team members. Comments on the proposal can then be contributed in the form of replies, linked to the proposal and to other related replies, so that the discussion can be followed and the evolution of objects and their descriptions can be traced. It is normally possible to reach a consensus by this method, but the facilitator may intervene if necessary. Tasks (i) and (ii) are the main tasks of the team members. Figure 1 gives a summary of the object analysis tasks.

Facilitating Social Interaction

In addition to brainstorming and analysis, the prototype also supports facilitation of social interaction between team members. This takes the form of specific support for a human facilitator. In particular, the facilitator will set the agenda for the group to follow, that is, what they should do,

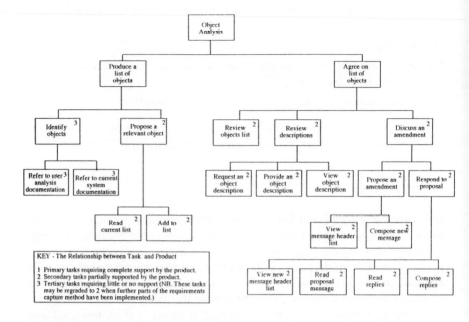

Figure 1 The relationship between task and product

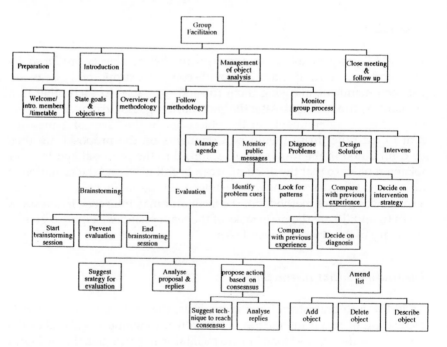

Figure 2 Task model for group facilitation

associated time constraints and outcomes or deliverables. The facilitator monitors the group progress through the task, getting feedback from the system as to the activity of the group members. In addition to monitoring the group, the facilitator may choose to intervene in order to resolve any problem that is occuring between team members. Figure 2 shows the task model for the facilitator.

SCHEMATIC OF THE CRC PROTOTYPE

The system consists of a central component—the *monitor*—which performs the routing of messages and the maintenance of the object and message bases. These are the repositories within which the objects and messages that have been generated by the team using the prototype are stored. There is also a distributed component of the prototype for each stakeholder that uses it. This runs locally on each stakeholder's machines, and provides them with functions for message exchange, and for interacting with the shared workspace. This distributed part of the system is known as the *interface*. The interface is identical for all of the stakeholders. The facilitator's interface provides a superset of the functionality of the ordinary stakeholder.

The primary difference between the two types of interface is that the facilitator's interface contains extra functions that can make use of the system activity data that is stored by the monitor. This provides the facilitator with aggregations of individual interactions taking place between the stakeholders and therefore enables trends in behaviour to be identified.

Figure 3 provides a schematic overview of the main features of the prototype showing several team members and a facilitator logged onto the prototype. The prototype has been designed using a client-server model from distributed systems design in which there is a central resource monitor through which all communications are sent and data is redirected to its intended destination.

One advantage of this design is that it allows the system to store and organise data relating to messages or to requirements; all data is stored persistently as CLOS (Common Lisp Object System) objects, thus facilitating their subsequent analysis and interrogation. The persistent storage of objects enables retrospective analysis of social interactions which could for example be used for facilitator training or minute taking or act as a permanent meeting record.

A second advantage is that this model is more amenable to the extension of the requirements capture team. Central to this approach is

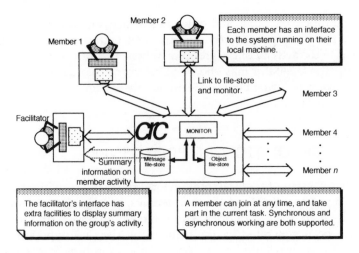

Figure 3   A Schematic of the CRC Prototype.

a linear relationship between the number of users (n) and the number of interactions, namely 2*n. Thus the size of the team will have less effect on the overall performance of the prototype than for example had we commissioned a model whereby each team member had a dedicated connection to every other member. This model would involve n*(n-1) connections and as such would quickly degrade the performance of the system.

A further feature of the design is that the user interfaces are designed as separate modules and hence when running the CRC prototype on a team member's workstation only the user interface module needs to be mounted. This will enable the user to simply open the CRC Window alongside other unrelated applications. In particular the design of the software is such that the interface modules could be written in different languages or mounted on different host machines. For example the user interface module may be written in hypertext on the Apple Macintosh. The CRC prototype was implemented on Sun workstations using Common Lisp and CLOS. An overview of the architecture and more details concerning its implementation are given in (O'Hare *et al.*, 1992), while (O'Hare *et al.*, 1995 to be published) describes the support provided for management of the social process.

DESCRIPTION OF THE USER INTERFACE

The CRC prototype is a single window, almost taking up the whole screen, which contains a number of child windows. Figure 4 shows a

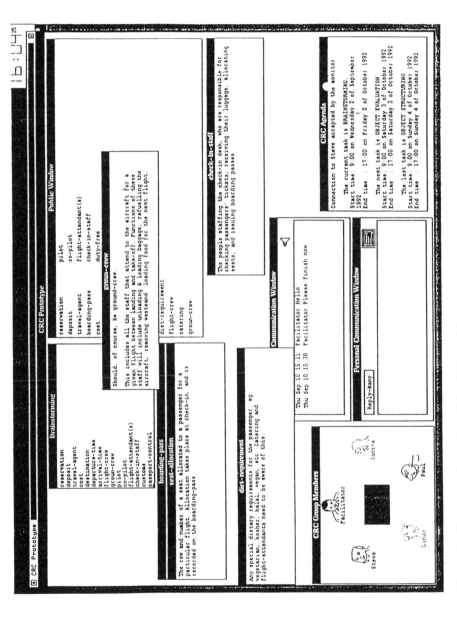

Figure 4   Group member's view of the CRC protype

typical group member's screen at the point where the brainstorming session has finished and the discussion or evaluation of objects is underway. All the windows are maintained in a consistent manner across each member's workstation.

The 'Personal Communication' Window

This window is situated in the middle of the main window at the bottom. It contains summary lines for the personal messages that you have received, i.e. messages addressed to you as an individual. The closest analogy to this in face to face communication is that of whispering to your neighbour, or passing a note to another group member. Each of the summary lines is a separate 'Message summary' region. Linked to this window is the Personal Communication Indicator, a small in-tray icon, shown as an address envelope, and situated on the right-hand edge of the main window.

The 'Group Communication' Window

This window is situated in the middle of the main window above the Personal Communication window. It functions in an identical way to the Personal Communication window, except that new messages are loaded in automatically as they arrive. A separate Message Viewer window is provided for displaying the contents of messages.

The 'CRC Agenda' Window

This window is situated at the bottom-right of the main window, and is used to display messages about the current and future tasks to be performed. Users have no need to interact with this window.

The 'Public Window'

This is the uppermost window on the right-hand side of the main window. Its purpose is to display items that are shared amongst the whole group. It therefore always displays the same information on each of the group members screens. The items that it displays are objects that have been generated as part of the brainstorming session, and are represented as active regions in the inner region of the window.

Description Windows

A description window is created for an object in the public window by selecting the object with the mouse. The windows are created in a 'stack' on the left-hand side of the main window, and the system provides a number of functions to help with managing them.

The 'Brainstorming' Window

This window is situated in the upper-middle of the main window, directly to the left of the Public Window. It is used during the brainstorming phase of a group session to allow group members to enter their ideas into the system, for display on the Public Window. It maintains a private copy of all the objects generated in a single session by that user.

The 'CRC Group Members' Window

This window appears bottom-left in the main window, and contains icons representing each group-member, the facilitator, and the group as a whole (the 'table'). There is a menu on each of the users, and on the 'table' icons.

Figure 5 shows the facilitators interface at the same point in the session as the group member's interface shown in figure 4.

The facilitator's interface to the CRC Group Members window differs from that of the group members in that additional information is available on individuals and group activity through selection of the appropriate icon. Selecting the table icon will invoke the Group Statistics window, which contains information about the group members' activities, and selecting an individuals icon will invoke an individual statistics window for that group member. The other difference for the facilitator is that current activity icons are displayed next to each group member's icon when they are logged on. These icons are: a light bulb, a pair of spectacles, a pen, and a question mark. They respectively indicate that the group member is: brainstorming, reading a message, composing a message, or the system cannot tell what the group member is doing.

Individual Statistics Windows (titled 'Paul' and 'Steve' in figure 5)

One of these windows is available for each of the group members. When one is created, it has the name of the individual that it refers to as

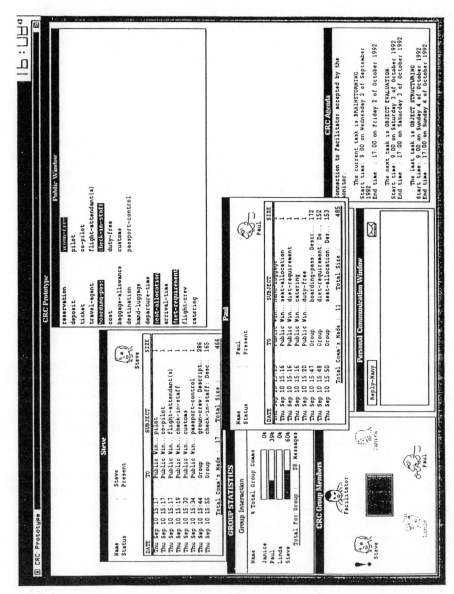

Figure 5   Facilitator's view of the CRC prototype

its title. These windows are very similar to the Group and Personal Communication windows in that they contain a list of message summaries that, when selected, allow the contents of the relevant message to be viewed. The difference is that the message summaries contained in these windows are for all the messages sent by the selected member during the current session. For reasons of privacy, you are only permitted to view the contents of messages that have been sent to the whole group, to which you would have access anyway.

The summaries contain information about who each message was addressed to, when it was sent, its subject, and its length (number of characters). The latter piece of information provides you with an additional measure of member participation that may be considered along with the number of messages sent. The total length of all the messages sent, including personal messages, is given at the bottom of the list. The alternative, graphical view shows the distribution of the messages that the member has sent amongst the rest of the group.

The 'Group Statistics' Window

This window provides a basic means for comparing the level of participation of the group members against each other. The number of messages sent by all the members can be displayed in a number of ways, selectable from the frame menu. Textual is the default view, and gives the number of messages sent for each member. Three graphical views are available, which present the information as a number of horizontal bars with percentages: total gives the same information as the textual view, with the length of each bar displaying the member's number of messages as a percentage of the total number of messages sent by the group; maximum displays each member's message count as a percentage of the member who sent the most; and average displays each member's message count relative to the average for the group.

EVALUATION OF THE CRC PROTOTYPE

An evaluation of the CRC prototype was performed at UMIST on the 23rd and 24th of September 1992. The design of the evaluation was developed over a number of reports and related meetings between project collaborators (see Internal Report CRC/229). This design was tested on September 2nd, and modified in the light of this experience. The resulting evaluation was carried out twice on the two days mentioned above, on two groups of subjects.

The purpose of the evaluation was to ascertain the usefulness of the prototype as a tool for supporting the kind of cooperative work that is typically encountered when performing requirements capture tasks. For this reason, the evaluation consisted of a number of tasks, each of which were intended to encourage a particular sort of cooperative behaviour by the groups of subjects.

Task 1: Competition: A warm-up task to familiarise the subjects with the message- passing capabilities of the system, and to encourage activity due to its competitive nature. The facilitator is provided with a piece of information that the group members must identify. They do so by asking questions and requesting clues.

Task 2: Document Creation: A cooperative task which requires each group member to separately compose one section of a document, and then for the group to agree on the wording of the text as a whole.

Task 3: Brainstorming and Analysis: This is the type of task that the prototype was specifically designed to support. The group first of all undertakes a brainstorming session in order to generate a list of objects that should be considered in the design of a particular computer system. Once this list has been generated, the group then analyses the objects, providing descriptions for them and agreeing on their inclusion in the final list.

The subjects were recruited mainly from ICL and Brameur, such that they were experienced in at least one of: requirements capture; team-work; or project management. Each was asked to reply to four questions that ascertained their experience in the above, as well as their use of Sun workstations. The subjects were also provided with some information about the prototype, and the purpose of the evaluation.

The evaluation was carried out in three rooms in the Computation Department at UMIST. A seminar/meeting room was used for the group briefing and de-briefing sessions; the group member workstations were housed in a laboratory, where training and briefings took place; and the facilitator's workstation was situated in a separate office, where the facilitator training and briefings took place. In the Sun laboratory, dividing screens were installed in order to isolate subjects from each other.

Data from the evaluation sessions was recorded via the system monitor. Each message and associated details were recorded. In addition, de-briefing sessions were held after tasks 1 and 3, and were recorded on audio tape.

The two sets of data were analysed in different ways. The transcript of the de-briefing sessions was analysed for comments and questions made by the subjects about the prototype. These comments were grouped into a number of classifications that were then used to drive the subsequent analysis. Graphical views of the raw system- recorded data were produced that enabled us to examine different aspects of the session, according to group member, objects, and type of activity.

An example of a graphical view is given in figure 6 which shows an analysis of the session by object. This table shows no information about who is responsible for the activity, but shows what happens to each object during the session on the prototype. A row is created for each object, in the order that they were added to the public window, and a box appears in the row each time an action is performed on the object. Time runs across the horizontal axis, in minute segments.

This table was created by hand from the data recorded by the system. It was not possible, however, to produce the table using only information gathered from the headers of messages. In order to classify messages as discussing certain objects, it is necessary to refer to the contents of each message. This could still be carried out by the system, if simple pattern-matching was used to recognise occurrences of the object names in message bodies as well as headers.

This view of the data allows the reader to see which objects have been concentrated on by the group, and which have been neglected. Recurring patterns of messages about objects can indicate, for example, where group members are comparing/contrasting objects (see for example evening meal and with-dinner in figure 6), with a view to possibly combining them, clarifying their differences, or removing one as a duplicate. With the added use of colour, it would also be possible to indicate which user had performed the actions on the objects.

The qualitative data that these sessions provided us with has been most useful in assessing the merits of the prototype, and our approach to cooperative requirements capture that it embodies. Despite the problems we encountered during the evaluation, the subjects felt that they had experienced enough of the system in order to make comments about the current state of the prototype, as well as about improvements that would make it more suitable for its proposed use. The best conclusions that we can can make, therefore, are those that can be drawn from the users' comments.

For example, the three primary areas with which the users concerned themselves throughout the de-briefing session on day two were: interacting with the prototype, group work via the prototype, and enhancements to the prototype. Within these areas of concern, the major points made were respectively: cognitive overloads placed on the users by the system, time pressures in particular; the need for a strategy for

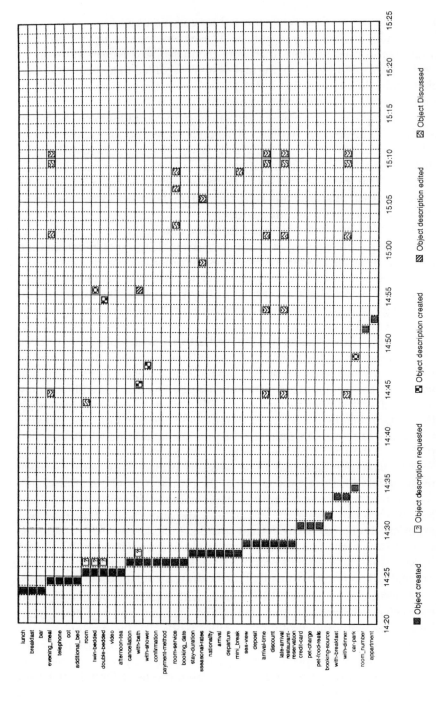

Figure 6   Timeline analysis of objects in an evaluation session

guiding group discussion; and the need for more feedback about the status of objects, messages, and other users of the system.

We have also demonstrated with the CRC prototype that recording some quite basic information about the activity of users on the system, enables us to perform various analyses on the group member's interaction with each other, and with the objects they have created during the session. This data can be produced in a graphical format, allowing a more abstract view of the data. The graphical views, in conjunction with the 'raw' data, allow feedback to be given to the group members on their performance as a group, as well as individuals.

The major achievements to date have been the design, implementation testing and evaluation of the CRC prototype. This process has enabled us to gain specific insights into the design and implementation of CSCW systems. We have recognised that supporting a team of people in the pursuit of a shared task is significantly different from that of supporting either an individual conducting the task or acting as an interpreter on behalf of a group who are conducting the task. The key requirement is that the group members can interact freely.

CONCLUSIONS

It is argued within the Cooperative Requirements Capture Project that requirements capture should be a collaborative and cooperative activity allowing the views, insights and needs of the representative stakeholders to be actively incorporated as part of the requirements capture process By definition, the representative stakeholders all have different 'stakes' in the resulting system and each 'team member' will want to discuss those issues which are of interest to them . Thus, simply identifying the stakeholders is not sufficient. Two further components are needed: firstly a mechanism for focussing the discussion of the 'team' and encouraging sharing of views and concerns; and secondly a structure is needed which will enable the team to address all the important issues and produce all the outputs needed by the commissioning organisation within resources allocated.

Thus computer support for Cooperative Requirements Capture must provide support not only the requirements capture method and communication between team members but also support facilitation of the group process.

ACKNOWLEDGEMENTS

The authors wishes to acknowledge their collaborators within the CRC (IED/1130) project, they are International Computers Ltd., Brameur Ltd. and Human Technology. The project received financial support from the Department of Trade and Industry and the Science and Engineering Research Council.

REFERENCES

Internal Report CRC/229 (1992) Overview of the Design of the evaluation of the UMIST Cooperative Working Platform, available from the authors on request.

Bales, R.F. & Cohen, S.P. (1979), SYMLOG: A System for the Multiple Level Observation of Groups, New York, NY, The Free Press.

Bentley, R., Hughes, J.A., Randall, D., Rodden, T., Sawyer, P., Shapiro, D. & Sommerville, I. (1992a), Ethnographically-informed systems design for air traffic control, In J. Turner & R. Kraut (Ed.) CSCW92, Toronto, Canada, ACM Press.

Bentley, R., Rodden, T., Sawyer, P. & Sommerville, I. (1992b), An architecture for tailoring cooperative multi-user displays, In J. Turner & R. Kraut (Ed.) CSCW92, Toronto, Canada, ACM Press.

Bly, S.A., Harrison, S.R. & Irwin, S. (1993), Media spaces: bringing people together in a video, audio, and computing environment, Communications of the ACM, 36 (1) :pp 28–46.

Conklin, J. & Begeman, M.L. (1988), gIBIS: a hypertext tool for exploratory policy discussion, In L. Suchman (Ed.) Proceedings of CSCW88, Portland, OR, ACM.

Cook, P., Ellis, C., Graf, M., Rein, G. & Smith, T. (1987), Project Nick: meetings augmentation and analysis, ACM Transactions on Office Information Systems, 5 (2) :pp 132–146.

Dennis, A.R., George, J.F., Jessup, L.M., Nunamaker, J.F.J. & Vogel, D.R. (1988b), Information technology to support electronic meetings, Management Information Systems Quarterly, 12 (4) :pp 591–624.

Dennis, A.R., Heminger, A.R., Nunamaker, J.F.J. & Vogel, D.R. (1990), Bringing automated support to large groups: the Burr-Brown experience, Information & Management, 18 (3) :pp 111–121.

Ellis, C.A., Gibbs, S.J. & Rein, G.L. (1990), Design and use of a group editor, In G.Cockton (Ed.) Engineering for Human-Computer Interaction., Amsterdam, Elsevier Science Publishers.

Ellis, C.A., Gibbs, S.J. & Rein, G.L. (1991a), Groupware: some issues and experiences, Communications of the ACM, 34 (1) :pp 38–58.

Gibbs, S.J. (1989), LIZA: an extensible groupware toolkit, In (Ed.) CHI89, ACM Press.

Greenberg, S. (1991a), Personalizable groupware: accommodating individual roles and group differences, In L. Bannon, M. Robinson & K. Schmidt (Ed.) ECSCW91—The Second European Conference on Computer Supported Cooperative Work, Amsterdam, Netherlands, Kluwer.

Greenberg, S. (1992a), GROUPLAB: The Computer-Supported Cooperative Work and Groupware research laboratory, Demonstration at CSCW92, Toronto, Canada.

Grohowski, R., McGoff, C., Vogel, D., Martz, B. & Nunamaker, J. (1990), Implementing electronic meeting systems at IBM: lessons learned and success factors, Management Information Systems Quarterly, 14 (4) :pp 369–383.

Hughes, J.A., Randall, D. & Shapiro, D. (1992), Faltering from ethnography to design, In J. Turner & R. Kraut (Ed.) CSCW92, Toronto, Canada, ACM Press.

Ishii, H. & Arita, K. (1991a), Clearface: translucent multiuser interface for TeamWorkStation, In L. Bannon, M. Robinson & K. Schmidt (Ed.) ECSCW91— The Second European Conference on Computer Supported Cooperative Work, Amsterdam, Netherlands, Kluwer.

Ishii, H., Kobayashi, M. & Grudin, J. (1992), Integration of inter-personal space and shared workspace: ClearBoard design and experiments., In J. Turner & R. Kraut (Ed.) CSCW92, Toronto, Canada, ACM Press.

Ishii, H. & Miyake, N. (1991b), Toward an open shared workspace: computer and video fusion approach of TeamWorkstation, Communications of the ACM, 34 (12) :pp 37–50.

Lai, K.-Y., Malone, T.W. & Yu, K.-C. (1988), Object Lens: a spreadsheet for cooperative work, ACM Transactions on Office Information Systems, 6 (4) :pp 332–353.

Macaulay, L.A., Fowler, CJH., Kirby, M., Hutt ATF., (1990) USTM: a new approach to requirements specification, Interacting With Computers, vol2 no.1, 92–117

Macaulay, L., O'Hare, G., Viller, S. & Dongha, P. (1993b), Cooperative requirements capture, In (Ed.) 1993 JFIT Technical Conference, Keele University, DTI.

Macaulay, L.A. (1993a), Requirements as a cooperative activity, In (Ed.) IEEE Symposium of Requirements Engineering, San Diego, CA., IEEE.

Malone, T.W., Grant, K.R., Lai, K.-Y., Rao, R. & Rosenblitt, D. (1987), Semistructured messages are surprisingly useful for computer-supported coordination, ACM Transactions on Office Information Systems, 5 (2) :pp 115–131.

Malone, T.W., Grant, K.R., Lai, K.-Y., Rao, R. & Rosenblitt, D.A. (1989), The Information Lens: an intelligent system for information sharing and coordination, In M.H. Olson (Ed.) Technological Support for Work Group Collaboration., Hillsdale, NJ, Lawrence Erlbaum.

Malone, T.W., Lai, K.-Y. & Fry, C. (1992), Experiments with Oval: a radically tailorable tool for cooperative work, In J. Turner & R. Kraut (Ed.) CSCW92, Toronto, Canada, ACM Press.

Neuwirth, C.M., Chandhok, R., Kaufer, D.S., Erion, P., Morris, J. & Miller, D. (1992), Flexible diff-ing in a collaborative writing system, In J. Turner & R. Kraut (Ed.) Proceedings of CSCW92, Toronto, Canada, ACM.

Neuwirth, C.M., Kaufer, D.S., Chandhok, R. & Morris, J.H. (1990), Issues in the design of computer support for co-authoring and commenting, In F. Halasz (Ed.) Proceedings of CSCW90, Los Angeles, CA, ACM.

Nunamaker, J.F., Dennis, A.R., Valacich, J.S., Vogel, D.R. & George, J.F. (1991b), Electronic meeting systems to support group work, Communications of the ACM, 34 (7) :pp 40–61.

O'Hare, G.M.P., Dongha, R.P., Macaulay, L.A. & Viller, S.A. (1992), Agency within CSCW: Towards the development of active cooperative working environments, In J.H. Connolly & E. Edmonds (Ed.) AI, Autonomous Agents and CSCW, Department of Trade & Industry, London, UK., To be published by Springer-Verlag.

O'Hare, G.M.P, Dongha, R.P. Macaulay, L/A and Viller, S.A., (1995) Computational Support for the Management of the Social Process within Organisational Teams, In Towards the Intelligent Organisation, Kim. S., & OHare, G.M.P (eds), to be published by Springer Verlag CSCW Series

Rein, G.L. (1991b), A group mood meter, In (Ed.) Proceedings of HICSS-24, Hawaii, IEEE.

Roseman, M. & Greenberg, S. (1992), GroupKit: a groupware toolkit for building real-time conferencing applications, In J. Turner & R. Kraut (Ed.) Proceedings of CSCW92, Toronto, Canada, ACM Press.

CCS, (1992), Oval Users Guide., Center for Coordination Science, Sloan School of Management, MIT, Cambridge, MA.

Sommerville, I., Rodden, T., Sawyer, P. & Bentley, R. (1992), Sociologists can be surprisingly useful in interactive systems design, In A. Monk, D. Diaper & M.D. Harrison (Ed.) People and Computers VII: Proceedings of the HCI92 conference, York, Cambridge University Press.

Stefik, M., Bobrow, D.G., Foster, G., Lanning, S. & Tatar, D. (1987), WYSIWIS revised: early experiences with multiuser interfaces, ACM Transactions on Office Information Systems, 5 (2) :pp 147–167.

Valacich, J.S., Dennis, A.R. & Nunamaker, J.F.J. (1991a), Electronic meeting support: the GroupSystems concept, International Journal of Man-Machine Studies, 34 (2), pp 261–282.

Viller, S.A. (1991) The Group Facilitator: a CSCW Perspective, in J.Bowers (ed.): ECSCW91. The Second European Conference on Computer Support for Co-operative Work, Amsterdam, Holland.

Westley, F. & Waters, J.A. (1988) Group Facilitation Skills for Managers, In Management Education and Development, vol 19, no.2, pp. 134–143.

Winograd, T. & Flores, F. (1986), Understanding Computers and Cognition: A New Foundation for Design, Norwood, NJ, Ablex Publishing Corp.

11

CSCW—A Stage Beyond Groupware

Garth Shephard

ABSTRACT

This paper will introduce the emerging technologies of Computer-Supported Cooperative Work (CSCW) and place them in the context of products and services currently marketed as groupware.

CSCW supports organisation transformation and process re-engineering by providing tools for collective management, consensus and decision making. Existing groupware products provide selective tool set and network facilities largely for local area networks and the developing client/server systems.

The most comprehensive collaborative development programme in CSCW started in the UK in late 1993. The discussion which follows will review the intentions and scope of this programme as well as the present market for groupware.

IT interfaces which enable cooperative working are being defined in the world of groupware and applications are being built out of the software packages currently available. Software engineering tools and infrastructure will emerge to create and integrate the new applications in CSCW.

The intention is to appraise the reader of the opportunities which may arise from these developments.

Computer Support for Co-operative Work. Edited by Kathy Spurr, Paul Layzell,
Leslie Jennison and Neil Richards
© 1994 John Wiley & Sons Ltd

A DEFINITION OF COMPUTER-SUPPORTED CO-OPERATIVE WORK (CSCW)

Most work is performed by people working together in groups of some kind. Computer Supported Co-operative Work (CSCW) is the generic term covering the application of information technology in support of such co-operative work-groups. The individuals in such groups use a wide range of computer-based support systems linked by various kinds of communication networks.

CSCW or Cooperative Technology is a new field of Information Technology (IT) which builds on capability emerging from software developers and network providers.

It has relevance to the ways in which members of the same team contribute to a shared objective.

THE NEED FOR CSCW

Most of the information upon which our actions depend already requires electronic retrieval of information.

The ease with which we currently access and comprehend this information can be greatly improved not just on behalf of the individual but also within a community of joint responsibility.

Individuals see the same information differently and can bring different expertise and value to it. CSCW involves 'multi-media' where computer representation of text and data are joined by graphics, image and voice. A single 'compound' document can already be created which includes all these media types.

Emerging IT systems can offer distributed applications as well as compound document transfer. CSCW is all about harnessing this for the benefit of group productivity.

THE CAPABILITY FOR CSCW

Slow-scan television and video-conferencing can bring others in on a site visit. Electronic mail systems can be supplemented by the transmission of associated pictures and voice annotation in real-time.

Wide area applications may be in 'distance learning' and the promotion of remote advisory services.

There are strong trends towards flattened hierarchies within large companies and the desire to involve more people in decision-making. This desire is facilitated by technologies built on local area networks and tele-working which promise to make group working more effective and open up new ways of organising work-flow and team structure.

A complex subject like co-operative working needs to be thoroughly researched. Seminars, conferences, market analyses and mixed-discipline centres are appearing in order to address the issues and educate the community.

THE COMMERCIAL ENVIRONMENT

Interest in CSCW is world-wide through the development of new products and services described as 'groupware, work-flow, intelligent messaging and information sharing'.

Market analysis companies have trumpeted these areas of IT variously:

- as the engine to support flattened hierarchies for the new breed of 're-engineered' organisations (Michael Hammer Associates);

- as the cost-effective replacement for office automation system which have offered little or no improvement in productivity (Business Intelligence 'The groupware report '93').

- as re-generating the fortunes of system and software vendors alike through a huge new market of 5.5 billion dollars in 1998. Figure 1 shows growth projections taken from the 1993 Ovum report 'Groupware: market strategies'.

The Spread of Groupware

Large organisations have generated case studies for the adoption of integrated groupware systems and work-group tools. Pilot implementations are running in most progressive organisations world-wide. Results have claimed pay-back periods of three months and productivity improvements frequently approaching 400% as indicated in figure 2 (KPMG survey on behalf of Lotus Development).

Small companies may feel that these issues are complex and that group working is not for them. The experience of other small companies is needed to convince them to invest in CSCW (DTI CSCW report 1993).

In 1991, small to medium-sized enterprises (SMEs) were the subject of case studies presented by City University Business School in association

- **15% + pa growth rates**

- **Revitalising desk-top software sales**

- **Building on PC-LAN infrastructure**

- **Bridging between IT and business processes**

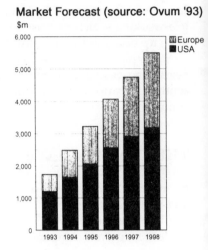

Market Forecast (source: Ovum '93)

Figure 1   Groupware: a new market area?

- **Nearly half of all Email users are managers or professionals**

- **They are twice as likely to originate groupware solutions than MIS**

- **Most implementations pay-back in 3 months**

- **Average pre-tax returns are almost 400%**

source: Lotus Development '93

Figure 2   Groupware in action

with Touche Ross, Lotus Development and the UK newspaper 'The Independent on Sunday'. Further examples are available of the use of groupware and access to remote workers on behalf of small companies and groups in association.

The new breed of British consultant, out-worker and SME can use seventy regional 'tele-cottages' (listed by the Telecottage Association) which enable individuals working from home and small groups to establish and maintain electronic channels of communication.

Many users and providers (large and small) are linked to international services which offer electronic mail and conferencing facilities through which they 'meet' and 'talk' (e.g. CompuServe, CIX, BT Gold and the Internet). There are believed to be 7,500 European on-line electronic services already available ('Teleworker' magazine November/December 1993).

'Teleworker' magazine, Ovum, Business Intelligence, the CSCW Special Interest group and many other sources are building a wide range of success stories.

THE JFIT CSCW PROGRAMME

In the UK, the Department of Trade and Industry (DTI) and the Science and Engineering Research Council (SERC) under the Joint Framework for Information Technology (JFIT) have recognised both the problem and the opportunity through a new thirteen million pound, three year programme in CSCW, which started in October 1993.

The programme intends to disseminate information on both the DTI/SERC Projects and on activities elsewhere through a DTI Awareness initiative which will be marshalling market and research intelligence as well as commissioning case studies which offer a guide through good (and bad) experiences.

The JFIT CSCW Programme includes eight consortia projects which are defining and addressing areas where they believe the next generation of products and services will be brought to bear. Some projects are taking existing groupware products and evaluating their relevance (benefits and limitations); others are developing tools and infrastructure which will support the development of all-embracing services.

Techniques ranging from virtual reality to ethnography are being exploited in the programme. Many projects contain SMEs and all plans exhibit the involvement of user organisations. Applications range from fashion to pharmaceuticals; from banking to brokering.

Defining the Problem Space

A pre-programme phase was conducted in order to give potential collaborators the opportunity to influence the call for proposals and to seek out other organisations with which they could work.

The pre-programme phase was important in generating and gauging the interest in such a programme. It also served to validate and refine the assumptions of the original Rationale Statement both through the contribution of participants and the exploration which proved possible of other influential initiatives and trends from user communities, industry and academia.

The potential consortia were given the following brief in The Technical Work-plan included in the call for proposals:

> The research and development of facilities to support groups of people working collectively offers the potential to transform the efficiency of computer-assisted group working and to transcend that which can be achieved today. Such developments will have a dramatic effect on the performance of future IT products, and promise levels of efficiency and achievement not attainable in current organisations.
>
> The future CSCW market will be a natural extension of the present market for IT products, but it will be characterised by new hardware platforms supporting more complex integrated software systems for which the adaptation of existing software packages will not suffice. This is because the basic principles and mechanisms underlying group interactions are significantly different from those applying to the present simple interactions of individuals using personal computers and sharing common centralised services. These factors, together with the availability of reliable transmission networks for people in the office or on the move using low-cost, multimedia work-stations, will create the environment in which CSCW products will evolve and expand over the next five to ten years.
>
> This programme will lay down the foundations for the commercial development and exploitation of this potential in the UK. It will capitalise on the rapidly developing market for new value-added services stimulated by the liberalisation of telecommunications achieved in the UK and in progress throughout Europe. It will incorporate new developments in computer network technology that promise a breakthrough in the effectiveness of new CSCW technologies over and above existing products. It will promote a further increase in the effectiveness and productivity of workers, through the use of multimedia information transfer techniques supporting improved organisational approaches.
>
> Although not a new area of research, CSCW is the subject of rapidly growing research interest. In the USA, a body of results produced in the 1980s under the banner of "Co-operation Technology" has led to the emergence of simple groupware tools which are helping to establish an awareness of the potential impact of CSCW. The developing new technologies of high-speed networks and multimedia work-stations offer radically different solutions to the broad

range of problems to be addressed, and these in turn are stimulating new and widespread academic and other long-term research.

The UK has been conducting basic research in a number of areas relevant to CSCW, but the technology is still in an embryonic state. This new programme will provide the focus to draw together the fragmented, multi-disciplinary threads of current research, to integrate existing and emerging technology in the engineering of generic CSCW software tools and methods with those for improved organisational approaches. It will produce application pilots for commercial development and exploitation by industry and commerce in key activities such as industrial design and manufacturing, tele-working, health-care, and education and training. It includes provision for the further collaborative research needed to increase the capabilities of CSCW systems and to underpin future developments in the topic.

The CSCW programme will be considered in three elements:

• Learning by Applying
• Enabling Technology
• Supporting People'

The call for proposals generated thirty-six consortia submissions of which eight were chosen.

The Chosen JFIT CSCW Consortia Projects

The chosen projects contain a broad range of topics in CSCW. They were submitted by an unusually comprehensive number of SMEs and end-user organisations. This establishes a framework of contribution which enables the results of the work to be marshalled together to appeal to a wide audience. The activities of the SMEs and end-users will act as an example to others and through appropriate channels of influence, encourage innovation in the development and use of CSCW tools, techniques and products.

The eight projects fall broadly in the areas of:

Business process re-engineering

Organisational modelling

Requirements analysis

Group design processes

Technical infrastructure and document-orientation

Social and behavioral issues.

The consortia tackling these areas contain:

9 Multi-national IT suppliers.

10 Corporate users active in banking, retail, pharmaceuticals, petrochemicals, manufacturing, aerospace and construction.

10 small to medium enterprise and software houses.

2 market-leading independent software vendors.

11 UK universities.

There are nine supported projects in the JFIT CSCW Programme, eight of which are consortia projects; as follows.

STARTED—Strategies, Tools and Resources for Team-based Early Design

This project is a collaborative R&D Project led by Cegelec Projects Ltd with the participation of Bristol University, the Rover Group, and Ove Arup and Partners.

The project will improve the early design process for large engineering projects, by providing a better framework for storage of large quantities of information, and graphical techniques for information presentation. STARTED will use an object based information management system to store the data, and hypertext and graphical user interfaces to speed browsing and retrieval.

STARTED will reduce the cost of up-front work, and increase the reliability of the results. This will reduce the waste on projects which do not proceed, and increase the confidence of profitability on those which go ahead.

More effective early design, and improved risk assessment, will lead to increased business profitability.

VIRTUOSI—Support for Virtual Organisations

The project will use virtual reality techniques to represent organisations in which collaboration takes place and to present to the user's powerful tools for design discussions. This aspect of the project will be strongly supported by Division Ltd who are a UK owned company specialising in the development of virtual reality (VR) systems.

The project will develop two application pilots. One will be concerned with improving communication between a number of BICC Cable factories within the UK and world-wide. A particular use of the system will be to enable technical experts to 'visit' a remote factory from their own desks and cooperate with people at the factory in solving production problems and other issues.

The other pilot will be based in the textile and clothing industry enabling cooperation within and between a number of Small/Medium Enterprises in the design and manufacture of fashion garments. This application will be part of Nottinghamshire County Council's programme to support the industry in its area.

Both BT, who is the lead partner for the project, and GPT will be involved in developing the telecommunications aspects of the project, supported by GEC Hirst Research Centre. A strong theoretical basis will be provided for the project by the academic partners. Three universities (Lancaster, Manchester, Nottingham and Nottingham Trent University) will bring expertise from computer science, sociology and psychology.

ICW—Integrated Cooperative Workspace

The partners will create a modular, integrated environment to support enterprise-wide CSCW and demonstrate this in health-care and financial applications.

The project outputs will be methods to support requirements capture, design of collaborative systems and a reusable tool set which is standards-based and scalable. This will enhance the partners' products, notably in business process re-engineering, work-flow and document management.

The industrial partners' specialities cover the spectrum of standards-based computing architecture and activities, e.g. client/server data-base (the Oracle Corporation); directory services (Nexor); process enactment (ICL Openframework); multiple data feeds (Micronics Telesystems); and information retrieval (Fretwell-Downing).

Collaborative Documents

The Collaborative Documents Project is producing technological aids for businesses which need to make the most effective use of their mobile and dispersed senior staff. The project uses work-flow technology as its base. The advances made within the project aim to empower a user with additional multi-media document capabilities which provide the ability to convey exactly what he or she has done during the performance of a task, why this has to be done and what the recipients should or should not go on to do with the results they are receiving.

Three multi-national corporations, from the foods, pharmaceutical and oil industry sectors, are participating in the project as end-users, ensuring that the technological solutions meet real business needs. The solutions are to be produced by Staffware plc, the prime contractor of this project, a market leader of work-flow systems and Brunel University's Centre for

Document Management, in association with Imperial College's Centre for Cognitive Studies.

Business Flight Simulator

Modelling organisations to reflect business options becomes possible when a number of the existing software tools are adapted and integrated into an environment which approximates to the organisation under study. Such an environment will allow "what-if" options to be examined and discussed by a wide range of those involved before they commit to a particular organisational structure.

The partners in the project provide strategic, business process, technical, research and information engineering services. They are led by ACT Business Systems with Bull Information Systems, City University Business School, PCL, Esmerk Informat and Touche Ross. The main partners are supported by a club of vendors for hardware, network and information services.

CORECT—COllaborative REquirements Capture Tool

This research project, being carried out jointly with Racal Research Ltd, Racal Instruments Ltd, the Universities of Edinburgh and Sussex and Intelligent Applications Ltd, seeks to investigate the automation of requirements capture and the creation of a database of information for systems specification and documentation. The project will develop a collaborative "Authoring Tool" for joint use by analysts and users to help ensure that specifications are complete and correct. The tool will also give designers rapid feedback and make requirements information immediately available, helping users, designers, managers and sales-people to work together by helping them communicate better.

SYCOMT—System Development and Cooperative Work: Methods and Techniques

Recent research by Digital Equipment Company has shown that companies waste millions of pounds developing computer systems that hinder rather than assist work procedures with the result of falling staff productivity, increased user frustration and management disillusionment. As companies look to implement groupware there is a risk of repeating the same mistakes again.

Digital are teaming with National Westminster Bank, the University of Lancaster and cybernetics specialists Syncho Ltd to undertake the research project called SYCOMT (Systems Development and Cooperative Work, Methods and Techniques). The project will look at the design and development of systems to support group working with a particular focus on problems in the retail banking industry where changing work practices and demands for improved customer service are stretching the current capabilities of IT systems.

DUCK—Designers as Users of Cooperative Knowledge

A computer tool-set which will allow simultaneous multiple access to a design and is 'project log', is being developed by a consortium of specialist organisations in the UK. The consortium comprises the University of Paisley, BAeSEMA and MARI Computer Systems Ltd (lead partner).

The project toolset will comprise a shared electronic design journal running over a distributed network of computers, allowing designers to work as if sharing a single office. The visible design will be the common access point, and pen computing techniques will give designers the flexibility to sketch on-line.

Since DUCK acknowledges that actual design as practised in the real world follows no set plan, no rigid prescriptive method is imposed by the system.

The full process by which the design was achieved will be recorded for re-use, quality assurance, product liability, and design management.

The Awareness Initiative—The Ninth Project

The Awareness initiative is an important addition which will promote technology transfer of CSCW research to enable UK industry to adopt and benefit from the new technology, support the penetration of UK products and services in CSCW and provide links to other DTI/European Commission umbrella awareness and technology transfer programmes.

As well as promotional activities, the Awareness Project will support a number of clubs, the CSCW and Tele-working Special Interest Groups, along with work in the area of standards and useability metrics. There will be an on-line information and management system using Groupware applications.

Further Work

There will be no further calls for proposals under the programme. However support will be given to self-funding consortia in the following areas:

Tele-working Applications
Distance learning
Distributed Computing and Vertical Applications.

THE MARKET FOR TOOLS AND SERVICES

Much of the current groupware products come from the independent software vendors and are based on local area networks of personal computers (see figure 3). The market-place is as yet immature and so these early products are setting the expectation for applications in CSCW.

Because they address a market driven by volume and associated licence policies, local area network technologies dominate their capabilities. The evolving technologies of distributed computing and digital telecommunications can offer substantial advantages if correctly exploited and are an obvious area in which to broaden cooperative applications.

Many of the partner organisations in consortia within the JFIT CSCW Programme and some involved in cooperative technology projects in the European Strategic Programme of Research in IT (ESPRIT) are attempting to create new cooperative network architectures and sophisticated tool sets.

• **Email penetration on PC LANs is 30% in Europe and 60% USA**

• **By 1998, it will be 93% in USA and 81% in Europe**

• **Software prices for messaging groupware will fall over the period by 30%**

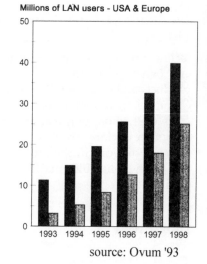

source: Ovum '93

Figure 3   E-mail as the enabler

The Open Software Foundation (OSF) has produced distributed computing platform software in the form of DCE (Distributed Computing Environment). This platform offers considerable benefit, primarily in terms of its client/server technology, allowing applications to be split across the network. It should be recognised, however, that the origins of this software lay in network technology components drawn from a number of leading commercial organisations and therefore it is limited to some extent by previous design assumptions.

Distributed systems research in Europe has produced equivalent platforms of greater potential for the purposes of CSCW research.

The reasons for this lie in the architectural elegance of the designs and in the number of parallel research initiatives which are currently being harnessed through initiatives within ESPRIT III to combine these technologies. ESPRIT Technical Week in Brussels in November 1992 illustrated a number of groupware application demonstrators which showed the way forward.

The technical features which are uniquely combined within European distributed system platforms include object orientation; persistence of information; 'trading' and 'agents' which together greatly facilitate CSCW. Researchers are recommended to investigate work done in the ISA, COMANDOS and HARNESS projects of ESPRIT (Project numbers: 2267, 2071 and 5279 respectively).

In looking at the distributed computing platforms available, European research has set new opportunities for CSCW not likely to be immediately exploited in the USA. By the same token, a rich high-level, open system networking platform must live alongside and be compatible with the platforms assumed to be available by those software and system vendors who are leading the groupware market.

Although the costs of software packages are falling in what is becoming a cut-throat market for personal packages, the planning and implementation costs for providing software on network systems are likely to be high. There is also concern that true work-group solutions will involve integration problems (DTI CSCW report 1993).

The nature and scope of concerns can be shown from research done by the DTI during the pre-programme phase. This highlighted the following issues:

- product positioning and the role of market analysts
- problems in establishing an effective network operation
- lack of compatible standards for products and platforms
- difficulties in providing coherent local and remote tools

- exaggerated claims for benefit and the need to be specific
- poor synergy with group working practices and behaviour
- assimilating contributions from the research community
- the limited scope of individual products
- the role of consultants
- snap judgements made about products and their use.

ALPHABET SOUP

It is the service sector which will come to the rescue of many implementation plans which search for a complete solution.

Areas where Ovum consider that tools and consultancy will be required to support effective use of CSCW are:

- coping with legacy systems
- integrating the infrastructure
- integrating the applications

From the DTI Survey in 1993 the most significant area of technical concern was in achieving the necessary product and platform integration (see figure 4).

Enhancements to network software are patchy and sometimes their facilities are duplicated in application software. However, through the available higher level local area network (LAN) interfaces and with security and resilience addressed, the smaller independent software vendor will tend to split between those providing rich server environments and those seeking to satisfy distributed peer or client support through personal assistants or work flow tools.

Regrettably, there is still a gap in the technical alphabet between the 'L' word and the 'M' word, with Lotus and Microsoft pursuing distinct application programming interfaces (APIs) such that not all servers and clients can meet.

There are also incompatibilities growing in terms of object characterisation for network entities between Microsoft and Novell. This 'M' to 'N' gap means that opportunities to capitalise on new-found resilience, security and server strengths is denied for those determined to build 'best of breed' network systems from multiple software and system vendors.

• 70% expected problems of product integration

• 72% expressed concern over whole-life costs

• 40% thought company structure would
  preclude tack-up

source: RSW ('93) on behalf of DTI

Figure 4   CSCW in prospect

Assumptions made and attitudes held by data-base suppliers, the network operating system vendors and the application writers lead to incompatibilities between the structure, access mechanisms and repository capabilities for stored information. We could extend the alphabet analogy by suggesting an 'O' gap. Oracle and Microsoft have recognised this gap but are approaching the bridge from different routes.

The lack of universal standards in the groupware world and the competing APIs created by the key software providers mitigate against the ease integration.

Providing 'exclusive architectures' as some key suppliers try to do merely locks users into a closed system community, much as the proprietary hardware systems used to do.

Whilst the international standards bodies and commercial consortia seek to develop open standards in many areas, they are ill-equipped to address the world of cooperative applications. They have so far failed to realise that groupware comes through LAN applications rather than CSCW growing out of distributed computing platforms (e.g., OSF DCE) and multi-media telecommunications capabilities (e.g., ISDN) which have been evolving through the 1980s.

Shared desk tops, co-authoring and remote interaction between local and remote applications may have to be deferred to a new generation of coherent applications which are usable at independent locations. Collaborative activities have, so far, had to observe a 'lowest common denominator' interchange via electronic mail, conference and whole-file transfer.

Even with electronic conference systems which provide both closed and open communities for interchange, we lack key technologies. Despite initiatives like those pioneered by the agreement to offer Lotus Notes through CompuServe, rich environments for information exchange still need sophisticated multi-media support and the ability to create a sense of process within the connected group.

These restrictions are in part responsible for the lack of apparent progress in allowing effective work from home by people who wish to contribute remotely to many interactive groups. Other factors relate to the lack of vision historically exhibited by the telecommunications providers who seem to believe that high usage comes before low tariff rates and high service levels. Having said this, there are many 'outworkers' who do work well within the 'legacy group' where they physically used to co-reside. They employ in many cases a secure and capable system for communication provided by their key client or employer. Membership of these 'clubs' requires observance to a restricted set of system and software tools and in some cases the use of proprietary techniques to achieve (e.g.) location transparency.

Some users thought open systems had arrived when the operating systems converged! But there is an ever-widening domain for standards observance.

SORTING OUT THE INGREDIENTS

So, what if this desired level of open integration does not happen? This is presumably the basic assumption behind the projected growth of consultancy services in the CSCW market. Ovum ascribes 60% of its projected 1998 groupware market to 'planning and implementation' services. Figure 5 shows the product market segments promoted by Ovum.

Within the established groupware market, the dominance of Lotus Notes has created a culture of use which exhibits two key expectations:

• that shared information is effectively enabled by the process of 'replication'
• that Notes is a basis for building applications.

The assumption that Notes is more of an environment than a solution has made it natural for users to expect to rely upon in-house

• **Email messaging products**

• **Work-flow products**

• **Groupware suites**

• **Team productivity tools**

• **Training and
Implementation services
(1.5 times product sales
but not included in charts)**

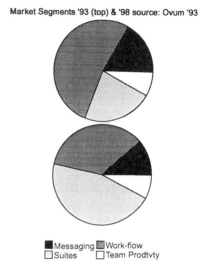

Market Segments '93 (top) & '98 source: Ovum '93

■ Messaging ▨ Work-flow
☐ Suites   ☐ Team Prodtvty

Figure 5   How to define the market?

or subcontracted programming and consultancy services to generate
the required applications. They can expect corporate installation and
application development to take up two years.

Of those users actively working with development tools, most are
piloting work-flow solutions. Less than half of these users are working
with their MIS Department to achieve these solutions!

The work-flow engine developed by Action Technologies is a
comprehensive development environment which incorporates many of
the technical options available for building server-based work-flow. ATI
Technology and other work-flow software like 'Staffware' are built in to the
products of system vendors and the tool sets of consultants who use them
to build application solutions. Through the use of standard interfaces like
STF (Standard Transaction Format), the application can be isolated from
the work-flow engine. APIs like this are the key to building groupware
suites.

Such standardisation may be a long time coming but some separation
and modularisation is to be seen in products like NetWare, Notes and
Workflo, e.g. the ATI work-flow engine contains three elements:

• a language interpreter
• work-flow processor
• agent processor.

Replication as undertaken within the Notes server network supports office-based information systems where conflicts of data update are rare and can be handled through relatively leisurely recovery procedures. For data-base vendors, used to the demands of transaction processing, such eventualities are more rigorously managed. Similarly, the ways in which a large user population is served, has led to data-base vendors approaching connectivity and networking issues from a different viewpoint. Oracle maintains a strict distinction between the application and the data storage functions and delivers applications as services rather than clients.

Microsoft has addressed the need for inter-operability amongst data-base systems in consultation with the SQL Access Group. It has specified the Open Database Connection (ODBC) standard which includes these features:

- SQL Query
- DBMS access lists (a directory of data bases)
- simultaneous connection to more than one DBMS
- an inter-program interface, DLL (supported by DBMS vendors)
- transaction controls.

ODBC can be viewed as the data equivalent of MAPI within the Windows environment.

Those developing the standards are currently seeking to evolve their capability to exploit emerging markets. It remains to be seen to what extent they will embrace international standard initiatives like PCTE for repositories, X.500 for directories and ODA for distributed computer architectures.

The SQL interface is being enriched to handle structured objects— inviting comparison with the compound document database offered in Lotus Notes. Oracle plans for text retrieval include fuzzy and context matching.

There is a move forecast by market analysts, to create divisions in the vendor market between the operating system suppliers and those marketing application suites. The lack of consistency between platforms may generate a class of vendor offering middleware tools. Ovum suggest that moves by companies like Oracle to address the groupware market facilitate the emergence of middleware to link between OS/NOS and robust enterprise-wide data storage.

Products are arriving which support an open choice of 4GL such as Floware from Plexus. Many of these are linked to graphical modelling front-ends or adapted case tools which ease design and implementation.

Groupware applications can be used to simplify options for IT system development through their use in rapid prototyping and pilot implementations.

CONCLUSION

The forgoing examination of current software and platforms for groupware and work-flow has recognised the predominance of the independent software vendors like Lotus whose Notes tool set invites the growth of application providers. It also has raised concerns relating to the different standards observed by these competing vendors and the growing distance between their solutions and those being explored by the international standards bodies.

In the medium term it seems likely that the potential market for exploiting local area network growth (over seventy million world-wide connections expected to be in place by 1998) will serve the software industry in license revenue. It will also serve to fuel a massive growth in those tool suppliers, software houses and consultancies which can make it all work together.

True object-oriented techniques would greatly assist in helping systems to be built along 'best of breed' lines. There is some emerging evidence to believe that many software suppliers will build packages, frameworks and suites along ever-more discrete lines, evolving towards object-oriented designs.

The future for CSCW lies in the challenge of multi-media, wide area networks and a recognition of the real requirements of people and teams. These requirements embrace the complete business process (only a part of which is currently served by groupware) and the enterprise as a whole (involving remote contribution, role management and other aspects).

Building such CSCW systems needs tool sets and methodologies to be incorporated, not just for information system design but for requirements analysis, organisational modelling and for the flexible inter-play of individuals and groups in interaction.

CSCW CONSORTIA PROJECTS

The following provides a contact list for projects in the JFIT CSCW Programme (all address are in the UK):

PROJECT TITLE: Strategies, Tools and Resources for Team-based Early Design—STARTED

PARTICIPANTS	CEGELEC Projects Ltd
	University of Bristol
	Rover Group
	Ove Arup and Partners
PROJECT MANAGER	Mr R M Watson
	CEGELEC Projects Ltd
	Boughton Road
	Rugby, Warks, CV21 1BU
Telephone	(+44) 788 563474

PROJECT TITLE: Support for Virtual Organisations—VIRTUOSI

PARTICIPANTS	BT
	BICC
	GPT
	Division
	Nottinghamshire CC
	University of Nottingham
	Lancaster University
	University of Manchester
PROJECT MANAGER	Dr A S Rogers
	BT
	BT Laboratories
	(B81/261)
	Martlesham Heath
	IPSWICH IP5 7RE
Telephone	(+44) 473 645600

PROJECT TITLE: Integrated Cooperative Workspace—ICW

PARTICIPANTS	Fretwell-Downing Data Systems Ltd
	ICL Open Framework Ltd
	Micronics Telesystems Ltd
	Nexor Services Ltd
	Oracle Corporation UK Ltd
	City University
	Sheffield Hallam University
	Supported by : ARIES User Group & Sheffield Health Information Project
PROJECT MANAGER	Mr Matthew Caunt
	Fretwell-Downing Data Systems Ltd
	861 Ecclesall Road
	Sheffield S11 7AE
Telephone	(+44) 742 686090

PROJECT TITLE: Collaborative Documents

PARTICIPANTS   BP Petrochemicals
                    Brunel University
                    Grand Metropolitan
                    Imperial College
                    Pfizer Pharaceuticals
                    Staffware plc

PROJECT MANAGER   Mr Jon Pyke
                    Staffware plc
                    6 Cricklade Street
                    Old Town
                    Swindon SN1 3EZ
Telephone   (+44) 793 541535

PROJECT TITLE: THE BUSINESS FLIGHT SIMULATOR (BFS)

PARTICIPANTS   ACT Business Systems
                    Bull Information Systems
                    City University Business School
                    Esmerk Informat
                    PCL
                    Touche Ross
                    In addition, industrial and academic consortia of clubs
                    including Cranfield, Loughborough & Strathclyde will
                    be created.

PROJECT MANAGER   Paul Ballard
                    ACT Business Systems Ltd
                    Technology House
                    Maylands Avenue
                    HEMEL HEMPSTEAD HP2 7DF
Telephone   (+44) 442 242277

PROJECT TITLE: Collaborative Requirements Capture Tool (CORECT)

PARTICIPANTS   Racal Research Limited
                    Edinburgh University
                    Sussex University
                    Racal Instruments Ltd
                    Intelligent Applications Ltd

PROJECT MANAGER   Dr J Walker
                    Racal Research Limited
                    Worton Drive
                    Worton Grange Industrial Estate
                    Reading RG2 OSB
Telephone   (+44) 734 868601
E-mail   jwalker@rrl.uucp

PROJECT TITLE: SYSTEM DEVELOPMENT AND COOPERATIVE WORK: METHODS AND TECHNIQUES (SYCOMT)

PARTICIPANTS   Digital Equipment Company Ltd.
                      National Westminster Bank Plc
                      SYNCHO Ltd
                      Lancaster University

PROJECT MANAGER   Geoffrey Darnton
                      Digital Equipment Co Ltd
                      1000 Parkway,
                      Solent, Business Park
                      Whiteley, Fareham,
                      Hampshire PO15 7AA
Telephone   (+44) 489 886688

PROJECT TITLE: DESIGNERS AS USERS OF COOPERATIVE KNOWLEDGE (DUCK)

PARTICIPANTS   MARI Computer Systems
                      University of Paisley
                      BAeSEMA

PROJECT MANAGER   Richard Lee
                      MARI Computer Systems
                      Old Town Hall
                      Gateshead
                      Tyne & Wear
                      NE8 1HE
Telephone   (+44) 91 490 1515

PROJECT TITLE: AWARENESS—Technology Transfer

PARTICIPANTS   Wide range of Contractors, Clubs and Special Interest
                      Groups

PROJECT MANAGER   Garth Shephard
                      Teknowledge
                      The Little House
                      2 School Lane
                      Welwyn Village
                      Herts, AL6 9DZ
Telephone   (+44) 43 871 8528
E-mail   CompuServe 100273,1203

REFERENCES

Raelene Stanley-Ware under contract to the DTI, *Perceptions of CSCW held by the informed community prepared by March 1993*

KPMG Management Consultants, *Lotus Notes User Group: Survey Highlights, September 1993*

Ovum Ltd report *Groupware: Market Strategies, 1993*

DTI/SERC Document *The CSCW Technical Workplan, JFIT Advanced Technology Programme, October 1992*

Section V

Selected Software for Supporting Co-operative Work

Leslie Jennison

The last section of this book contains overviews of software (and some hardware) demonstrated at the seminar. The use of some software is also described in the preceding papers. The intention is to provide enough information for you to decide if you are interested in evaluating or using any of these products, and to give you the UK and USA contact points so that you can obtain further details. Details appear in product name sequence, and the information is as given at the time of going to press in March 1994.

The editors would like to thank the staff of suppliers for supplying the information (sometimes at short notice). For each product there is a short description giving:

- The name of the originating organisation
- The status of the product: whether it is commercially available, for proprietary use only, or a research tool
- The year of introduction
- An indication of the price: where possible giving the price per user,

Computer Support for Co-operative Work. Edited by Kathy Spurr, Paul Layzell,
Leslie Jennison and Neil Richards
© 1994 John Wiley & Sons Ltd

or assigning the price per user to one of the following bands—lower (less than £500 or $500), medium (around £2000 or $2000) or upper (£5–8000 or $5–8000). Some suppliers have chosen to provide prices on application.

- The name and address of the supplier in the United Kingdom, and in the USA

- The key features as stated by the supplier

- The supplier's brief description of any development methodology used or supported

- Operating environments in which the software can be used for development and operation

- Interfaces to other development and operational tools

- A short illustration, provided by the supplier, of how development is achieved or how a typical developed application operates.

The inclusion of products in this book is for informational purposes only, and constitutes neither an endorsement nor a recommendation of quality or fitness for purpose. The publisher and editors assume no responsibility with regard to the performance or use of these products.

This is not intended to be a complete catalogue of products that can be used. In particular we have not concerned ourselves with free-standing electronic mail software. The editors are happy to receive information about other automated aids to co-operative working.

DESKTOP CONFERENCING

Originator: Fujitsu Networks Industry, Inc.

Status: Commercially available

Year of introduction: 1993

Price details: Five-user pack £995

Supplier in United Kingdom:

Fujitsu Networks Industry, Inc.
2 Longwalk Road, Stockley Park
Uxbridge, Middlesex, UB11 1AB
Tel: (+44) 81 573 4444, Fax: (+44) 81 561 2468

Supplier in USA:

Fujitsu Networks Industry, Inc.
Soundview Plaza, 1266 East Main Street
Stamford, CT 06902-2546
Tel: (+1) 203 326 2700 Fax: (+1) 203 964 1007

Key features:

Real-time, multi-party PC data conferencing package with electronic white board, real-time application sharing and remote application control
    Electronic documents, pre-printed forms, drawings, images and faxes, may be used, all of which can be worked on and annotated in a workflow environment.

Methodology support:

Use of an application development methodology is not applicable. There is a lifetime free help line for advice on use.

Operating environments:

Microsoft DOS 3.x (or later), Microsoft Windows 3.0 (or later), and Novell IPX

Interfaces to other tools:

DDE interface to control DeskTop Conferencing application

Using DeskTop Conferencing

One person using a PC creates a conference (the chairperson) and other colleagues join the conference. Once the participants have joined the conference, any image appearing on the chairperson's screen is automatically displayed on all other participants' screens. The live application is conferenced, but it only needs to be resident on the chairperson's PC. The role of the chair may be transferred to other participants in the conference, and a participant can take over remote control of the chairperson's application.

An electronic white board is provided for brain-storming and the result may be stored as flip chart pages. These may be loaded in a subsequent conference. A companion application is provided for archiving the pages of the electronic white board.

Formal and informal conferences may be created and access control features are provided.

DRAMS—DATA REGISTRY AND MANAGEMENT SYSTEM

Originator: Intergraph Corporation

Status: Commercially Available

Year of Introduction: 1992

Price: Price is on application as it will depend on the software modules purchased.

Supplier in United Kingdom:
Intergraph UK Ltd
Delta Business Park, Great Western Way
Swindon, Wiltshire, SN5 7XP
Tel: (+44) 793 619999 Fax: (+44) 793 618508

Supplier in USA:
Intergraph Corporation
Corporate Headquarters
Huntsville, AL 35894-0001
Tel: (+1) 205 730-2000 Fax: (+1) 205 730-3300

Key features:
Data indexing, searching and retrieval
Workflow management
Change management
Departmental or enterprise wide solution
Fully customisable
Database independent

Operating environments:
DRAMS uses a Client/Server Architecture based on an RDBMS of customer choice, Oracle, Informix, DB2, Sybase, DEC RDB or Ingres.
   Client interfaces are available for X-Windows and Microsoft Windows 3.1 and NT.

Interfaces to other tools:

DRAMS is easily integrated with application tools for the office and engineering departments. By incorporating Intergraph's viewing and redlining technology, files can be viewed in their native format throughout the corporation.

Through customisation, DRAMS can be linked to other corporate databases to provide a single point of entry to a wealth of corporate information.

DRAMS—Module Overview

Registry

The registry module is used to populate and maintain a digital library of document and data information.

It goes on to provide a file management capability so that files associated with the data, e.g. word processed files, drawing files, scanned images, text files, etc., can be located from a file vault and automatically delivered to a user in order that they may carry out some activity with them, e.g. edit, view or replicate, wherever they are on the network.

Revision Control

The revision control module allows current activity may be grouped into projects or jobs, so that by selecting a project, an operator only sees a list of documents that they need to work on.

Structured workflow allows data to be passed through a state cycle so that the issue of information and access to it can be controlled.

The notify and alarm feature will monitor the length of time that a document remains at a state. If that period exceeds a time-out value, a mailing list will then be notified so that appropriate actions may be taken.

Change Management

The Change Management module allows change requests to be categorised in order of importance. The information that will be affected by any change needs to be associated with that change request. The change request may then formally reviewed and approved in order that proposed changes may take place. Once a change request has been authorised it will then be turned into a change order.

A change order will allow several change requests to be grouped together. Only when a change order is approved may the revision role take place. This will create a new revision record for each document that is associated with the change order. The newly created document revisions may be updated.

Configuration Control and Distribution

Configuration control is provided with the use of a document control list. This will be used to define a list of particular documents and their purpose for which they should be used.

Document control lists and/or individual documents may then be put into a package of work.

It is the work package that is then distributed to the members of the distribution list via a transmittal.

DRAMS will log the contents of the package, the date that it was sent, the format that the contents of the work package were distributed in and also create a transmittal notice to cover this information. Each transmittal will have a number that will allow the system to track it.

DRAMS will distribute the work package either via the postal system or via the network directly to other DRAMS systems.

DRAMS will also log all transmittal dates, times and content in order that this information may be used to resolve any contractual issues that might arise during the life of a project.

Proposal Data Management

Proposal data management will be used when the system must track multiple concurrent document proposals that are being undertaken to a base document revision, e.g. three proposals to an as-issued document.

The Proposal Management module is intended for those organisations whose workflow is governed by regulatory authorities, e.g. the nuclear and oil industry.

FLOWMARK FOR OS/2

Originator: International Business Machines Corporation (Vienna Software Development Laboratory)

Status: Commercially available

Year of introduction: 1994

Price details: One copy of all three components (server, build-time client, run-time client) is £9559. Price for each extra run-time client is £1600.

Supplier in United Kingdom:

Workflow & Image Solutions Centre
IBM United Kingdom Limited
Rosanne House, Bridge Road
Welwyn Garden City, AL8 6TZ
Telephone +44 707 363196

Supplier in USA:

International Business Machines Corporation
1133 Westchester Avenue
White Plains, NY 10604
Call 1-800-IBM-3333 for the contact point of the nearest marketing representative.

Key features:

Definition facilities enable you to define processes graphically, assign programs to activities and allocate staff.

A process animation facility allows you to simulate the execution of process models.

A process execution facility allows you to start and manage defined processes.

The work list manager provides users with on-line to-do lists.

The system administrator can specify audit trails to record all process and activity related events.

The FlowMark server co-ordinates build-time and run-time clients and the FlowMark database.

Methodology support:

Generic workflow modelling and design
  Modellers build, test and document processes, using an understanding of the staff requirements, programs and data structures used in the programs they are modelling.
  System administrators install FlowMark, set up a database, register programs and define data structures used in process models.

Operating environments:

FlowMark client and server components can use:

- OS/2 2.1 and above
- IBM Communications Manager/2
- IBM DATABASE 2 OS/2

Support is planned for multiple LAN OS/2, AIX and Windows.

Interfaces to other tools:

Export and import processes, staff, program, data structure to flat files.
Access programs running under CICS, IMS, TSO.
Applications Programming Interface, used to modify programs attached to process models.

Using FlowMark for OS/2

Sample process models are provided that are based on workflow scenarios for insurance, banking, and application development.
  The user can interactively define, test, modify, document, and run processes.
  For example, a credit application model is delivered with FlowMark as an on-line model. It demonstrates basic workflow concepts. The model defines the path for a request for personal credit through the credit department of a bank.
  Inquiries gather the customers name and ID, and the amount of credit requested. If the amount requested is less than a figure specified by the bank, credit is granted. If the amount is higher than the specified figure, a bank employee is requested to approve or reject the credit application. A bank employee is notified whether the application has been accepted or rejected. Throughout the process, bank employees are assisted by the credit workflow and its dialogs.

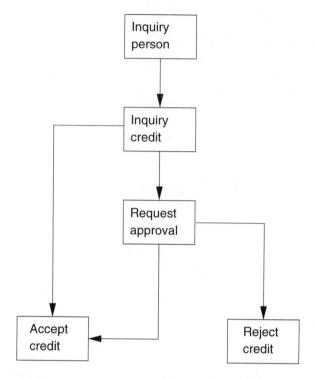

A Banking Solution

Activities

Inquiry person
A program activity. Gets personal information about an applicant (name and person ID). The person ID is passed to the Inquiry credit, Accept credit, and Reject credit activities.

Inquiry credit
A program activity. Gets the amount of credit requested. If the amount is less than a figure specified by the bank, the application is accepted, and control is passed to the Accept credit activity, along with the person ID and amount. If the amount is more than the requested figure, control is passed to the Reject credit activity, along with the person ID and amount.

Request approval
A program activity. Prompts a bank employee to approve or reject the credit amount. If it is approved, control is passed to the Accept credit

activity, along with the person ID and amount. If it is rejected, control is passed to the Reject credit activity, along with the person ID and amount.

Accept credit
A program activity. Displays notification of credit approval.

Reject credit
A program activity. Displays notification of credit rejection.

INFOIMAGE FOLDER

Originator: Unisys Ltd.

Status: Commercially available

Year of Introduction: 1992

Price: Prices on application

Supplier in United Kingdom:

Unisys Ltd.
Stonebridge Park
London, NW10 8LS
Tel: (+44) 81 965 0511 Fax: (+44) 81 961 2252

Supplier in USA:

Unisys Corporation
Jolly Road & Township Lane
Bluebell, PA 19424
Tel: (+1) 215 986 4011 Fax: (+1) 215 986 6850

Key features:

InfoImage Folder is a document image processing application which provides both workflow and the storage and retrieval of document images. Based on a client/server architecture, it can be tailored and configured to provide comprehensive business solutions for any market sector. Configuration is performed using Windows based tools and menu systems. Extensive integration and extension facilities are available to ensure that the InfoImage Folder solution is fully integrated into the business processes of the organisation.

InfoImage Folder is based on open systems platforms, using UNIX servers for document management and Windows PC workstations for presentation. Systems can be configured to support as few as eight users through to multi-server enterprise-wide systems supporting hundreds of users.

Unisys can provide complete business solutions, including consultancy, design, implementation, training, support and project management services from our dedicated team of professionals.

Methodology support:

Unisys has its own preferred development methodology, but is also often mandated on its products to use the customer's own methodology. Unisys has successfully used: James Martin Information Engineering, SSADM in government, LSDM/System Engineering, Method 1, and IEF in its commercial customers.

Operating environments:

InfoImage servers operate under UNIX System V.4. Client software requires DOS and Windows.

TCP/IP is the required communication protocol, over Ethernet or Token ring.

Interfaces to other tools:

InfoImage provides full multi-media support. Any file type, including word processing, spreadsheet, sound and video can be incorporated into an InfoImage solution.

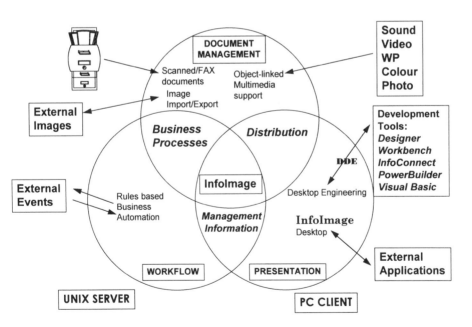

InfoImage Folder Integration Interfaces

One of the key strengths of InfoImage Folder is the richness and variety of opportunities for integration with other information systems. These range from the ability to import image document based information to and from the server, through to the ability to create totally unique client applications using standard tools.

KEYFILE

Originator: Keyfile Corporation

Status: Commercially available

Year of introduction: 1991

Price: From £595; 20 user system with workflow £30,000

Supplier in United Kingdom:

NBI Limited
Breckenridge House, Stoke Gardens
Slough, Berkshire, SL1 3QD

Supplier in USA:

Keyfile Corporation
22 Cotton Road
Nashua, NH03063

Key features:

Keyfile is a Windows based integrated document management system, which allows users to file, retrieve, mark-up, share, distribute, print, fax, copy, route, process, shred and archive all types of documents.

These may consist of electronic documents, pre-printed forms, drawings, images and faxes, all of which can be worked on and annotated in a workflow environment.

Methodology support:

Keyfile is a fully open object oriented, client/server architecture developed in C and C++

Operating environments:

True client (Windows) with Server (OS/2, UNIX, NT) architecture

Interfaces to other tools:

Keyfile is totally open, with links to Visual Basic, Powerbuilder, 4GL databases. It is fully compliant with OLE and DDE links.

LINKWORKS AND TEAMLINKS

Originator: Digital Equipment Corp.

Status: Commercially available

Year of introduction: LinkWorks: 1993, TeamLinks: 1992

Price: LinkWorks is £299 per user plus £299 per server (10 clients+1 server=£3289).
TeamLinks is from £47 per user for the mail component.

Supplier in United Kingdom:

Digital Equipment Co. Ltd
Worton Grange,
Reading, RG2 0TE
Tel: (+44) 0734-868711 Fax: (+44) 0734-202129

Supplier in USA:

Digital Equipment Corporation
146 Main Street
Maynard, MA 01754-2571
Tel: (+1) 508 493 5111   Fax: (+1) 508 493 8780

Key features of LinkWorks:

LinkWorks is an open client/server, object-oriented framework based on industry standard relational technology.

Out of the box, LinkWorks provides basic groupware capabilities such as mail and information filing. Beyond this, LinkWorks meets the needs of business managers for customised solutions to solve structured and often critical business problems.

Features of LinkWorks include:

- Object-oriented graphical user interface
- Flexible client/server architecture
- Open desktop approach giving a choice of: desktop and server platform, database repository, LAN transport
- Electronic mail (X.400)
- Group sharing and co-authoring

- Workflow (routing)
- Document management
- Group administration and management
- Security (DoD C2 compliant)
- Ability to integrate and customise applications
- Built on standards (X.400, POSIX, Motif, Microsoft OLE)

Key features of TeamLinks:

TeamLinks applications meet the needs of teams looking to work better together on ad hoc, relatively unstructured problems. TeamLinks makes organising, accessing and sharing information easy, not matter how large or small the group of users.

Features of TeamLinks include:

- Electronic mail (X.400)
- Electronic filing
- Ad hoc routing
- Database access
- Group conferencing
- Electronic library
- Group scheduling
- Ability to integrate popular PC applications

Interfaces to other tools:

TeamLinks interfaces with ALL-IN-1 IOS

Operating environments:

Clients supported by LinkWorks and TeamLinks: Macintosh, Microsoft Windows
Clients supported by LinkWorks: OS/2 Presentation Manager, OSF/1 Motif
Servers supported by LinkWorks and TeamLinks: Open VMS, OSF/1
Servers supported by LinkWorks: ULTRIX, SCO UNIX, HP UX, IBM AIX
Databases supported by LinkWorks: ORACLE, INGRES, INFOMIX, Rdb.

LOTUS NOTES

Originator: Lotus Development Corporation

Status: Commercially available

Year of introduction: 1989

Price: £375 per user

Supplier in United Kingdom:

Lotus Development UK Ltd,
Lotus Park, The Causeway
Staines, Middlesex, TW18 3AG
Tel: (+44) 784 455445 Fax: (+44) 784 469345

Supplier in USA:

Lotus Development Corporation
55 Cambridge Parkway
Cambridge, MA 02142
Tel: (+1) 617 577 8500

Key features:

Single Consistent User Interface to all people, resources and information
located on the network
    Compound Document Architecture containing multiple data types
Rapid Application Development Environment for rapid development of
work group applications
    Replicated Architecture to give all users located anywhere within the
extended enterprise access to up-to-date information
    Scalability to support any size of work group

Methodology support:

Lotus Notes is a robust secure application development environment
through which developers can quickly create cross-platform client-server
applications. These knowledge sharing applications allow multiple users
to manage compound documents, communicate effectively, and take
advantage of business process automation over geographically dispersed
and even remote regions.

Operating environments:

Windows, OS/2, Macintosh, UNIX

Interfaces to other tools:

Uses operating system standards, such as DDE, OLE, OCE and has an open published API for interfacing to other systems.

The architecture of Lotus Notes:

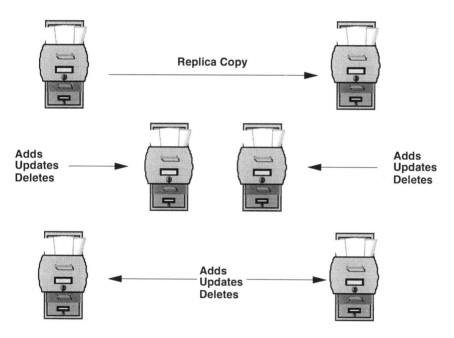

Lotus Notes is a replicated architecture.

Replication is the process through which a Notes database with copies on multiple servers is synchronised. Notes allows databases on different servers to be synchronised at intervals scheduled by the system manager, even if these servers are only occasionally connected over telephone lines. Notes uses the process of database Replication to distribute and update copies of the same database stored on different servers. This allows users on different networks, in different time zones, or even different countries to share information (even if they are only occasionally or remotely connected). The servers connect to each other at scheduled intervals, and the databases replicate changes to documents, access control lists, and design elements such as forms and views.

Replication makes all copies of a database essentially identical, over time. If a user makes changes in one copy of a database, replication ensures that those changes are added to all copies across the network, as long as the Replication options are set up to do so.

Lotus Notes also provides Replication between the desktop client and the server. With this feature, employees in the field can use Notes by dialling in at regular intervals, and the server will resolve differences between the desktop copy of the database and the server copy. Even if the user is only occasionally connected to the network, replication provides them with virtually the same functionality as users permanently connected to the LAN.

PENANALYSIS

Originator: Hitachi Software Engineering America

Status: Commercially available

Year of introduction: 1993

Price: From £900 per user to £24500 per meeting system according to hardware and software options included

Supplier in United Kingdom:

Virtual Software Factory Ltd.
Crest House, Embankment Way
Ringwood, Hants, BH24 1EU
Tel (+44) 425 474484 Fax (+44) 425 474233

Supplier in USA:

Hitachi Software Engineering America, Ltd
1111 Bayhill Drive, Suite 395
San Bruno, CA 94066
Tel: (+1) 800 624 6176 Fax: (+1) 415 615 7699

Key features:

• Direct entry of diagram and text with pen-based devices.

• Incorporates a recognition capability of hand written text and graphical symbols

• Supports pen-based applications (e.g. spreadsheets)

• Individual TabletStyle for personal or one-to-one interaction and a MeetingStyle for the facilitation of dynamic group sessions

Methodology support:

Process Modelling, Data Modelling

Operating environments:

Uses the PenPoint operating system running on 32-bit PCs (e.g. 386 or above), IBM Thinkpad and OE tablet. In MeetingStyle, uses also a digitising white board (WACOM MS2000 series).

Interfaces to other tools:

Virtual Software Factorys VSF-based products, Knowledgeware's Application Development Workbench (ADW), spreadsheets (CSV format), word processors (RTF format).

Using PenAnalysis

PenAnalysis software recognises drawing with an electronic pen on a tablet computer or digitising white board, and interprets symbols as data stores, processes or external agents, arrows as data flows, and hand-written text as text strings. This allows you to draw intelligent data flow (DFD) diagrams and decomposition diagrams that are linked together, stored in an integrated database and exchanged directly with a CASE tool.

With the MeetingStyle configuration, multiple users can easily interact in group or meeting environments to create diagrams on the fly and capture them in Hitachi Softwares Pen Analysis Process Modeling software running on a PC-compatible computer. Using a digitising white board and LCD overhead projector display allows the conduct of interactive joint application design (JAD) or business process re-engineering (BPR) sessions.

The Tablet Style configuration can be used either individually or in on-on-one sessions, using a pen-based computer. The results can then be downloaded into a desk top PC.

These method of working are designed to produce rapid, accurate capture of validated results and reduced modeling and design cycle times.

PROCESSIT

Originator: AT&T Global Information Solutions (formally NCR)

Status: Commercially available

Year of introduction: 1993

Price: Price on application. Pricing is dependant on functionality required. Approximate base pricing would start at £700 per seat for Workflow application software only (including client and server software).

Supplier in United Kingdom:

AT&T Global Information Solutions
206 Marylebone Road
London, NW1 6LY
Information Centre: Tel: (+44) 071-724-4050 Fax: (+44) 071-724-6519

Supplier in USA:

AT&T Global Information Solutions—Software Products Division
3245 Platt Spring Road
West Columbia, SC 29170
Tel: (+1) 803-939-7930 Fax: (+1) 803-939-7745

Key features:

As ProcessIT remains completely separate from the applications that perform tasks, it can facilitate the use of best in class applications plus dynamic change of work flows without disruption to the business process evolved.

Users can be allocated a number of Roles so the most appropriate and available person is allocated a job item thus optimising current resources.

Workview, NCRs electronic to-do list, can present a choice of appropriate work to the individual, or alternatively, display the next available job item.

ProcessIT is not e-mail based, but built on a transaction engine making reporting and monitoring facilities more flexible and responsive to management needs.

ProcessIT has the ability to span the enterprise to allow corporate allocation of resources to world-wide work flows.

ProcessIT can workflow any data format and is not limited just to images. Through the use of folders ProcessIT can allow the workflow of and reference to text, image, voice, fax and so on.

The application independence of ProcessIT allows the integration of existing applications and systems (protection of investment) as well as the use of best in class applications.

Operating environments:

ProcessIT can run as a Standalone solution or integrated with NCR Document Management System (DMS) and/or NCR COOPERATION.

For hardware operating environments—Server—UNIX V.4 and Client—DOS/Windows 3.0 or higher

Interfaces to other tools:

ProcessIT Open APIs: NCR ProcessIT API Library allows customers to embed ProcessIT function calls into any 3GL or 4GL application language or development environment that can interface to the C language. The following development environments are certified with ProcessIT:

- C (Borland, Metaware, Microsoft)
- C++ (Borland, C Front, Glockenspiel, Microsoft)
- Gupta SQL Windows
- Informix UNIX 4GL
- Micro Focus COBOL/2
- OBJECTVISION
- Oracle Card
- Progress
- REI/Plexus 4GL
- SmallTalk/V Windows
- Visual Basic

Support for the above application development software helps protect customers' investment in legacy systems (application programs and data repositories) and resources, (people, skills, and training).

Using MapBuilder for workflow in ProcessIT

MapBuilder is a client/server development tool designed to create and maintain workflow paths defined by an organisation. It gives developers

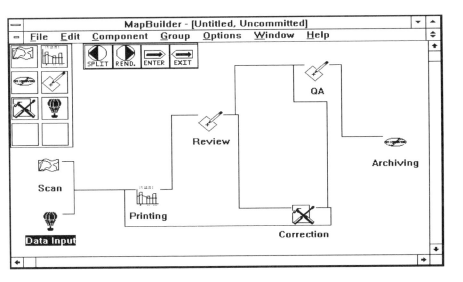

MapBuilder

familiar with one or more business processes a graphical environment to define and layout a particular workflow or set of workflows known as Process Maps.

MapBuilder—Windows Development Tool

This can be installed as a standalone version on any 386/486 PC with MS-Windows. Mapbuilder is commonly used as a standalone tool to assist process re-engineering or redesign efforts. The tool is an effective means to capture and visualise a process. A process owner can use the tool as a communication device to review what a process is or could be with organisations and/or departments participating in the process.

Running under MS-Windows 3.1, MapBuilder provides an intuitive, graphical method for drawing Process Maps. Process Maps describe the flow of work through user-defined processes and consist of activities and the routes between activities. The Process Maps are used by the Process Activity Manager (another module of ProcessIT) to control the flow of work through a defined workflow.

To build a Process Map, a user can select Activity icons from an available list displayed on the workstation screen. This list is a pre-compiled library that is defined by the user. Each Activity is represented by a Windows bit mapped icon and an abbreviated step title. These bit mapped icons come within MapBuilder's library of icons; but the customer can also add customised bit mapped icons to this library using commercial packages such as MS-SDK Paint. A user can react quickly to procedure changes by changing routes (how steps are connected), adding new processing steps, or icon representations to those already supplied. MapBuilder is able to print the Process Map to any output device supported by the environment.

ProcessIT can accommodate an unlimited number of Process Maps. SubMaps representing a sequence of activities that appear in more than one process can be developed and used repeatedly.

MapBuilder enables the user to create Activity and subMap icons for the component library.

As a visual management and communication tool, MapBuilder helps illustrate where systemic problems exist in a process and provides the means to easily and quickly modify the process.

SAROS DOCUMENT MANAGER AND SAROS MEZZANINE

Originator: Saros Corporation

Status: Commercially available

Year of introduction: Saros Document Manager: 1993; Saros Mezzanine: 1989

Price: Price per user—lower band (i.e. under £500), entry level 30 users

Supplier in United Kingdom:

Saros (UK) Limited
7 Wellington Business Park, Dukes Ride
Crowthorne, Berkshire, RG11 6LS
Tel: (+44) 0344 750321 Fax: (+44) 0344 750322

Supplier in USA:

Saros Corporation
10900 N E 8th Street, Suite 700
Bellevue, WA 98004
Tel: (+1) (206) 646 1066 Fax: (+1) (206) 462 0879

Key features:

Easy to use, out-of-the-box Document Manager
   Saros Document Manager is based on Saros Mezzanine—foundation of Enterprise Library Services and provides:

- network-wide searching
- version control
- access control
- on-line backup and restore

Manages ANY document format (text, graphics, video, voice. . .)
Supports ALL Windows applications.
Searches on document attributes or contents.
Allows document sharing between PCs and Macs.

Provides inside-out and outside-in integration.
Supports laptops and portables.
Manages hard-vopy documents.
Supports server to server communication, enabling access to documents from any location.
Provides server extendibility, giving limitless capacity and load balancing by the addition of extra servers.
Includes complete security and audit capabilities.

Methodology support:

Open

Operating environments:

Hardware: PC, Macintosh, UNIX
Client operating systems: Windows, DOS, Macintosh, OS/2
Server operating systems: OS/2, UNIX (HP, DG, IBM, AT&T GIS)
Windows NT and Novell NLM
Networks: LAN Manager, LAN Server, Novell, Banyan Vines, UNIX
Mezzanine-based solutions run on DOS, Windows, OS/2 and Macintosh workstations and are network OS independent.

Interfaces to other tools:

Saros Document Manager is fully integrated with over one hundred of the most commonly used desktop applications.

SAROS API: makes full capability of Mezzanine available through a complete set of object-oriented C subroutine calls. With the API, an entire custom user interface to the network can be developed that is independent of any existing application. The Saros API provides the building blocks to integrate applications under Windows, DOS, OS/2 or UNIX.

DDE INTERFACE: makes full capability of Mezzanine available through macros written in macro programming languages of Windows applications that support DDE commands. A powerful object metaphor passes information between macros and the DDE Interface. Windows applications can become Mezzanine front ends that are tailored to fit an existing work environment.

AML INTERFACE: works with macros written in the macro programming languages built into DOS applications such as WordPerfect. DOS application users deal with the system from within their familiar PC system, using only a few additional commands to gain transparent access to the network.

Saros Document Manager
Everything in One Convenient Place!

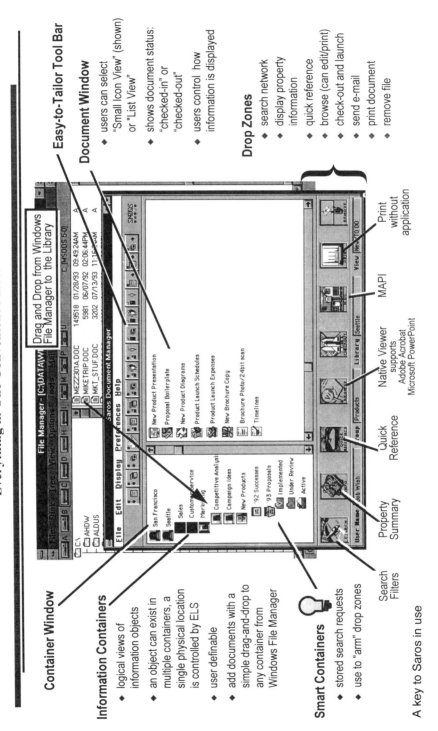

Container Window

Information Containers

♦ logical views of information objects

♦ an object can exist in multiple containers, a single physical location is controlled by ELS

♦ user definable

♦ add documents with a simple drag-and-drop to any container from Windows File Manager

Smart Containers

♦ stored search requests

♦ use to "arm" drop zones

A key to Saros in use

Search Filters

Property Summary

Quick Reference

Native Viewer supports Adobe Acrobat Microsoft PowerPoint

MAPI

Print without application

Easy-to-Tailor Tool Bar

Document Window

♦ users can select "Small Icon View" (shown) or "List View"

♦ shows document status: "checked-in" or "checked-out"

♦ users control how information is displayed

Drop Zones

♦ search network

♦ display property information

♦ quick reference

♦ browse (can edit/print)

♦ check-out and launch

♦ send e-mail

♦ print document

♦ remove file

Drag and Drop from Windows File Manager to the Library

MEZZANINE OLE: provides query, security, version control, backup and other services. Operates with any OLE client application such as Microsoft Mail; cc:Mail; Lotus Notes 3.0, Microsoft Excel; WordPerfect for Windows.

Using Saros Document Manager

Saros Document Manager is a ready-to-use document management system based on Saros Mezzanine. Saros Document Manager allows end users to transparently tap into the power of Mezzanine through a complete document management system that is easy to install, use, and maintain.

Mezzanine enterprise library services enable document management, document image processing, workflow and other such enterprise applications across large enterprise LANs. Mezzanine is client/server software that manages the life cycle of information objects, ensuring the right information is always at the right fingertips. Mezzanine does this by providing a range of services (version control, access control, search, back-up, archiving, network load-balancing, and more) commonly referred to as enterprise library services.

Saros Document Manager is designed to accommodate user preferences. The system operates from within popular Windows applications such as WordPerfect for Windows and Microsoft Excel (inside-out integration), as well as directly from the Windows desktop (outside-in integration).

Saros Document Manager brings significant benefits to end users, information managers, system integrators, and developers. MIS managers can provide enterprise users with an easy to learn, easy to use product that profoundly improves the efficiency of system administration while ensuring security and data integrity. End-users have a superior way to organise and access information and a way to automate many routine tasks. System integrators and developers have an enhanced foundation on which to build very focused enterprise solutions.